Ontario BICYCLE *Touring Atl*

**Get out your bicycle and enjoy touring in Ontario!
Cycle the shore of Lake Ontario, Lake Erie, Lake Huron, Georgian Bay,
the St. Clair River, Niagara River, St. Lawrence River and more.**

These routes were developed over nineteen years of selecting quiet scenic roads for enjoyable cycling and from responding to requests for routes through various areas. This publication puts all of these routes together with added published route information from regions throughout Ontario. You will find useful information on towns, attractions, bicycle repair shops, and libraries for washrooms, water, and internet access and rest stops while you are travelling plus selection of the most conveniently located and best restaurants, bed and breakfasts, inns, motels and camping. Also included is information on wineries, theatre, festivals, beaches, natural areas, historic sites, Mennonite and Native Canadian communities. There are long distance linear routes across the province and loop routes, suitable for day trips or weekends.

In this new edition over thrity five percent of the maps have new paved road or bike trail routes added. This includes the Ontario Greenbelt cycling route in the Toronto centred region, the K&P Trail in Frontenac County (north of Kingston) and extensive on road routes in Simcoe County (Barrie and Orillia area), Lennox and Addington (north of Napanee), Haliburton and the Ottawa Valley (north and west of Ottawa). All of the Bike ON Tours Package Routes as they exist in 2015 are shown in the mapping. The Community Index has been totally updated. To improve the usefulness and accessibility of this information it is now periodically updated and available on the internet with links at: http://www.bicycleontario.ca/destinations.html.

CONTENTS

PHOTOS COURTESY OF
HOWARD PULVER ©2009

Credits:
Maps ©2016 LUCIDMAP
Bicycle routes & touring information compiled and written by Howard Pulver, ©2016 Bike On Tours

Seventh Edition
ISBN 978-1-927391-648

For more detailed information and customized trip planning, contact:

Bike ON Tours
45 Chestnut Drive
Belleville, ON K8N 4Z5
E-Mail info@bicycleontario.ca
www.bicycleontario.ca

Designed & Published By:
LUCIDMAP
222 Islington Ave., Suite 227
Toronto, ON M8V 3W7
Tel: 416-244-7881
Fax: 416-244-5422
E-Mail: info@lucidmap.ca
www.lucidmap.ca

Touring Areas by Howard Pulver

THAMES - AVON

STRATFORD - LONDON - ST. MARYS

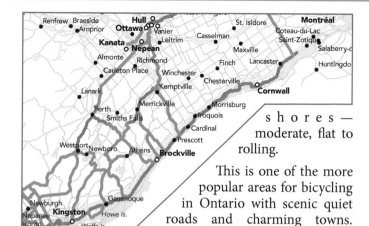

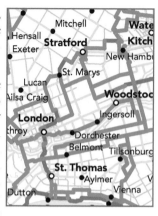

Features: London Bike Paths, historic, river valley, Theatre [Shakespeare Festival] - moderate, flat to rolling.

Go for the Theatre at the Stratford Festival and stay to bicycle. Every year from May to early November Stratford attracts visitors from Canada, the United States and around the world to the Stratford Festival for Theatre on four stages. The gardens, lakeside parks, restaurants and downtown shopping area make this an attractive place to stay a while and enjoy bicycling on tree lined country roads through scenic farmland.

Bicycle 25 kilometres from Stratford to visit St. Marys with a wonderful main street of Victorian stone buildings, Canada's largest outdoor swimming pool in an old quarry, the Canadian Baseball Hall of Fame and Museum and a scenic riverside promenade.

There are a number of bicycling options in this area including a 60 kilometre ride, which takes you to London and Fanshawe Park Conservation Area where you can camp, swim and visit the pioneer village. Continue into London and enjoy the outdoor festivals in the downtown area amid the Thames River parks and tree-lined streets.

Theatre lovers might also wish to try a bike route with a special appeal! Take a tour between the Shaw Festival in Niagara-on-the-Lake and the Shakespearian Festival in Stratford. A package route guide is available for a 5-day "Theatre to Theatre Ride" with 110 kilometre average distance per day. The package includes turn-by-turn directions, accommodation suggestions and attractions. Start at Niagara-on-the-Lake or Stratford. You bike through Six Nations First Nation, along the Grand River through Brantford, then northwest to Stratford. From Stratford you ride to Lake Erie to Port Dover along the Niagara Parkway past Niagara Falls.

You can also bicycle from London south to the Waterfront Trail along the Lake Erie shore and east toward Woodstock. For Information see:
www.bicycleontario.ca/theatre-to-theatre.html

ST. LAWRENCE - RIDEAU

GANANOQUE - KINGSTON - OTTAWA - BROCKVILLE - PRESCOTT - MERRICKVILLE

Features: Waterfront Trail, Ottawa Bike Paths, Rideau Canal, ferries, history, river valley, summer theatre, scenic

shores — moderate, flat to rolling.

This is one of the more popular areas for bicycling in Ontario with scenic quiet roads and charming towns. Kingston is a popular historic waterfront city with a ferry to Wolfe Island and New York State. Bike 30 kilometres east on the Waterfront Trail to Gananoque, the gateway to the Thousand Islands. Along the way you can take a short ferry ride to Howe Island. Gananoque has a lively waterfront featuring the riverfront Heritage Centre, island boat cruises, theatre at the Thousand Islands Playhouse and the Festival of The Islands in August.

Enjoy the 70 kilometre scenic Thousand Islands Parkway bikeway and Waterfront Trail between Gananoque to Brockville. Brockville's Riverfest offers many days of concerts and entertainment starting the last week of June but there are also lots of regular attractions at this historic city on the St Lawrence River including the farmers market, historic railway tunnel, Theatre Brockville, the Brockville Museum and Fulford House 1900's Edwardian mansion.

From Brockville you continue on the Waterfront Trail 50 kilometres to Prescott with historic Fort Wellington, on the St. Lawrence River.

Follow quiet historic routes north to Kemptville leading to the wonderful old stone buildings and Blockhouse Museum in the historic Rideau Canal town of Merrickville. Continue along the Rideau Canal from Kemptville to Parliament Hill in Ottawa. The nation's capital has a great system of bike paths and an unequalled array of attractions, museums, restaurants and accommodation. It is 40 kilometres from Brockville to Kemptville and an additional 30 kilometres to Ottawa.

A package route guide is available for a 5 day "St. Lawrence and Rideau Canal Ride" with 58 kilometre average distance per day including turn-by-turn direction, accommodations suggestions and attractions. Starting at Gananoque, you bike east along the Thousand Island Parkway and then north to Rideau Canal visiting several canal lock towns. Luggage transfer and accommodation reservations are available.
For information see:
www.bicycleontario.ca/st-lawrence-and-rideau-canal.html

PORTS OF LAKE ERIE

PORT DOVER - PORT ROWAN - PORT BURWELL - PORT STANLEY

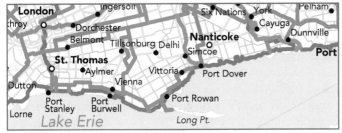

Features: Beaches, bird watching, historic, summer Theatre, waterfront - moderate, flat with a few short hills.

This is one of the best areas for bicycle touring in Ontario. It is a place that time forgot; a gem of historic lakefront ports and an easy ride on traffic free paved roads making it truly a cyclists' paradise.

Bike close to the Lake Erie shore with many newly added options for shorter distances and loops. It is about the same distance - 40 kilometres - between Port Dover, Port Rowan and Port Stanley.

The settlements, which date from the early 1800's include the early regional capital at Vittoria, Port Burwell with an 1840 lighthouse and the picturesque hamlets of Normandale and Port Ryerse. You can rest on the Lake Erie beaches and camp at the Provincial Parks at Long Point, Turkey Point or Port Burwell. Long Point is also a UN designated natural area. The Backus Conservation area near Port Rowan has a heritage village with an original operating 1798 water powered mill and camping facilities.

Both Port Stanley and Port Dover have summer Theatre. Port Dover is a tourist centre with restaurants featuring fresh Lake Erie perch and pickerel. Should you happen to visit there on any Friday the thirteenth you will find yourself a part of as unique celebration with hundreds of recreational motorcyclists from near and far.

For a longer ride which combines the most scenic section of the Lake Erie shore with the rail trail through Waterford and Simcoe to Port Dover and includes London, Ingersoll and Woodstock you might enjoy the four day, 275 kilometers Ports of Lake Erie package tour with an average of 71 kilometers (44 miles) per day.

For information see:
www.bicycleontario.ca/ports-of-lake-erie.html

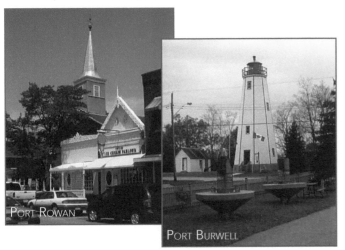

PORT ROWAN

PORT BURWELL

GLENORA FERRY, PICTON

BAY OF QUINTE

PICTON - BELLEVILLE - DESERONTO - NAPANEE

Features: Waterfront Trail, beaches, bird watching, cheese factories, ferry, historic, First Nations, waterfront, wineries - moderate, flat to rolling.

This is one of the most popular areas for bicycling in Ontario, centered on the peninsula of Prince Edward County. Enjoy scenic rolling countryside, waterfront views, sand beaches, camping and great restaurants. Sample the wines and cider near Wellington, Waupoos and Milford. Bike on quiet country roads, explore historic villages and visit cheese factories. Stop at Lake on the Mountain to enjoy the panoramic view of the Glenora Ferry.

Take the bridge across the Bay of Quinte to visit the native craft shops of the Tyendinaga First Nation near Deseronto, to see Belleville's revitalized waterfront and the Glanmore Victorian mansion National Historic Site. The Glenora Ferry takes you across the bay to continue east to Napanee or historic Kingston.

Picton is a great starting point for multiday bike ride loops going west or east on the Waterfront Trail and then north to Rice Lake, Campbellford and Tweed. Package route guides are available for three different rides – "Bay of Quinte" 30 kilometers (19 miles) per day including Belleville, Frankford, Brighton and Deseronto; "Bay of Quinte and Northumberland" 55 kilometers (36 miles) per day including Brighton, Cobourg, Gores Landing and Campbellford and "Lake Ontario and Trent Canal" 100 kilometers (60 miles) per day including Port Hope, Gores Landing, Tweed and Kingston.

For information see:
www.bicycleontario.ca/bay-of-quinte.html
www.bicycleontario.ca/bay-of-quinte-and-northumberland.html and
www.bicycleontario.ca/lake-ontario-and-trent-canal.html

WELLAND CANAL

NIAGARA

NIAGARA FALLS - NIAGARA-ON-THE-LAKE - FORT ERIE
PORT COLBORNE - DUNNVILLE - GRIMSBY

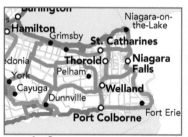

Features: Niagara Parkway, Friendship Trail and Welland Canal Trails, beaches, historic, ships on Welland Canal, Theatre [Shaw Festival], waterfalls, lakeshore, wineries—moderate, mostly flat except escarpment hills.

The Niagara Falls region is one of the best areas for bicycling anywhere in North America as a result of the unrivalled scenery of Niagara Falls, the Niagara Parkway and many bike paths. Niagara is also Ontario's oldest wine producing area with a growing number of wineries welcoming visitors. The terrain is quite flat except for where you climb and descend the Niagara Escarpment.

Starting on the shore of Lake Ontario in the charming and historic town of Niagara-on-the-Lake, you can bike 60 kilometres through the manicured parkland of the Niagara Parkway. The Niagara-on-the-Lake to Niagara Falls section is best enjoyed if you can avoid the busy holidays and summer weekends. The parkway is a limited speed roadway, with a bike path beside it, following the Niagara River through Niagara Falls all the way to Fort Erie, on Lake Erie, across from Buffalo, New York.

From there the Friendship Trail takes you 25 kilometres to Port Colborne where you can join the Welland Canals Parkway. You will see ocean going ships travel through the locks and you can ride across the canal on the pedestrian ferry at Port Robinson. Follow the bike paths along the canal for 40 kilometres to return to Lake Ontario. For a longer ride, bicycle west to Dunnville and take the scenic River Road along the edge of the Grand River to York, then cross the Niagara Peninsula to Lake Ontario at Grimsby.

You might wish to try out the bike route with a special appeal for Theatre lovers, between the Shaw Festival in Niagara on the Lake and the Shakespearian Festival in Stratford. A package route guide is available for a 5 day "Theatre to Theatre Ride" with 110 kilometre average distance per day including turn-by-turn directions, accommodation suggestions and attractions is available. Starting at Niagara on the lake you bike through Six Nations First Nation, along the Grand River through Brantford and Paris north and west to Stratford.

You return along Lake Erie and the Niagara Parkway through Port Dover, Fort Erie and Niagara Falls with stops in Ohsweken, Stratford, Port Dover and Port Colborne.

A package route guide is available for a 4 day "Grand Niagara Ride" with 65 kilometre average distance per day including turn-by-turn directions, accommodation suggestions and attractions.

For information see:
www.bicycleontario.ca/grand-niagara.html

HURON SHORE

GODERICH - BAYFIELD - IPPERWASH BEACH - GRAND BEND - SARNIA

Features: St. Clair Parkway and Sarnia Lakeshore Trails, beaches, ferries, history, First Nations, ships on St. Clair River, waterfront –moderate, rolling to flat.

Historic Bayfield Village, although a lively port for small boats, looks pretty much as it did in the 1840's with its quaint main street including two historic hotels. You can check out the nearby Folmar Windmill, flea markets or shop for fresh and smoked fish. A back road route takes

BLUE WATER BRIDGE, SARNIA

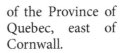
CHANTRY ISLAND, SOUTHAMPTON

you 20 kilometres to Goderich, with its unique octagonal town square, lighthouse and beaches on Lake Huron. The town square is the location of the Saturday Farmers Market. The restored mills of Benmiller provide a scenic and peaceful luxury resort. There are a number of loop routes in this area.

Enjoy peaceful roads with cottages along Lake Huron, a back road connection to Pinery Provincial Park and the Rotary Trail (adjacent to Highway 21) to Grand Bend, the Kettle Point First Nation community and fruit growing areas; away from heavy motor vehicle traffic on Highway 21.

Ipperwash Beach is a broad sand beach with a shallow shoreline and spectacular sunsets. Best of all, you can enjoy it all day and park your motor vehicle at no charge. Take the 80 kilometre loop route to Arkona and the adjacent Rock Glen Conservation Area, the scenic centre of a tender fruit growing area, with cherries, peaches and apples.

The Sarnia area has bike paths from Errol on Lake Huron continuing 20 kilometres under the Blue Water Bridge. Heading south, the St. Clair Parkway is a 40 kilometre route all the way to Wallaceburg. Small ferries connect to the Bridge to Bay Trail in Michigan at Sombra [Marine City] and Walpole Island [Algonac].

WATERFRONT TRAIL

WINDSOR - NIAGARA-ON-THE-LAKE - HAMILTON TORONTO - COBOURG - KINGSTON BROCKVILLE - CORNWALL

Features: Bike paths, beaches, historic, theatre, ferry, waterfront along Lake Erie, Lake Ontario and St. Lawrence River, moderate— flat to rolling.

This wonderful greenway traverses the largest urban areas in Ontario, yet is still very scenic and follows the shore of Lake Erie, Lake Ontario and the St. Lawrence River. You can bicycle all the way from Niagara to the border

of the Province of Quebec, east of Cornwall.

Starting in Windsor the route is mostly a signed on road route close to the shore of Lake Erie. From picturesque and historic Niagara-on-the-Lake, you'll pass through Toronto's Harbourfront, attractive beachfronts, and residential neighbourhoods, to quiet lakefront roads, farmland and small historic towns including charming Port Hope & Cobourg, Bloomfield, Picton, and on to the Glenora Ferry. Enjoy the bike paths of the Loyalist Parkway and Thousand Islands Parkway, Kingston, "the Limestone City", Fort Henry and historic Brockville and Prescott. This is wonderful ride with all of the tourist services that you could desire. Easy, flat to slightly rolling.

The Waterfront Trail is also a great starting point for multiday bike ride loops going west or east on the Waterfront Trail and then north to Rice Lake, Campbellford, Perth and all the way to Ottawa. Route information packages with turn-by-turn route guides are available at:

www.bicycleontario.ca/bike-tour-guides.html

BRUCE PENINSULA

OWEN SOUND - COLLINGWOOD - PORT ELGIN - KINCARDINE - PAISLEY - MARKDALE

Features: Georgian Trail, Saugeen Trail, beaches, breweries, First Nations, Mennonite, waterfalls, waterfront — easy to difficult, flat to rolling hills.

A quiet and scenic area which goes from the port of Owen Sound, past the rugged rocky shores and clear water of Georgian Bay and Colpoys Bay, to miles of quiet sand beaches on Lake Huron, and through peaceful farming areas. See the cascading eighty foot high waterfall at Inglis Falls near Owen Sound and visit the home of Wiarton Willie, the world famous groundhog weather forecaster who makes his prediction each February. It is a pleasant 80 kilometre ride from Owen Sound to Southampton and Port Elgin on Lake Huron.

Enjoy the popular Summerfolk Music and Craft Festival, late August in Owen Sound and check for local special events happening most summer weekends in the resort towns of Port Elgin and Southampton.

The Beaver Valley is unique and scenic with steep hills on each side, which meet at Kimberley. This is a beautiful

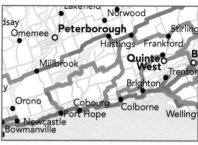

area which suits cyclists at all levels–an easy ride on the hard packed gravel Georgian Trail with access to beaches on Georgian Bay between Meaford and Collingwood, a moderate 20 kilometre ride up the scenic valley to Kimberley or a challenging 40 kilometre ride on to Flesherton and Markdale.

The Saugeen River valley is a rural countryside experience with small towns, quiet roads and an Amish Mennonite farming area. Bicycling between Paisley, Chesley, Hanover, Mildmay and Formosa makes a pleasant 100 kilometre ride. The reminders of the past are everywhere with rushing water past mills and mill ruins. Visit and sample the brew from two historic breweries still in operation on the route, the 1859 Neustadt Springs Brewery and the 1870 Formosa Springs Brewery. The area is also well known as a great place for canoeing and kayaking.

A package route guide is available for a 4 or 6 day "Bruce Peninsula Ride" with a 57 or 85 kilometre average distance per day including turn by turn directions, accommodation suggestions and attractions. Starting from Owen Sound, you bike close to the shore of Georgian Bay and Colpoys Bay through Wiarton to the shore of Lake Huron traveling south to Kincardine and Point Clark. Return through Mennonite farming countryside and historic mill towns on the Saugeen River. For information see:

www.bicycleontario.ca/bruce-peninsula.html

NORTHUMBERLAND - KAWARTHAS

COBOURG - PORT HOPE - RICE LAKE - COLBORNE - BRIGHTON

Features: Waterfront Trail, Trent Canal, apple orchards, beaches, historic, First Nations, waterfront - moderate to difficult, hilly north of Lake Ontario.

You can enjoy an easy ride along Lake Ontario through the old fashioned main streets of delightful heritage towns. In Port Hope enjoy Theatre and music at the atmospheric Capitol Theatre; visit the Canadian Firefighters Museum or shop for antiques and collectibles on the unique mid-19th century main street. Cobourg, with its beach and boardwalk on Lake Ontario, offers Theatre at the 1860 Victoria Hall. Continue on the Waterfront Trail to visit the landmark "Big Apple" in Colborne, with a charming town square. Near Brighton, Presqu'ile Provincial Park offers beaches and natural areas to explore. It is 14 kilometres from Port Hope to Cobourg, a further 25 to Colborne and an additional 15 to Brighton.

You'll encounter picture perfect rolling farmland with wooded hills on your way to naturally beautiful Rice Lake and the Alderville First Nation community. Try the 150 kilometre challenging loop route from Cobourg through Port Hope to Rice Lake and Warkworth, returning under Highway 401 along scenic Shelter Valley Road.

You'll encounter picture perfect rolling farmland with wooded hills on your way to naturally beautiful Rice Lake and the Alderville First Nation community. Try the 150 kilometre challenging loop route from Cobourg through Port Hope to Rice Lake and Warkworth, returning under Highway 401 along scenic Shelter Valley Road.

The lakeshore towns of Northumberland are great starting points for multiday bike ride loops. This area is included in the "Bay of Quinte and Northumberland" 55 kilometers (36 miles) per day including Brighton, Cobourg, Gores Landing and Campbellford and "Lake Ontario and Trent Canal" 100 kilometers (60 miles) per day including Port Hope, Gores Landing, Tweed and Kingston package tours.

For information see:
www.bicycleontario.ca/bay-of-quinte-and-northumberland.html and
www.bicycleontario.ca/lake-ontario-and-trent-canal.html

ERIE SHORES

WINDSOR - LEAMINGTON - KINGSVILLE - CHATHAM - PELEE ISLAND

Features: Chrysler Greenway Trail, beaches, bird watching, ferry, French Canadian, historic, waterfront,

POINT PELEE BOARDWALK

wineries–easy, flat.

You can bike through the most southerly part of Canada, close to the shore of the Detroit River, Lake St. Clair, the 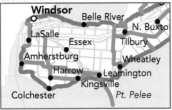 Thames River and Lake Erie. This area is very flat, making it perfect for an easy early or late season rides since it is frost free a month longer than the rest of Ontario.

The Chrysler Canada Greenway Trail follows an abandoned rail line from the paradise of Colisanti's Tropical Gardens to the Colio Winery in Harrow and the south side of Windsor.

Leamington makes a great centre for exploring this area and a number of loop routes are available. From there you can bicycle 15 kilometres to Point Pelee, 50 kilometres to Amherstburg, 70 kilometres to Windsor or 80 kilometres to Chatham.

Enjoy scenic countryside including the French Canadian community of Pain Court as well as the settlements of black slaves who escaped from the United States at North Buxton. Learn about the history of this area by visiting the restored Buxton National Historic Site and Museum, 1850 John Park homestead on the lake at Colchester, and Fort Malden on the river in historic Amherstburg.

This area is home to one of Ontario's oldest wineries, the Pelee Island Winery in Kingsville, as well as a growing number of new ones close to Lake Erie. This unique natural area produces an abundance of fresh fruit and vegetables from the fields and acres of greenhouses.

Explore the boardwalk, nature trails and beaches of Point Pelee National Park, featuring a tree canopied paved road down to the tip. Pelee Island makes an interesting day trip from Leamington or Kingsville harbour along quiet lakefront roads.

A package route guide is available for a 4 or 5 day "Erie Shores and Pelee Ride" with a 63 kilometre average distance per day including turn by turn directions, accommodation suggestions and attractions. Starting from Windsor or Amherstburg, you bike close to the shore of Lake Erie, the Thames River and Lake St. Clair including Point Pelee National Park. The 5th day is an optional day trip travelling by ferry to bicycle Pelee Island.

For information see:
www.bicycleontario.ca/erie-shores--pelee.html

GRAND RIVER

BRANTFORD - PARIS - SIX NATIONS TERRITORY
ST. JACOBS - ELORA

Features: Grand River Trails, Hamilton - Brantford Rail Trail, covered bridge, historic, First Nations, Mennonite, river valley–moderate, rolling.

Encounter horses and buggies and cross Ontario's last remaining covered bridge at West Montrose. You are certain to see Mennonites at work in the fields, travelling to town or to the meetinghouses on Sunday in Elmira, near Floradale and near Linwood. This is one of the few areas in Ontario where the Amish and old order Mennonites are living much as they did when they first settled in the early 1800's.

A 130 kilometre loop route takes you from St. Jacobs across the covered bridge to Fergus, returning through Elmira and Wellesley. Follow the Grand River and see the scenic Elora Gorge from the 1870 Elora Mill – now an inn and restaurant – or explore the gorge by taking a short walk from town.

There is a 160 kilometre loop route centred the Grand River towns around Brantford including Paris, Ancaster and the Six Nations Territory.

The Grand River is a designated Canadian Heritage River and it's a wonderful natural resource for hiking, canoeing, bird watching, fishing and camping as well as bicycling. Enjoy the scenic valley towns, lush rolling countryside and the large Six Nations native settlement of loyalist natives who relocated from the Mohawk valley of New York State in 1784.

The family home of Alexander Graham Bell overlooks the Grand River, where he developed the principle of the telephone in 1874. From here, the first long distance telephone call was made, to Paris, ON. Other attractions in Brantford include a native cultural centre, replica 17th century Iroquoian village, a restored 1919 performing arts centre, military heritage and motorcycle museums.

MENNONITE TRANSPORT

Ten Tips For Enjoyable Bicycle Touring

1. Wear A Helmet - Helmets save lives and prevent serious injuries. While other injuries can heal, a head injury can lead to disability or death.

2. Check Your Bike - Use a bike with a lightweight alloy frame and have it checked out by a trained bicycle mechanic if you are not certain that it is in good condition. Carry an inner tube to fit your tires, a tire pump and tools to change a flat.

3. Train To Enjoy The Ride - Ride 30 kilometers (20 miles) or more several times each week. Ride the distance that you plan to ride in a day at least once prior to the trip

4. Ride Safely And Be Visible - Always follow the rules of the road. Wear bright colours to increase your visibility. Use a headlight and rear light at night.

5. Be Alert - Look ahead constantly for hazards including turning vehicles, rail tracks, sewer grates, road debris and broken pavement.

6. Drink Water - Take a large water bottle and drink before you are thirsty to avoid dehydration.

7. Pack A Snack - Carry your favourite snack such as fruit, fruit juice and granola bars to eat on the road. Eating dairy products (other than yogurt) and large meals on a strenuous ride may cause indigestion.

8. Dress For Comfort - Wear purpose designed bike shorts to protect the bike seat contact area (available in styles that look like walking shorts or form fitting lycra shorts). Dress in layers on cool days so that you can adjust your clothing to stay comfortable.

9. Lock Your Bike - When your bike is out of sight lock the rear wheel, frame (and front wheel if possible) to a secure object. A "U" shaped security lock is best.

10. Reserve Ahead - Always reserve needed overnight accommodation in advance. Be certain that you will have a comfortable place to rest and a secure place for your bicycle at the end of the ride.

> For a complete marked Route Map and turn by turn Route Description with Attractions, Accommodation, Restaurant and Bike Repair Shop List; customized to meet your specific needs and the locations that you want to travel, contact **Bike On Tours**.
> E-mail to info@bicycleontario.ca

WELLAND CANAL

Touring Resources

You may also find the following list of resources useful when planning a bike trip in Ontario. For live links and additional resources including current weather, regional and city route maps, organized rides, cycling clubs and cycle tourism information go to www.bicycleontario.ca/online-resources.html

Ontario Travel Information
 www.ontariotravel.net/en/home
 Tel: (800) 668-2746

Parks & Conservation Areas for Biking and Camping
Ontario Provincial Parks
 www.ontarioparks.com
Ontario Conservation Areas
 ontarioconservationareas.ca

Cycling Advocacy
Share the Road
 www.sharetheroad.ca

Information for Cycling in Ontario
Welcome Cyclists - Bicycle friendly places to eat, visit and sleep
 welcomecyclists.ca

Bicycling Travelogues
Open Directory Project - Travelogues - Cycling In Canada
 www.dmoz.org/Sports/Cycling/Travel/Travelogues/North America/Canada

Bicycle Repair
Total Bike - Bicycle Repair Guide
 www.totalbike.com/web/repair

Training, Nutrition and Health
Cycling Performance Tips - Practical Advice on Training and Diet
 www.cptips.com

Share Your KNOWLEDGE
With your feedback, we can make this atlas even better!
E-mail your comments to
info@lucidmap.ca

Map Section Contents

Ontario BICYCLE *Touring Atlas*

Legend

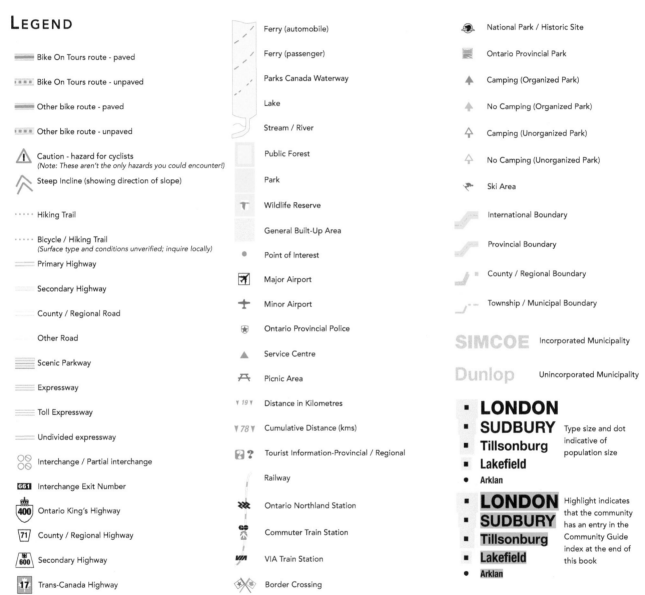

- Bike On Tours route - paved
- Bike On Tours route - unpaved
- Other bike route - paved
- Other bike route - unpaved
- ⚠ Caution - hazard for cyclists *(Note: These aren't the only hazards you could encounter!)*
- Steep Incline (showing direction of slope)
- Hiking Trail
- Bicycle / Hiking Trail *(Surface type and conditions unverified; inquire locally)*
- Primary Highway
- Secondary Highway
- County / Regional Road
- Other Road
- Scenic Parkway
- Expressway
- Toll Expressway
- Undivided expressway
- Interchange / Partial interchange
- **661** Interchange Exit Number
- **400** Ontario King's Highway
- **71** County / Regional Highway
- **600** Secondary Highway
- **17** Trans-Canada Highway

- Ferry (automobile)
- Ferry (passenger)
- Parks Canada Waterway
- Lake
- Stream / River
- Public Forest
- Park
- Wildlife Reserve
- General Built-Up Area
- Point of Interest
- Major Airport
- Minor Airport
- Ontario Provincial Police
- Service Centre
- Picnic Area
- 19 Distance in Kilometres
- 78 Cumulative Distance (kms)
- Tourist Information-Provincial / Regional
- Railway
- Ontario Northland Station
- Commuter Train Station
- VIA Train Station
- Border Crossing

- National Park / Historic Site
- Ontario Provincial Park
- Camping (Organized Park)
- No Camping (Organized Park)
- Camping (Unorganized Park)
- No Camping (Unorganized Park)
- Ski Area
- International Boundary
- Provincial Boundary
- County / Regional Boundary
- Township / Municipal Boundary
- SIMCOE Incorporated Municipality
- Dunlop Unincorporated Municipality

- ▪ **LONDON**
- ▪ **SUDBURY**
- ▪ **Tillsonburg**
- ▪ **Lakefield**
- ● **Arklan**

Type size and dot indicative of population size

- ▪ **LONDON**
- ▪ **SUDBURY**
- ▪ **Tillsonburg**
- ▪ **Lakefield**
- ● **Arklan**

Highlight indicates that the community has an entry in the Community Guide index at the end of this book

WARNING AND DISCLAIMER:

⚠ Cyclists are solely responsible for risks encountered and for their own safety. The following are potential safety hazards: weather, poor road surface, heavy traffic, reduced visibility, physical or mental well-being, damaged equipment, speed, knowledge or technique, food or drink, road position, improper procedure, protection, scheduling, new or unexpected situation, fatigue, distraction, peer pressure. Neither Bike On Tours, nor the authors and publishers assume any responsibility for the accuracy of this guide and associated maps, the safety or fitness of the suggested routes or any damages and/or claims whatsoever associated with use.

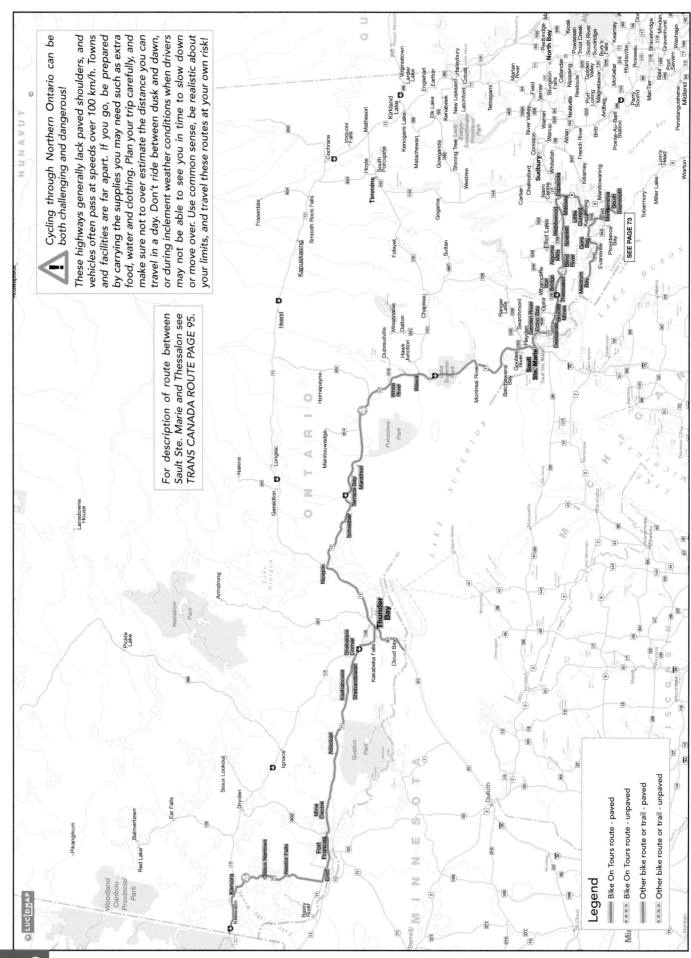

Cycling through Northern Ontario can be both challenging and dangerous!

These highways generally lack paved shoulders, and vehicles often pass at speeds over 100 km/h. Towns and facilities are far apart. If you go, be prepared by carrying the supplies you may need such as extra food, water and clothing. Plan your trip carefully, and make sure not to over estimate the distance you can travel in a day. Don't ride between dusk and dawn, or during inclement weather conditions when drivers may not be able to see you in time to slow down or move over. Use common sense, be realistic about your limits, and travel these routes at your own risk!

For description of route between Sault Ste. Marie and Thessalon see TRANS CANADA ROUTE PAGE 95.

Legend

▬▬▬	Bike On Tours route - paved
▬▬▬	Bike On Tours route - unpaved
▪▪▪▪	Other bike route or trail - paved
▪▪▪▪	Other bike route or trail - unpaved

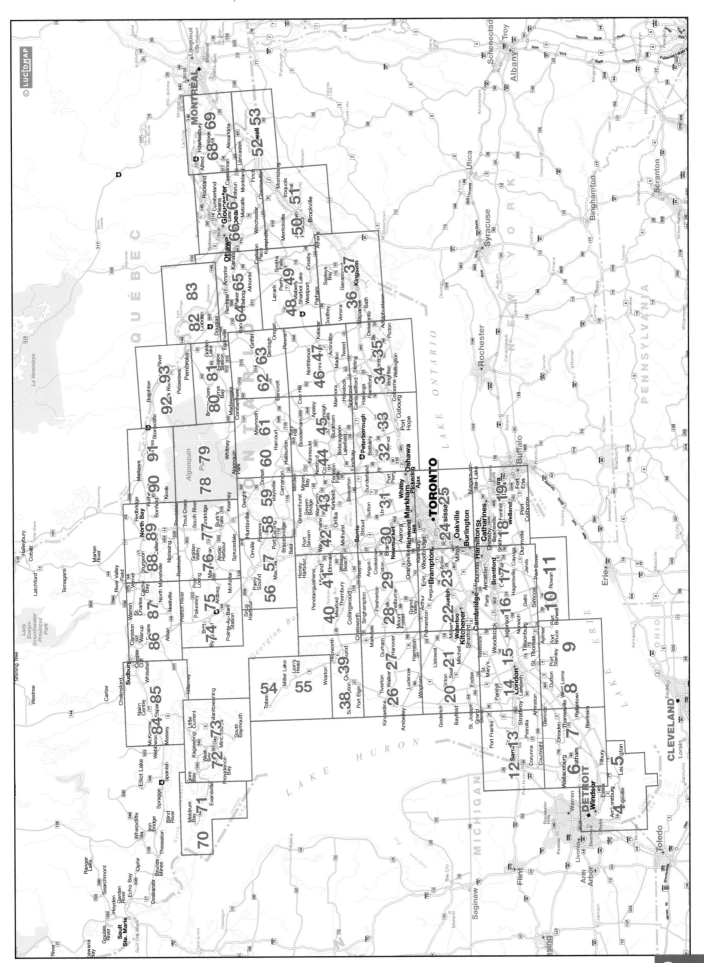

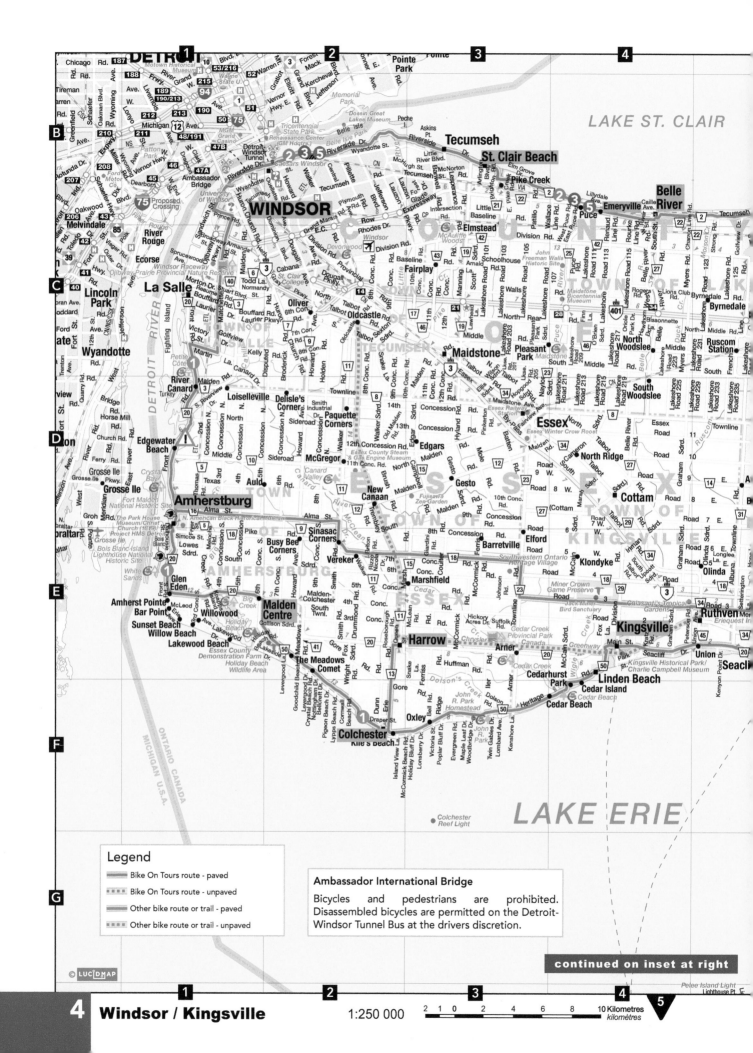

Legend

Bike On Tours route - paved
Bike On Tours route - unpaved
Other bike route or trail - paved
Other bike route or trail - unpaved

Ambassador International Bridge

Bicycles and pedestrians are prohibited. Disassembled bicycles are permitted on the Detroit-Windsor Tunnel Bus at the drivers discretion.

continued on inset at right

2 1 0 2 4 6 8 10 Kilometres
kilomètres

© LUCIDMAP

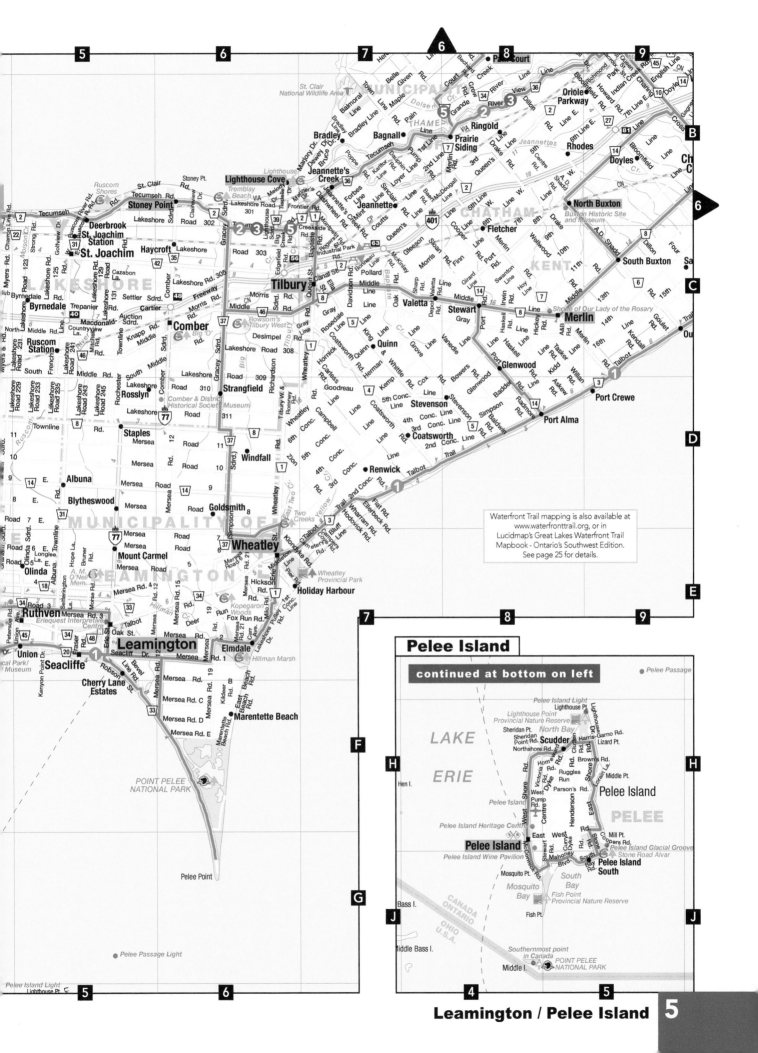

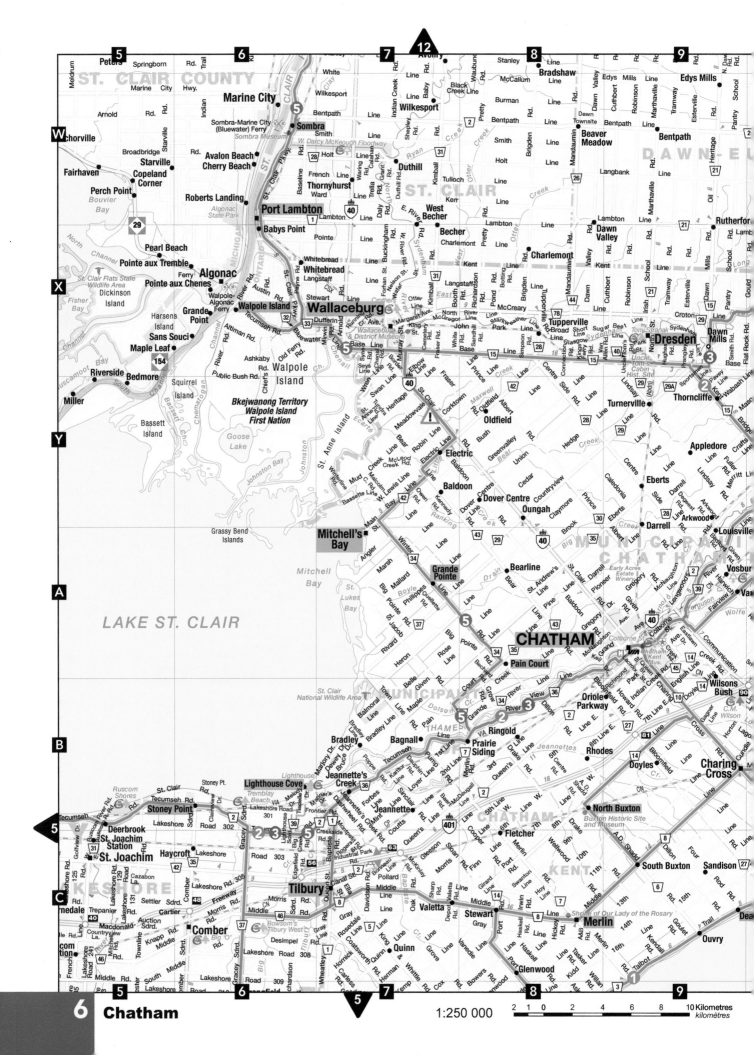

1:250 000

LAKE ERIE

Legend

Bike On Tours route - paved
Bike On Tours route - unpaved
Other bike route or trail - paved
Other bike route or trail - unpaved

Waterfront Trail mapping is also available at
www.waterfronttrail.org, or in
Lucidmap's Great Lakes Waterfront Trail
Mapbook - Ontario's Southwest Edition.
See page 25 for details.

© LUCIDMAP

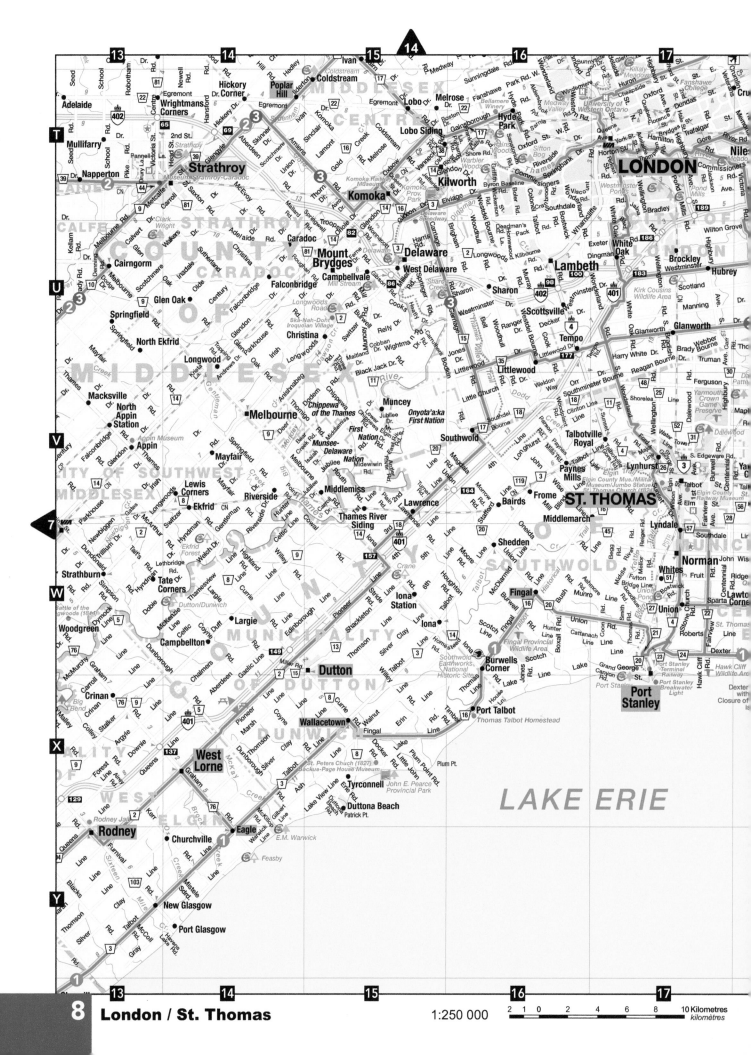

1:250 000

2 1 0 2 4 6 8 10 Kilometres
kilomètres

LAKE ERIE

LONDON

ST. THOMAS

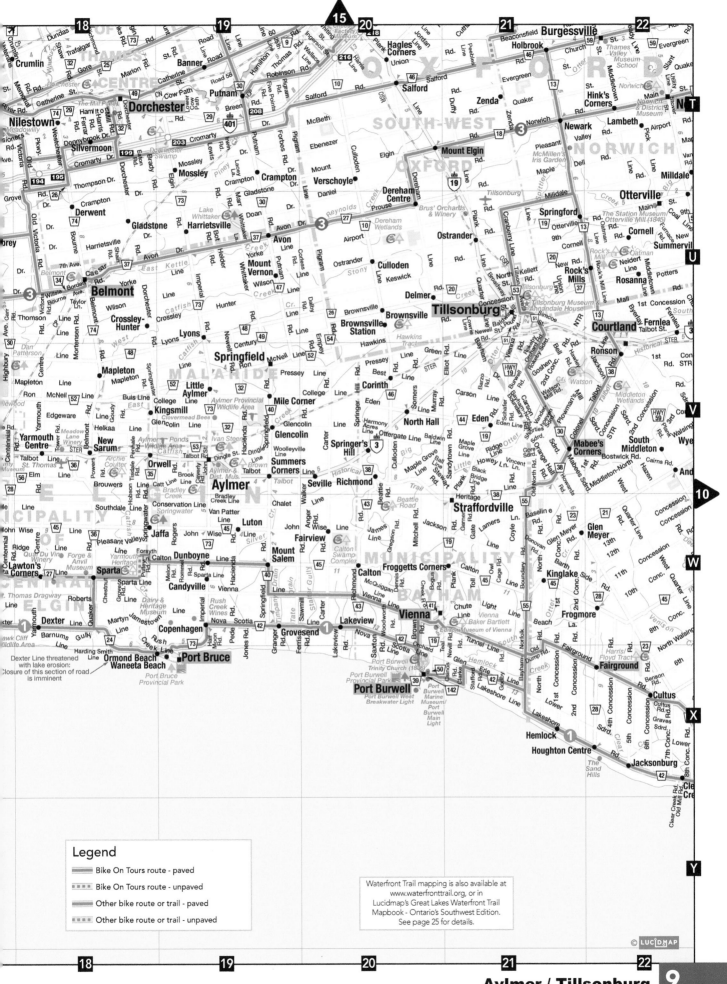

Legend

Bike On Tours route - paved
Bike On Tours route - unpaved
Other bike route or trail - paved
Other bike route or trail - unpaved

Waterfront Trail mapping is also available at
www.waterfronttrail.org, or in
Lucidmap's Great Lakes Waterfront Trail
Mapbook - Ontario's Southwest Edition.
See page 25 for details.

© LUCIDMAP

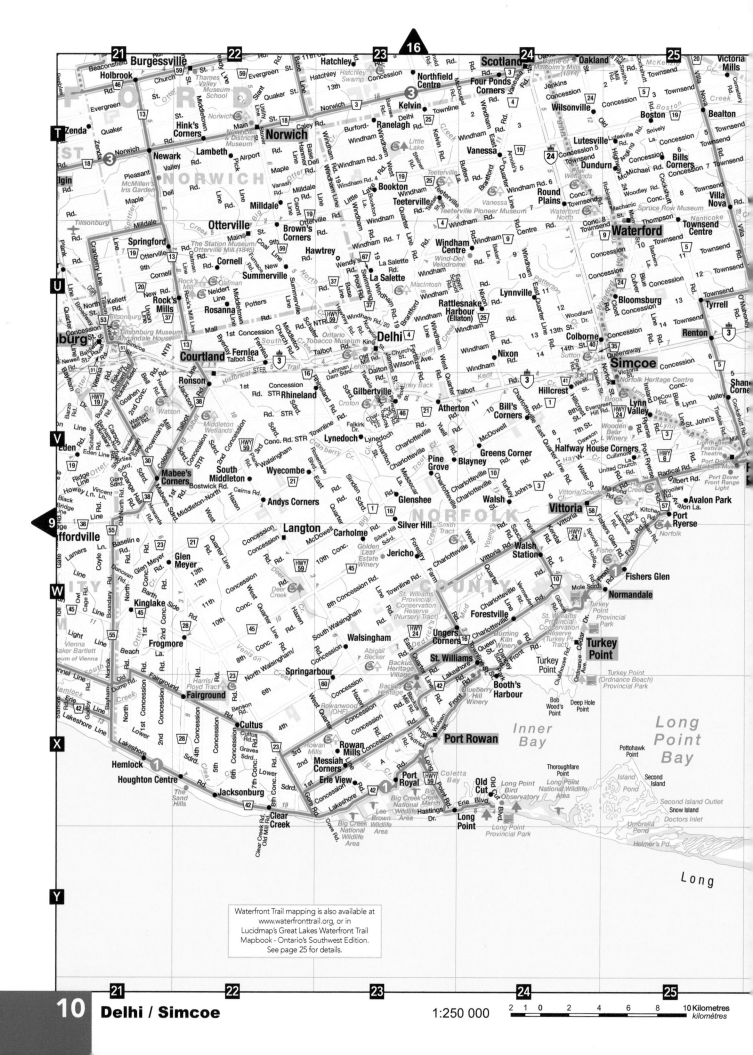

1:250 000

2 1 0 2 4 6 8 10 Kilometres
kilomètres

Waterfront Trail mapping is also available at
www.waterfronttrail.org, or in
Lucidmap's Great Lakes Waterfront Trail
Mapbook - Ontario's Southwest Edition.
See page 25 for details.

Legend

- Bike On Tours route - paved
- Bike On Tours route - unpaved
- Other bike route or trail - paved
- Other bike route or trail - unpaved

LAKE ERIE

© LUCIDMAP

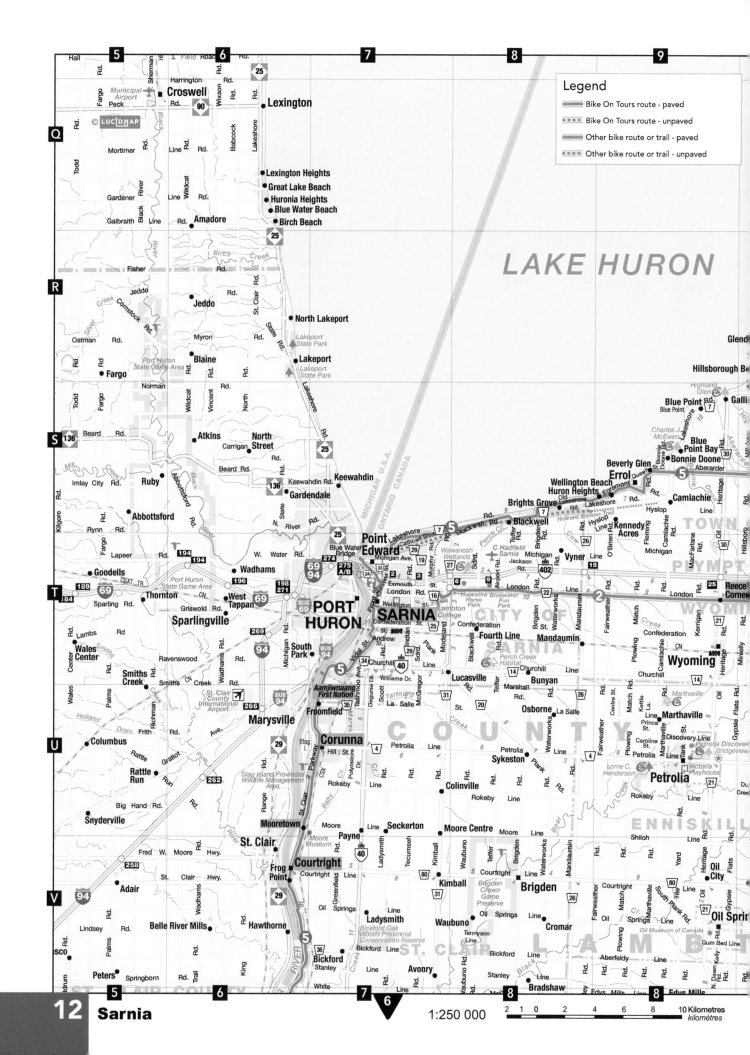

LAKE HURON

Legend
- ━━ Bike On Tours route - paved
- ┅┅ Bike On Tours route - unpaved
- ━━ Other bike route or trail - paved
- ┅┅ Other bike route or trail - unpaved

1:250 000

2 1 0 2 4 6 8 10 Kilometres
kilomètres

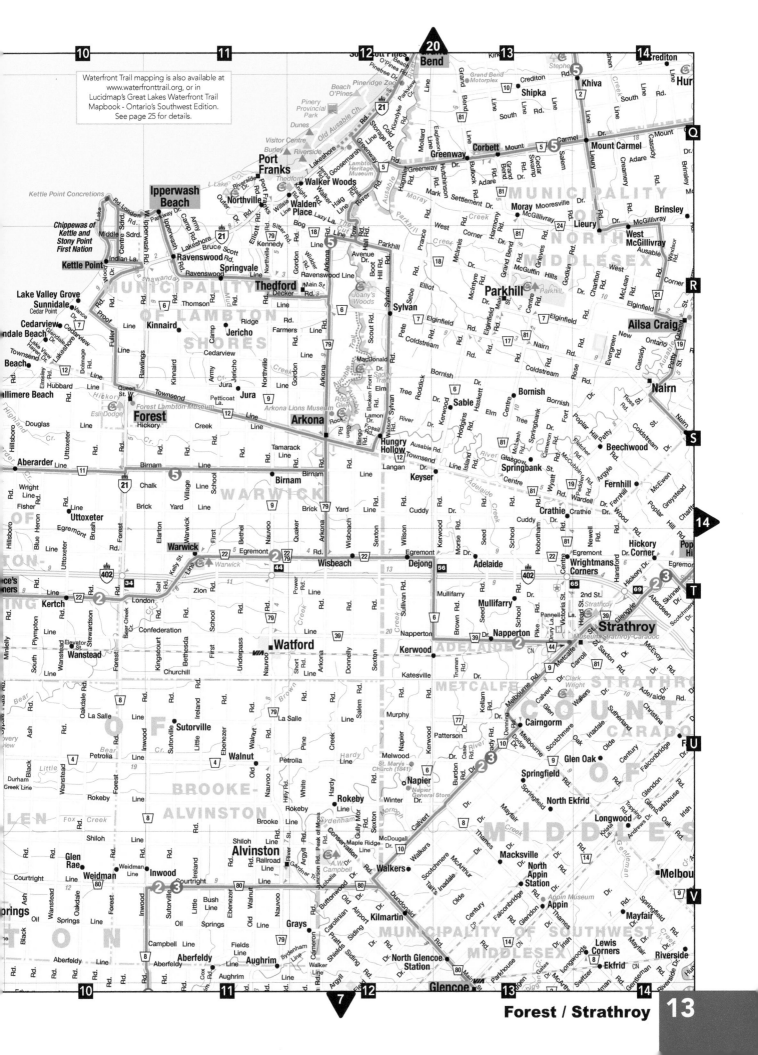

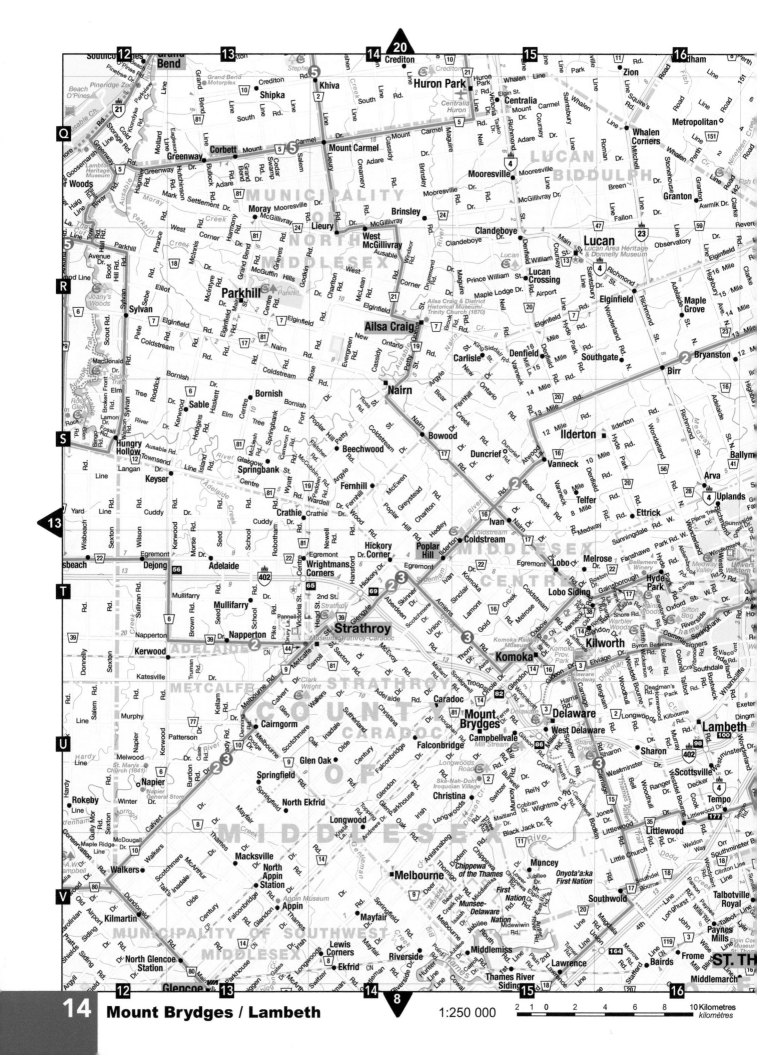

2 1 0   2   4   6   8   10 Kilometres
kilométres

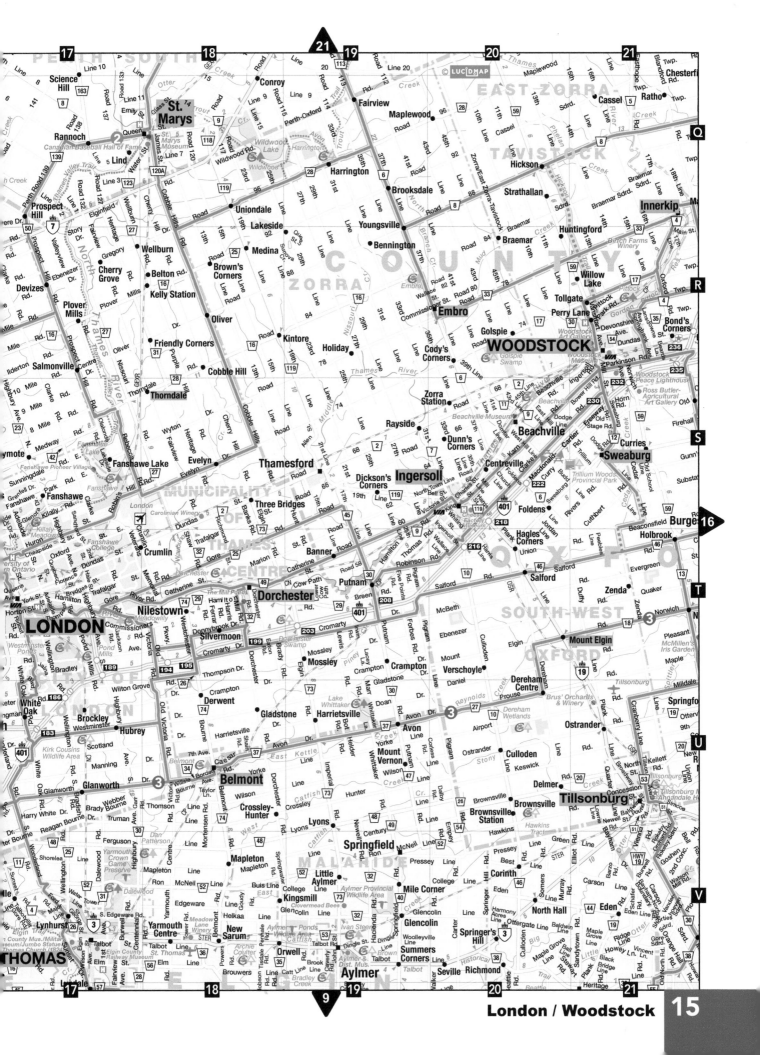

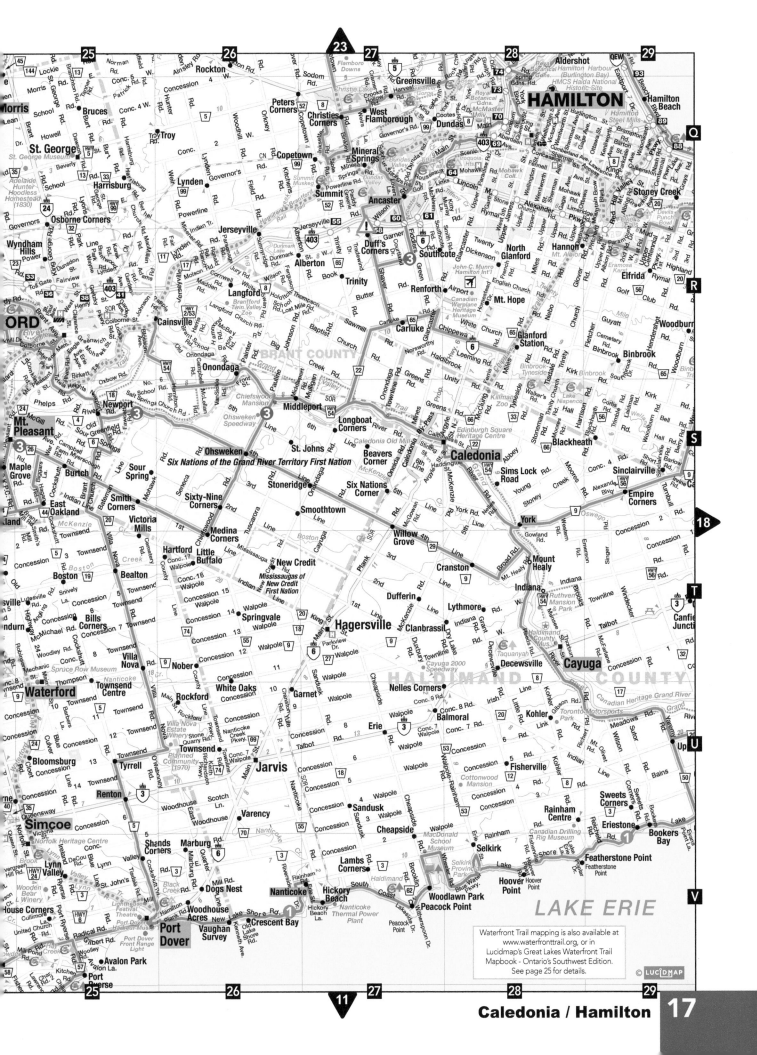

Waterfront Trail mapping is also available at
www.waterfronttrail.org, or in
Lucidmap's Great Lakes Waterfront Trail
Mapbook - Ontario's Southwest Edition.
See page 25 for details.

© LUCIDMAP

LAKE ERIE

Legend

- Bike On Tours route - paved
- Bike On Tours route - unpaved
- Other bike route or trail - paved
- Other bike route or trail - unpaved

LAKE ONTARIO

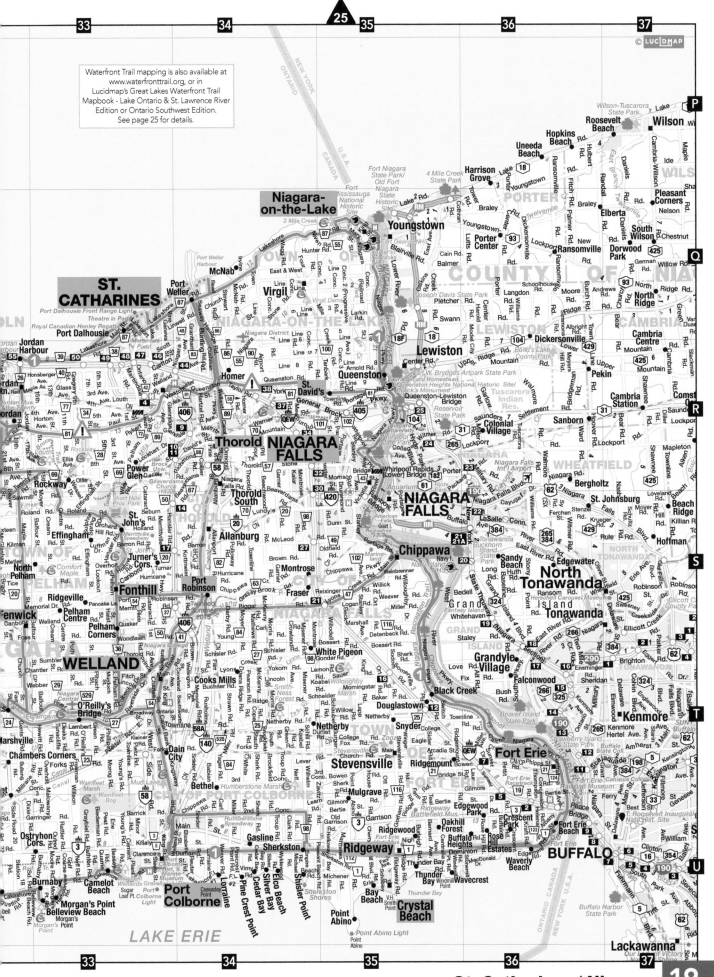

Waterfront Trail mapping is also available at www.waterfronttrail.org, or in Lucidmap's Great Lakes Waterfront Trail Mapbook - Lake Ontario & St. Lawrence River Edition or Ontario Southwest Edition. See page 25 for details.

© LUCIDMAP

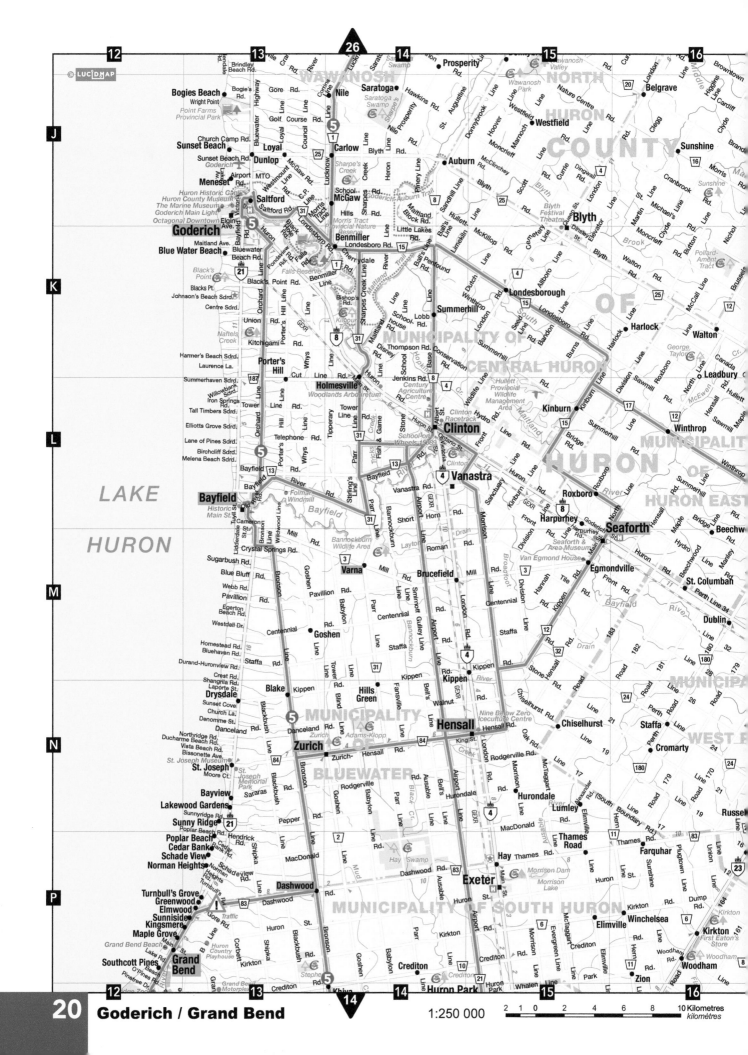

LAKE

HURON

1:250 000

2 1 0   2   4   6   8   10 Kilometres
kilométres

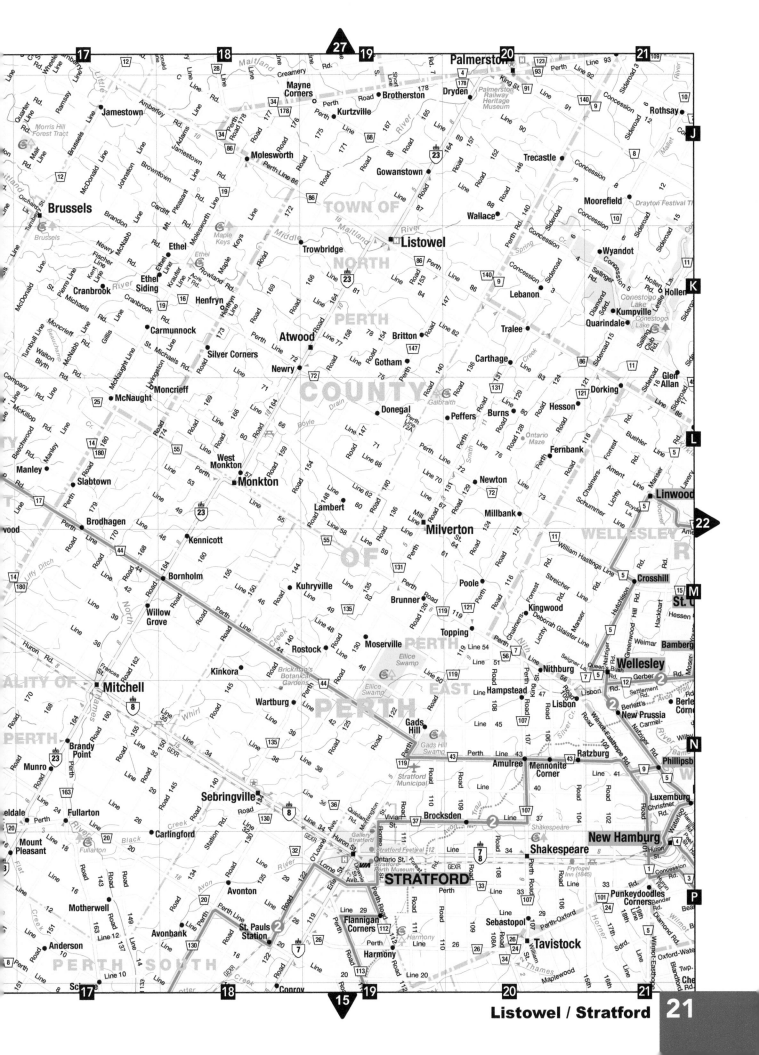

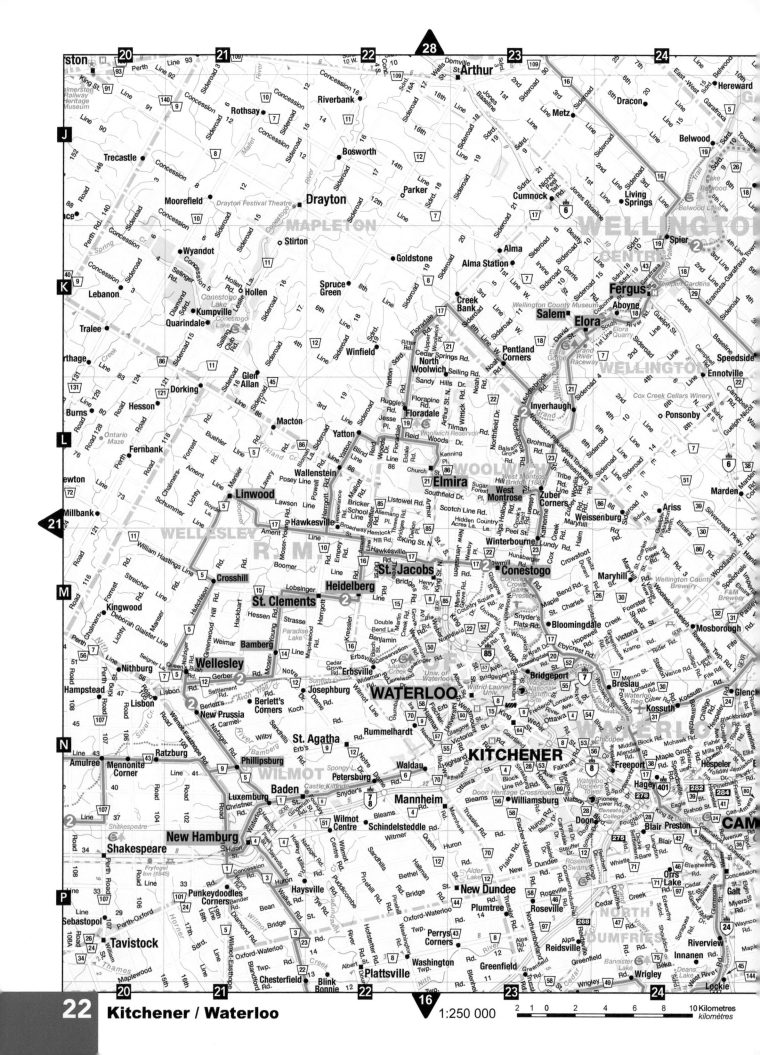

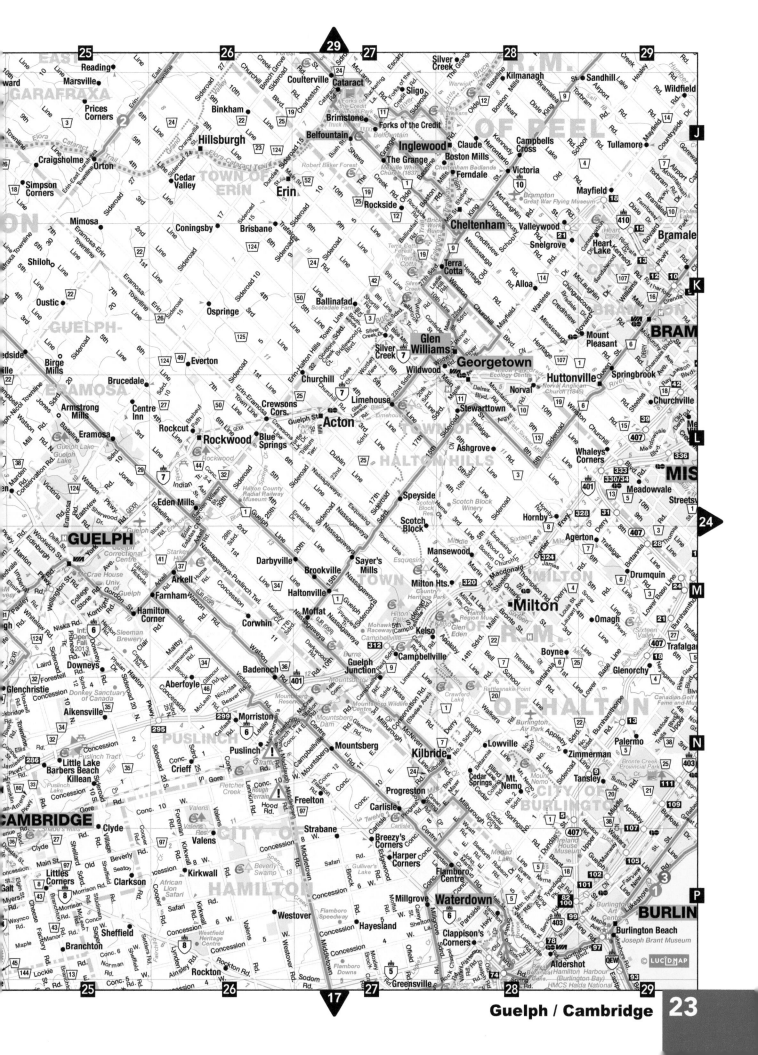

1:250 000

2 1 0 2 4 6 8 10 Kilometres
kilomètres

Legend

Bike On Tours route - paved

Bike On Tours route - unpaved

Other bike route or trail - paved

Other bike route or trail - unpaved

© LUCIDMAP

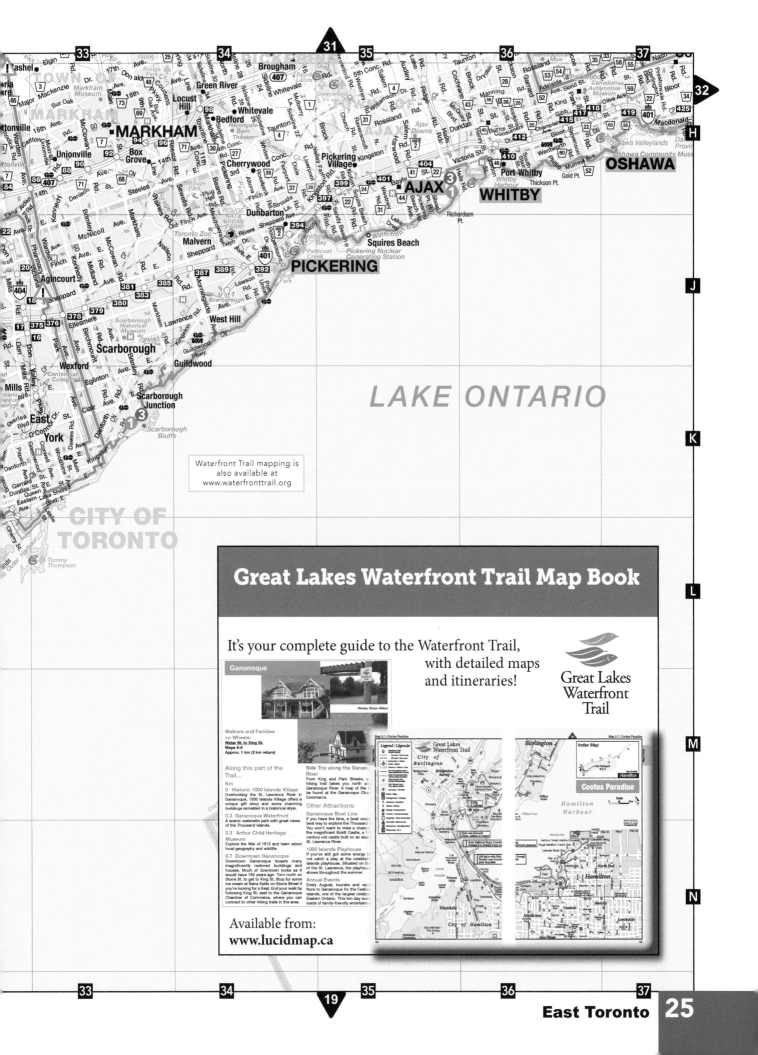

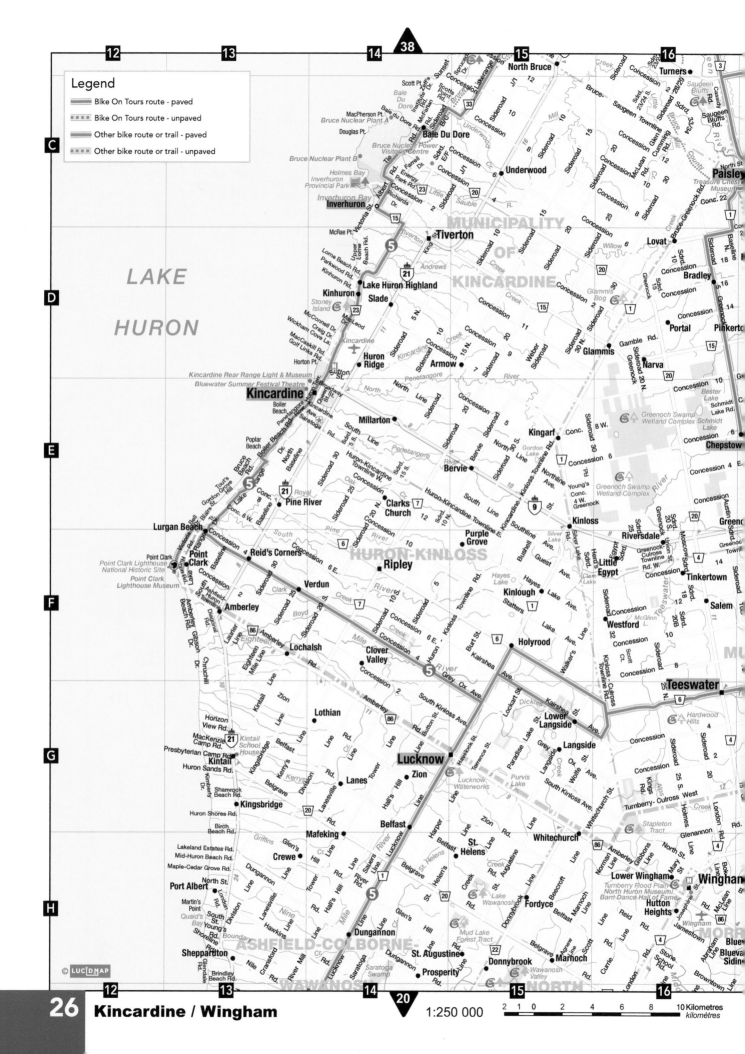

1:250 000

2 1 0 2 4 6 8 10 Kilometres
kilomètres

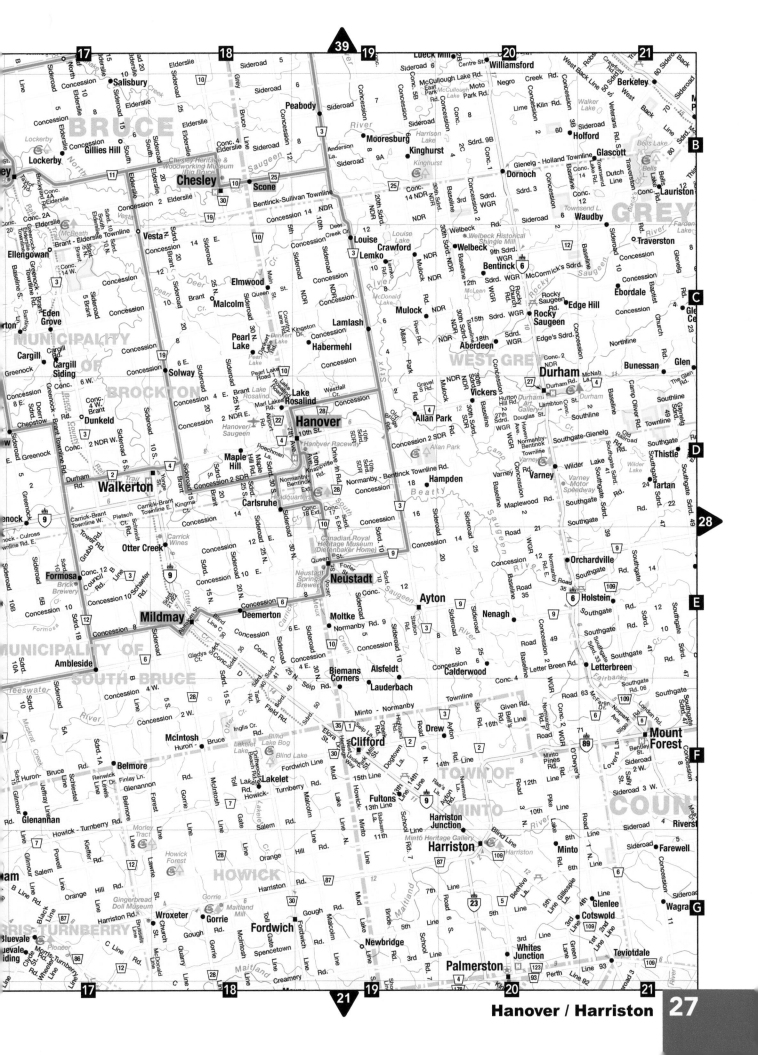

1:250 000

2 1 0 2 4 6 8 10 Kilometres
kilomètres

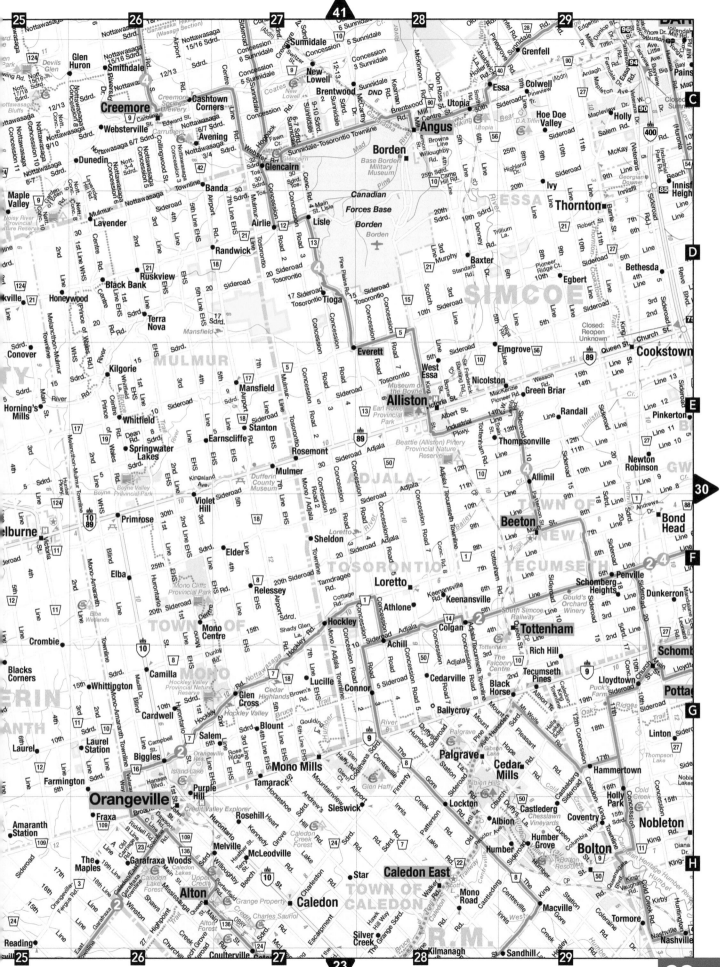

1:250 000

2 1 0 2 4 6 8 10 Kilometres
kilométres

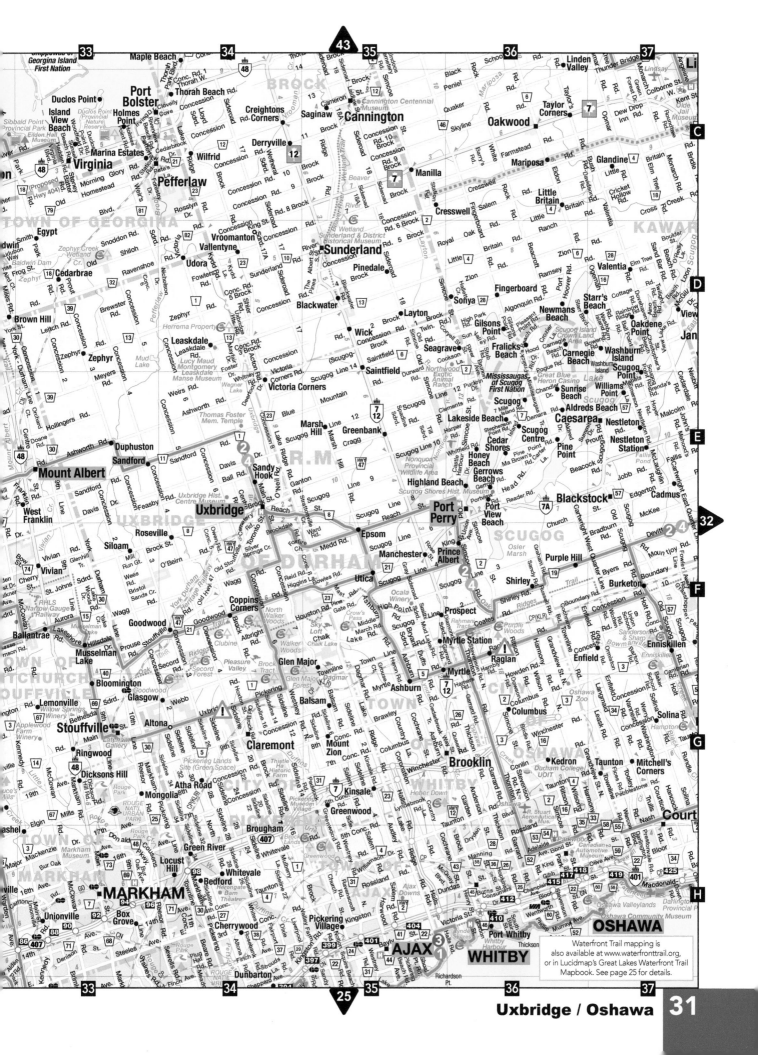

1:250 000

Legend
Bike On Tours route - paved
Bike On Tours route - unpaved
Other bike route or trail - paved
Other bike route or trail - unpaved

LAKE ONTARIO

COUNTY OF NORTHUMBERLAND

1:250 000

2 1 0   2   4   6   8   10 Kilometres
kilomètres

Legend

Bike On Tours route - paved

Bike On Tours route - unpaved

Other bike route or trail - paved

Other bike route or trail - unpaved

Waterfront Trail mapping is
also available at www.waterfronttrail.org,
or in Lucidmap's Great Lakes Waterfront Trail
Mapbook. See page 25 for details.

LAKE ONTARIO

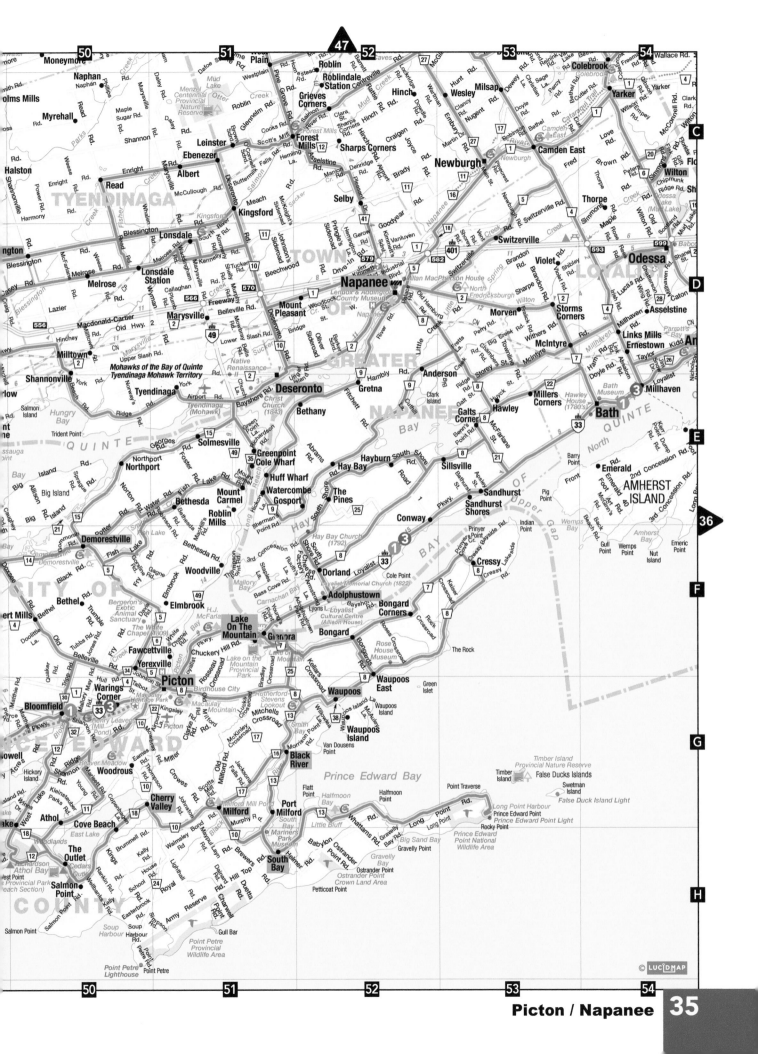

1:250 000

2 1 0 2 4 6 8 10 Kilometres
kilomètres

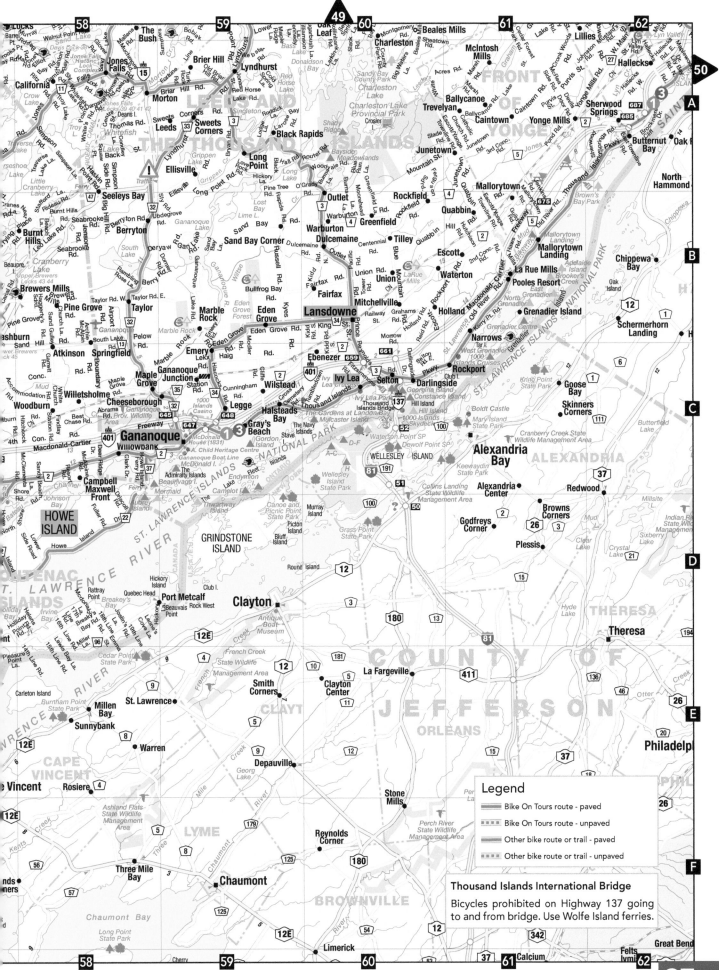

1:250 000

2 1 0   2   4   6   8   10 Kilometres
                                    kilomètres

Legend
━━━ Bike On Tours route - paved
┄┄┄ Bike On Tours route - unpaved
━━━ Other bike route or trail - paved
┄┄┄ Other bike route or trail - unpaved

LAKE HURON

© LUCIDMAP

GEORGIAN BAY

Legend
- Bike On Tours route - paved
- Bike On Tours route - unpaved
- Other bike route or trail - paved
- Other bike route or trail - unpaved

GEORGIAN BAY

NOTTAWASAGA

1:250 000

2 1 0 2 4 6 8 10 Kilometres
kilomètres

1:250 000

2 1 0 2 4 6 8 10 Kilometres
kilomètres

Legend

Bike On Tours route - paved
Bike On Tours route - unpaved
Other bike route or trail - paved
Other bike route or trail - unpaved

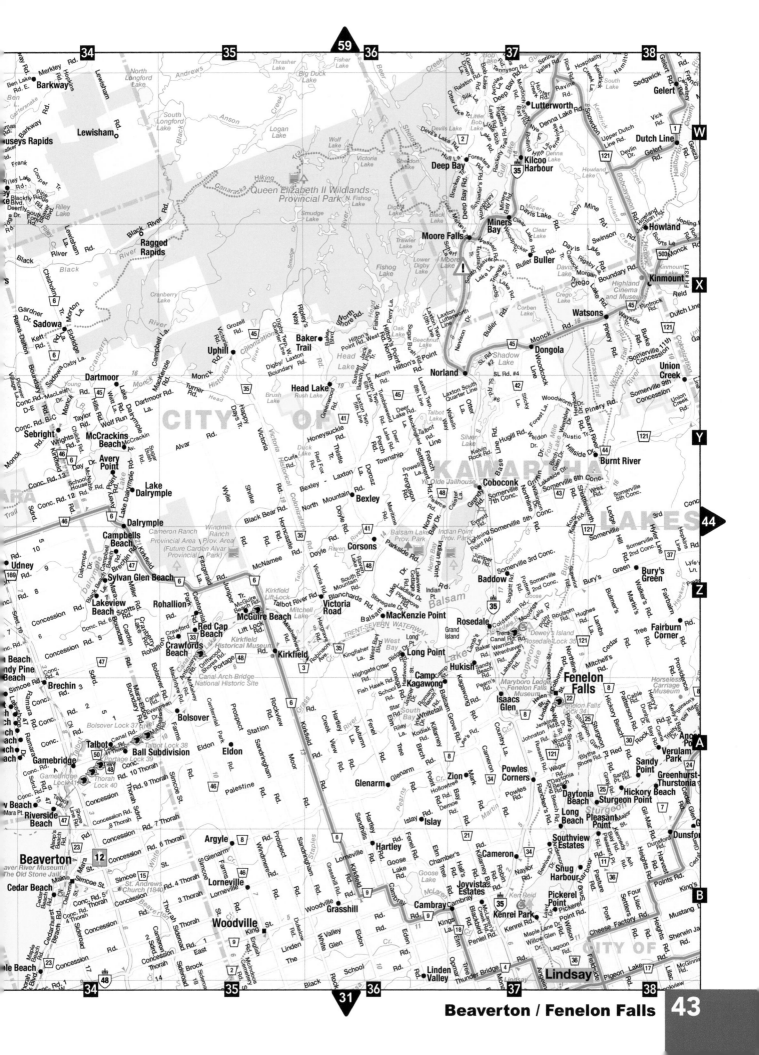

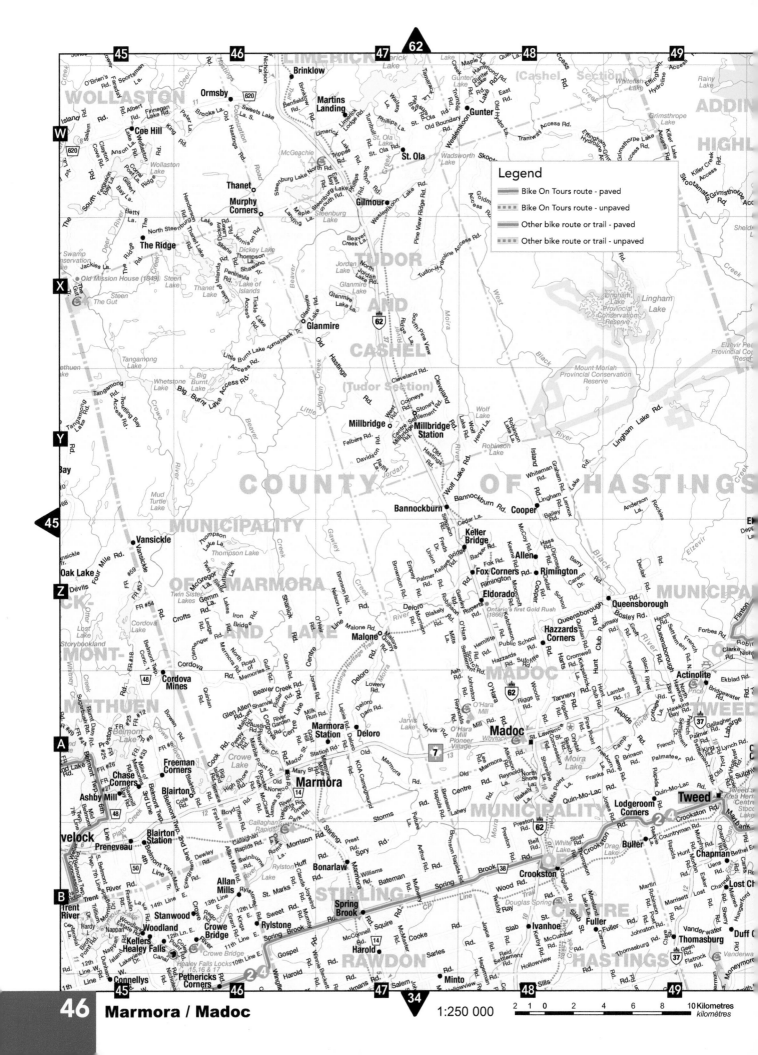

1:250 000

2 1 0 2 4 6 8   10 Kilometres
kilomètres

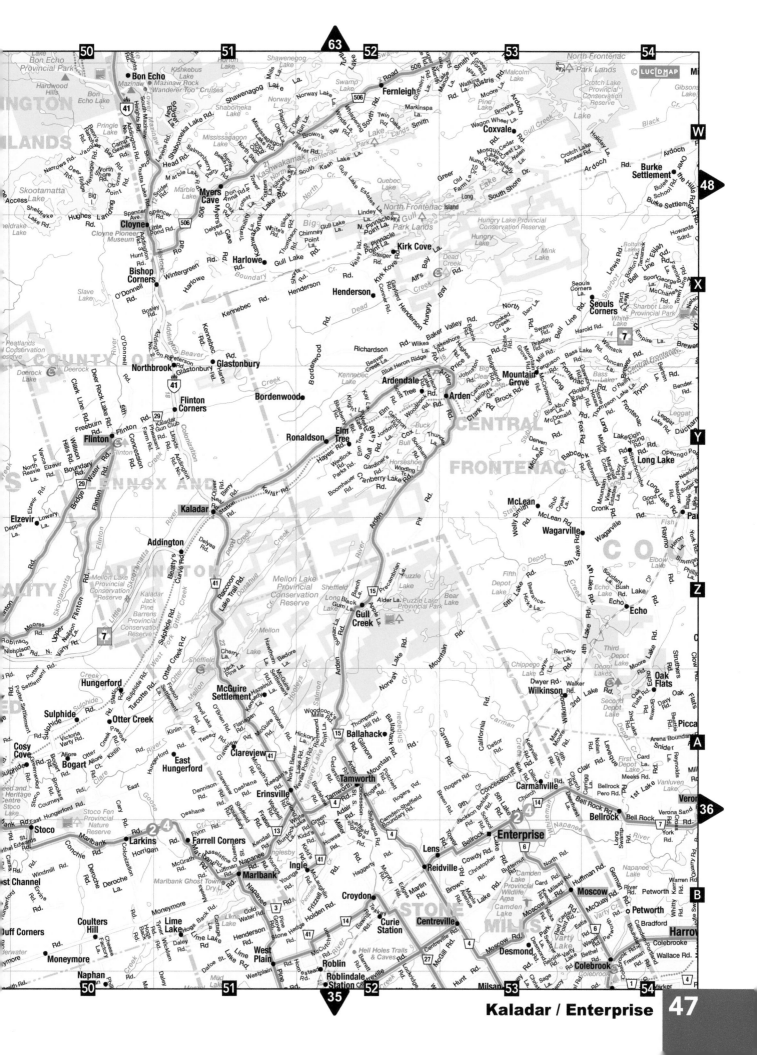

1:250 000

2 1 0 2 4 6 8 10 Kilometres
kilomètres

© LUCIDMAP

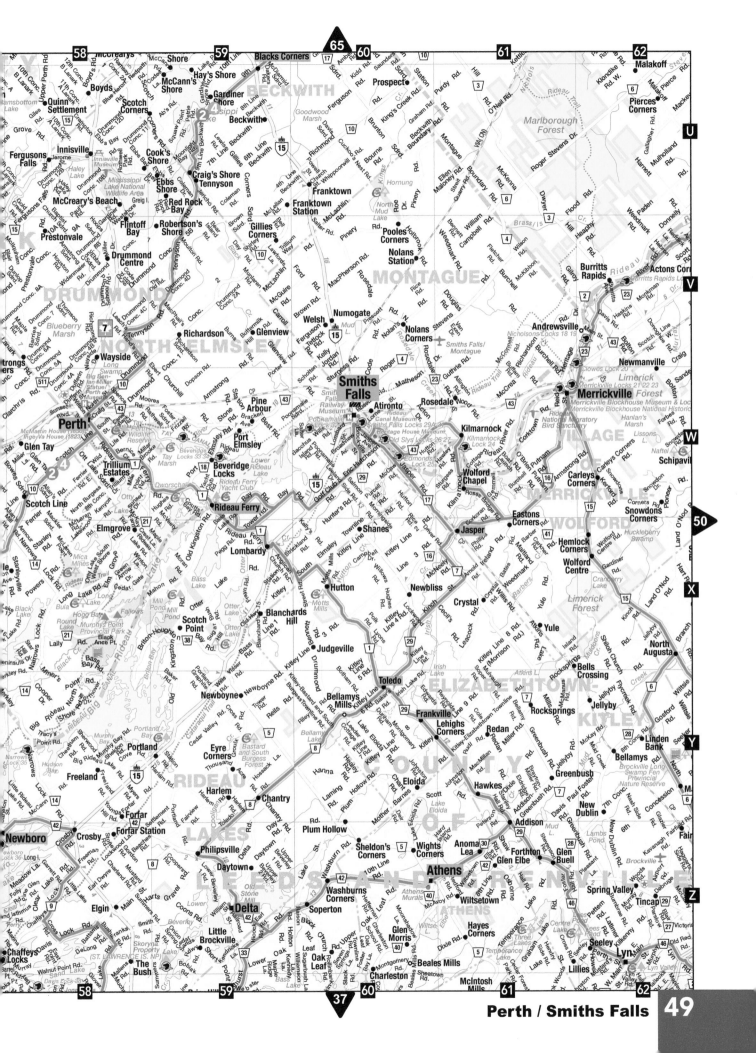

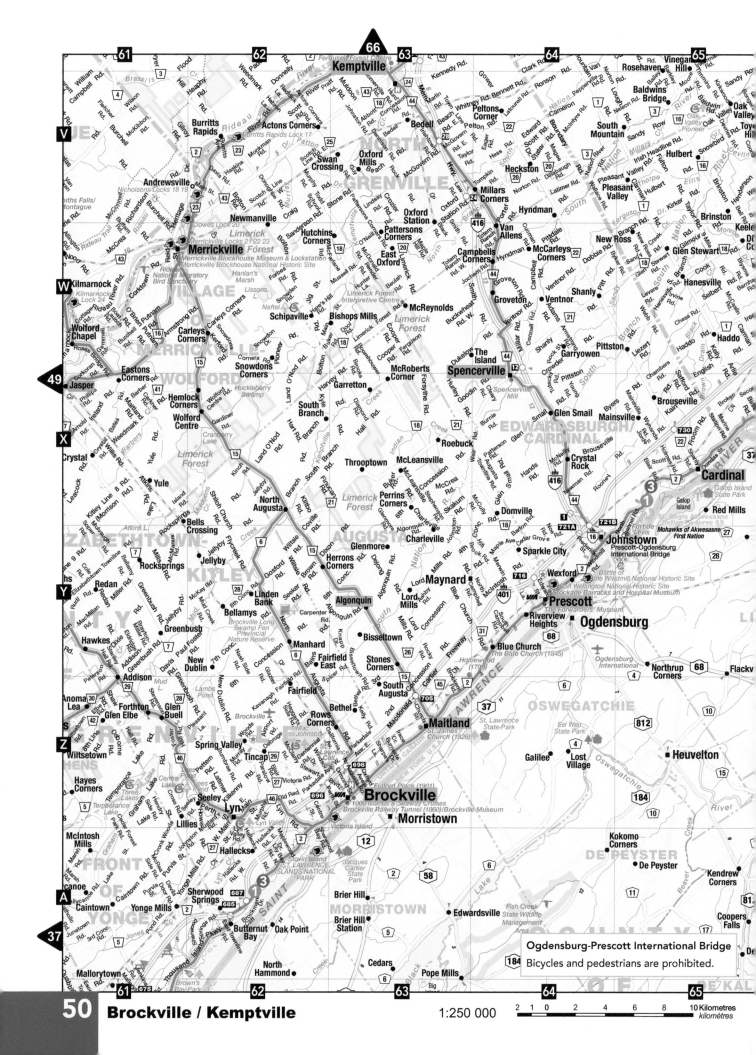

1:250 000

2 1 0 2 4 6 8 10 Kilometres
kilomètres

Ogdensburg-Prescott International Bridge
Bicycles and pedestrians are prohibited.

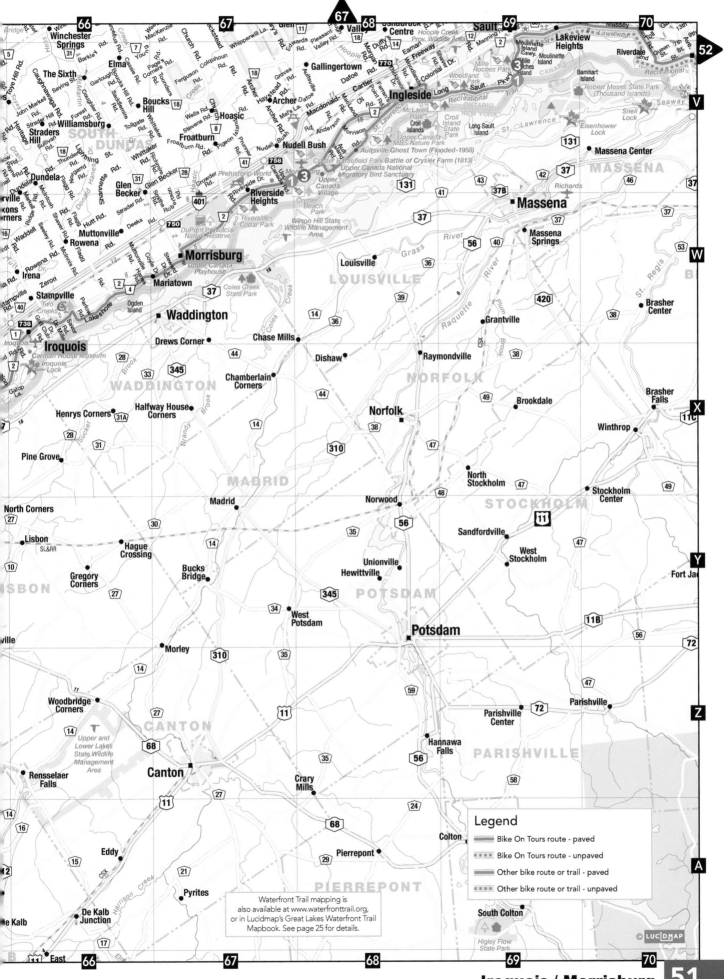

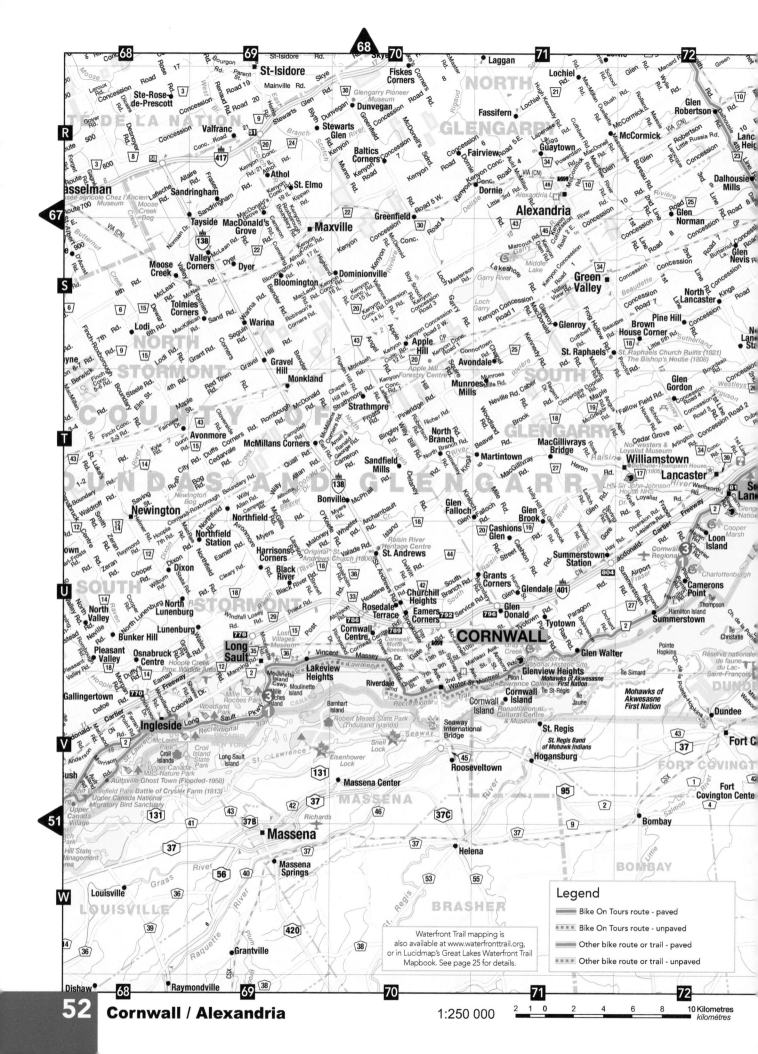

Legend

━━━━ Bike On Tours route - paved

▪▪▪▪ Bike On Tours route - unpaved

━━━━ Other bike route or trail - paved

▪▪▪▪ Other bike route or trail - unpaved

Waterfront Trail mapping is
also available at www.waterfronttrail.org,
or in Lucidmap's Great Lakes Waterfront Trail
Mapbook. See page 25 for details.

2 1 0   2   4   6   8   10 Kilometres
                                        kilométres

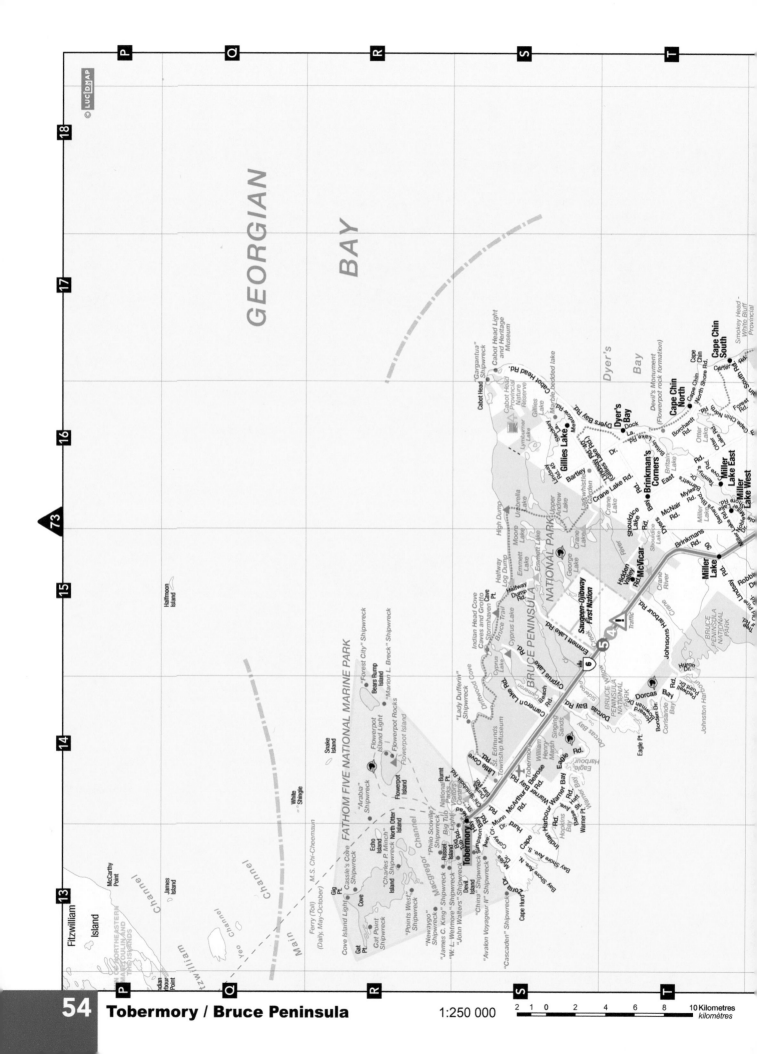

GEORGIAN

BAY

FATHOM FIVE NATIONAL MARINE PARK

"Forest City" Shipwreck

Bears Rump Island

"Marion L. Breck" Shipwreck

Flowerpot Island Light

Flowerpot Rocks

Snake Island

White Shingle

Halfmoon Island

M.S. Chi-Cheemaun

Ferry (Toll) (Daily, May–October)

Main Channel

Yeo Channel

Channel

"Arabia" Shipwreck

Cove Island Light

Cassie's Cove Shipwreck

Gig Pt.

Gat Pt.

Cove

Gat Point Shipwreck

Echo Island

"Charles P. Minch" Shipwreck

North Otter Island

"Points West" Shipwreck

"Newaygo" Shipwreck

"James C. King" Shipwreck

"W. L. Wetmore" Shipwreck

"John Walters" Shipwreck

"Avalon Voyageur II" Shipwreck

"Cascaden" Shipwreck

Macgregor Channel

Russel Island

Devil Island

"China" Shipwreck

Zora Cr.

Cape Hurd

Flowerpot Island

Burnt Pt.

National Parks Visitors Centre

Big Tub Light

Tobermory

"Philo Scoville" Shipwreck

"Lady Dufferin" Shipwreck

Driftwood Cove

Indian Head Cove Caves and Grotto

Stormhaven Cave Pt.

Bruce Trail

Cyprus Lake

Cyprus Lake Rd.

Cameron Lake Rd.

St. Edmunds Township Museum

Little Cove Rd.

Little Cove

Cyprus Lake Beach Rd.

Cabot Head "Gargantua" Shipwreck

Cabot Head

Cabot Head Provincial Nature Reserve

Cabot Head Light and Heritage Museum

Cabot Head Rd.

Marble bedded lake

Dyer's Bay

Gillies Lake

Lymburner Lake

High Dump

Moore Lake

Umbrella Lake

Emmett Lake

Halfway Log Dump

Halfway Dump Rd.

George Lake

Crane Lake

Crane Lake Rd.

BRUCE PENINSULA NATIONAL PARK

Saugeen-Ojibway First Nation

Emmett Lake Rd.

Upper Andrew Lake

Gillies Lake Rd.

Stokes Lake

Dyers Bay Rd.

Dock La.

Dyer's Bay

Devil's Monument (Flowerpot rock formation)

Smokey Head – White Bluff Provincial

Cape Chin South

Carter

Cape Chin

Cape Chin North Shore Rd.

Cape Chin North

Borchardt Rd.

Otter Lake

Miller Lake East

Miller Lake West

Brinkman's Corners

Bartley

Lindsay

Glen

McNair Rd.

Shouldice Lake Rd.

Shouldice Lake

Hidden Valley Rd.

McVicar

Crane River

Brinkmans Rd.

Miller Lake

Miller Lake Rd.

Johnsons

Dorcas

Dorcas Bay Rd.

Dorcas Bay

Bordern Dr.

Singing Sands

William Henry Rd.

Eagle Rd.

Eagle Bay

Eagle Pt.

Warner Bay

Warner Bay Rd.

Warner Pt.

Hopkins Bay Ave.

Harbour Rd.

McArthur Rd.

Hay Bay Rd.

Indian Cape

Bay Shore Ave. N.

Bay Shore Ave. S.

Corey Ct.

Cape Hurd Rd.

Myles

Hurd

Johnston Harbour

Huron Dr.

Pedwell Point Dr.

Constande Dr.

BRUCE PENINSULA NATIONAL PARK

Howard Bowman Point Rd.

Bruce Willow Point Rd.

96

5 4 !

6

Traffic

Harbour Rd.

Lindsay

Fitzwilliam Island

NORTH CHANNEL OF LAKE HURON – NORTHEASTERN MANITOULIN ISLAND AND THE ISLANDS

McCarthy Point

James Island

Indian Harbour Point

Fitzwilliam

continued in inset

LAKE

HURON

Legend

Bike On Tours route - paved

Bike On Tours route - unpaved

Other bike route or trail - paved

Other bike route or trail - unpaved

continued from far right

Legend

Bike On Tours route - paved
Bike On Tours route - unpaved
Other bike route or trail - paved
Other bike route or trail - unpaved

© LUCIDMAP

1:250 000

2 1 0 2 4 6 8 10 Kilometres
kilomètres

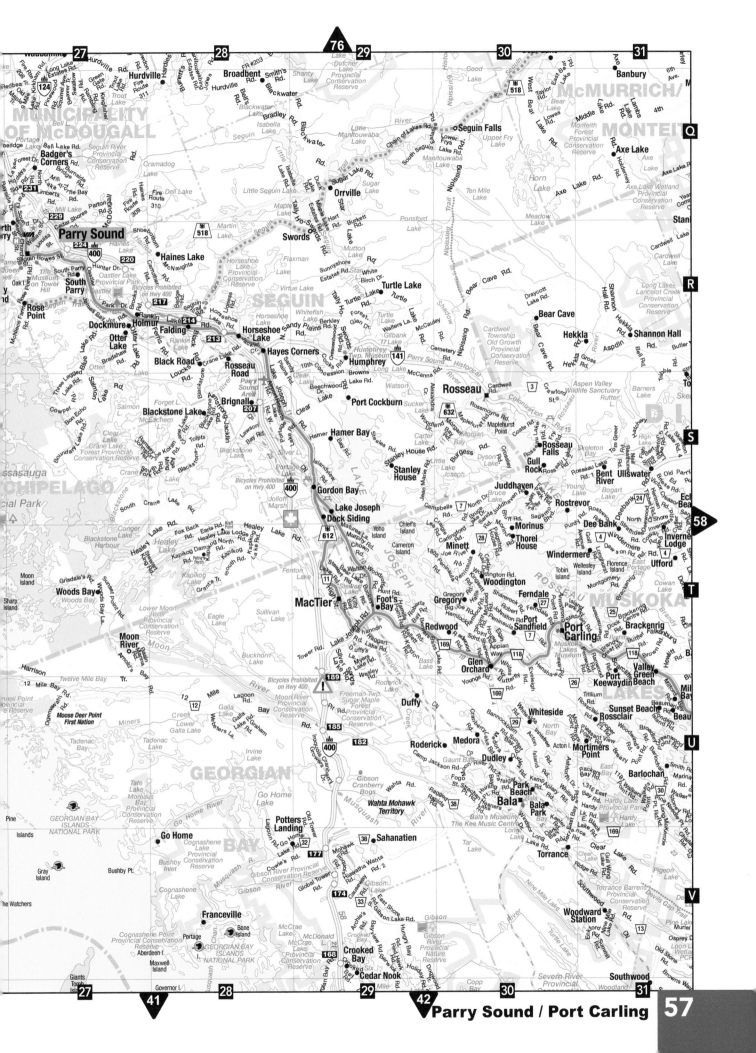

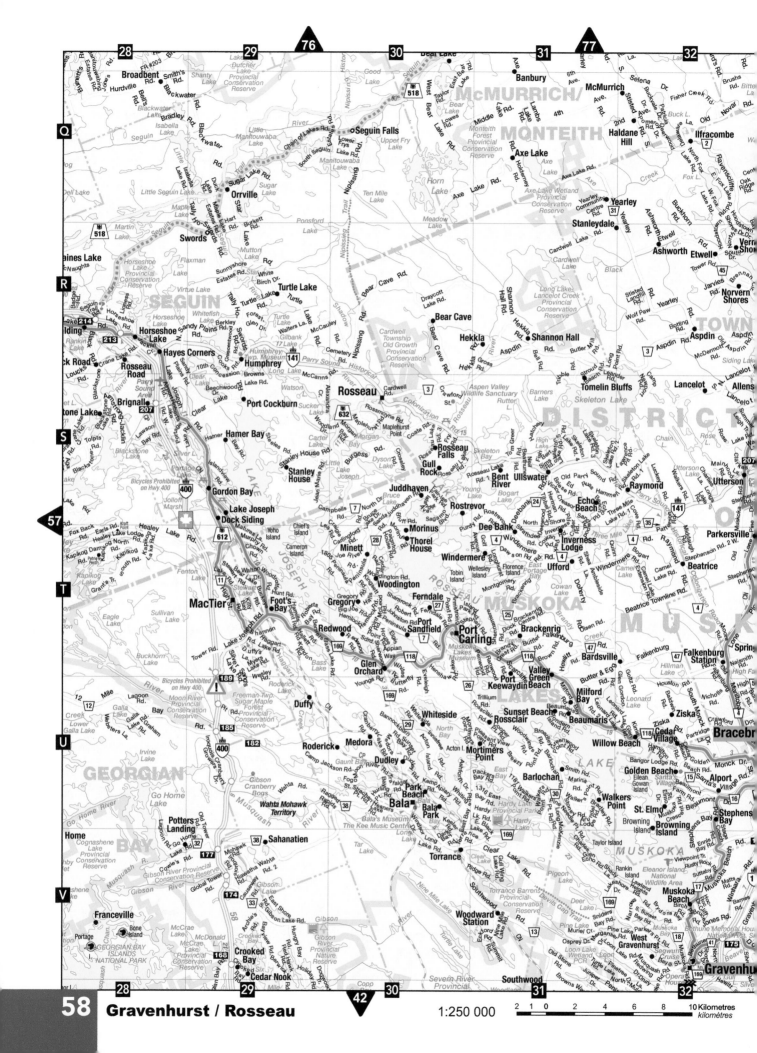

1:250 000

2 1 0 2 4 6 8 10 Kilometres
kilomètres

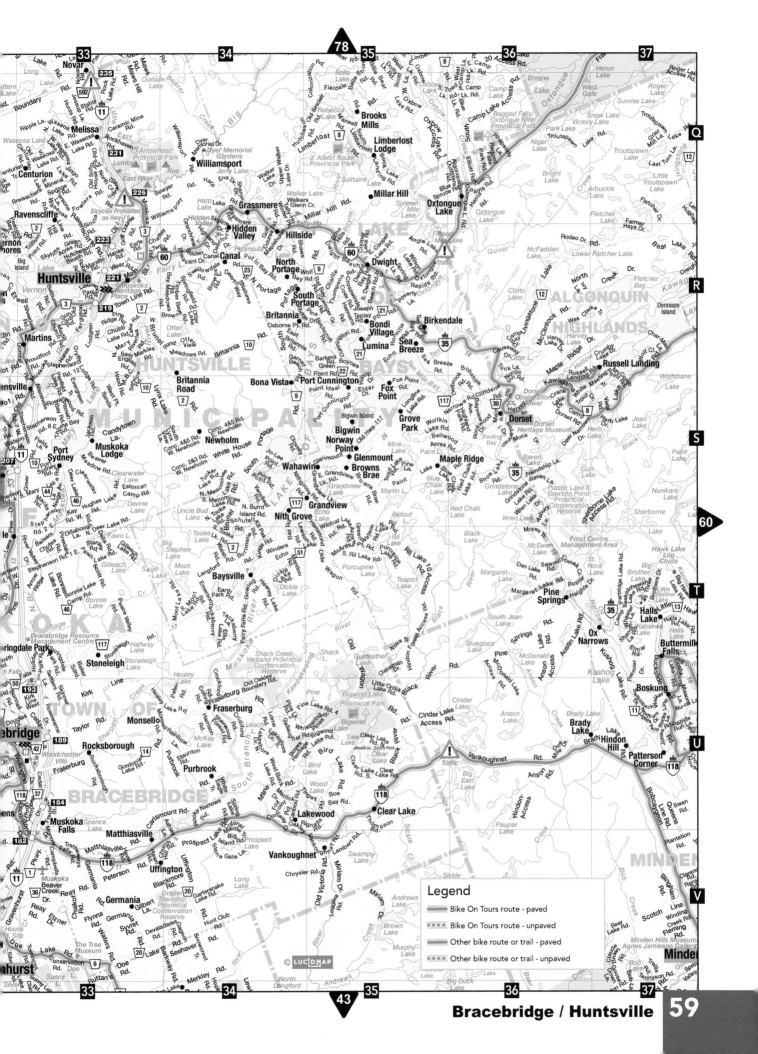

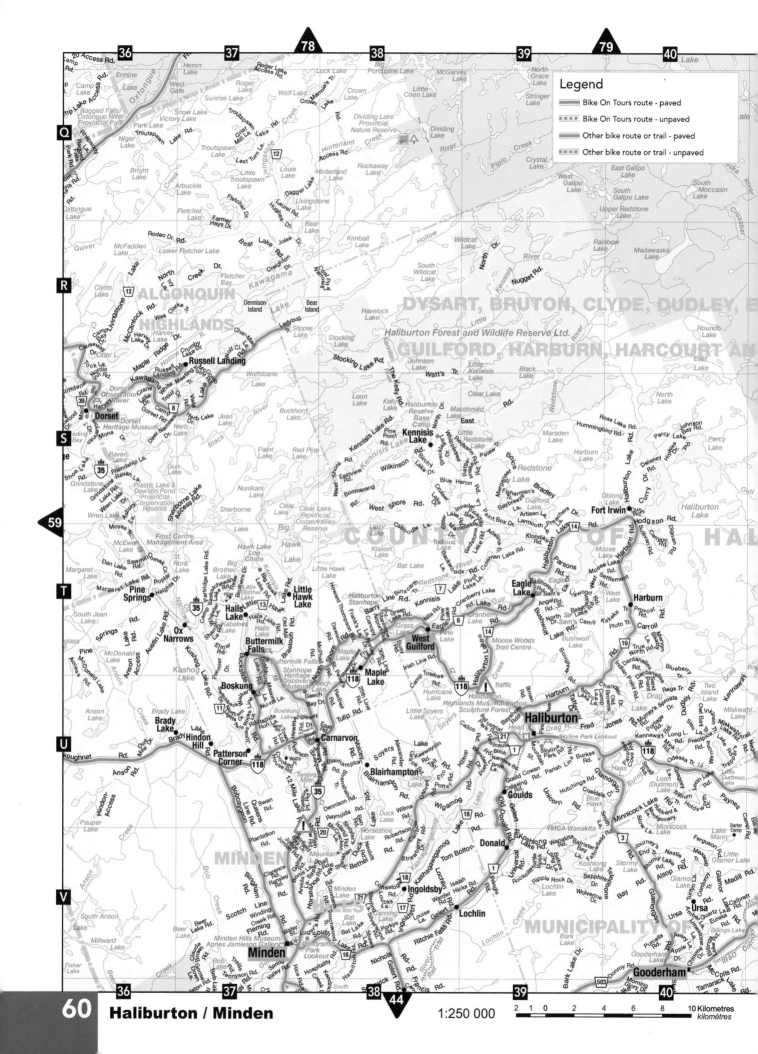

1:250 000

2 1 0   2   4   6   8   10 Kilometres
                                                        kilomètres

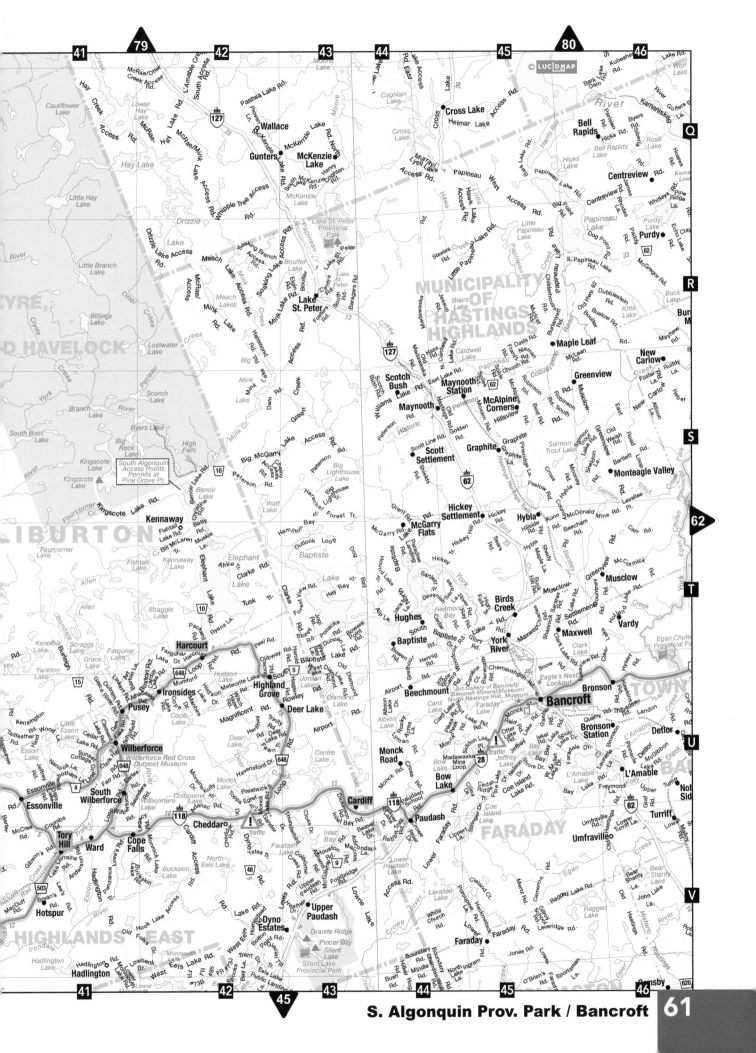

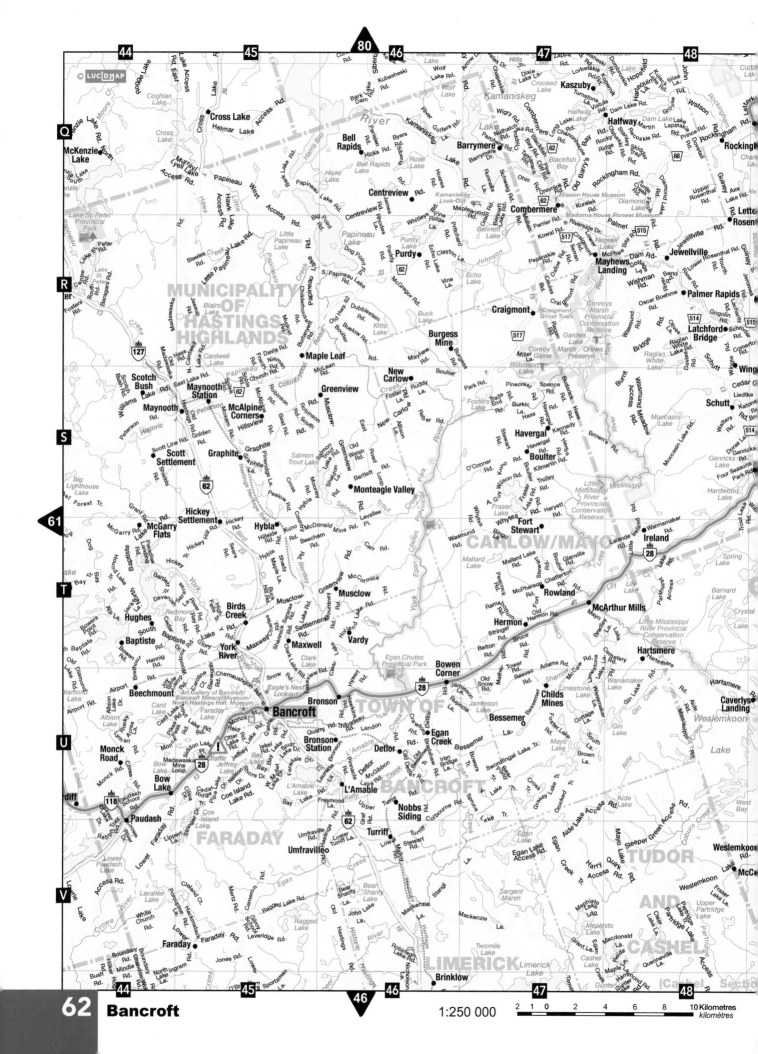

1:250 000

2 1 0   2   4   6   8   10 Kilometres
kilomètres

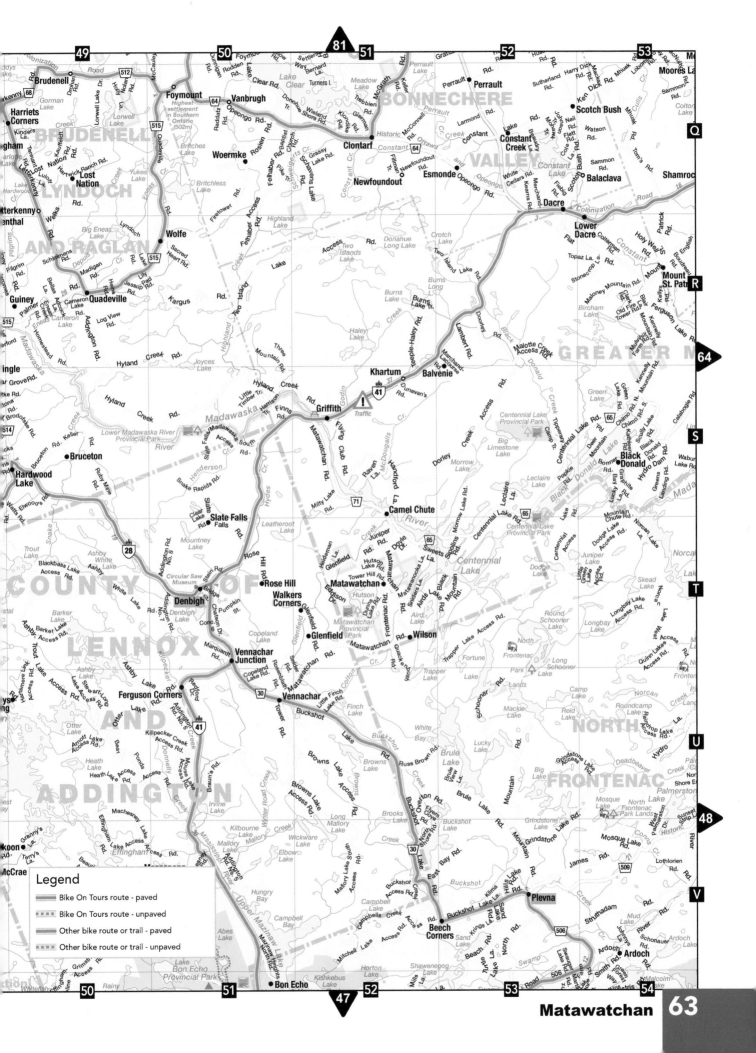

Legend

Bike On Tours route - paved
Bike On Tours route - unpaved
Other bike route or trail - paved
Other bike route or trail - unpaved

Matawatchan 63

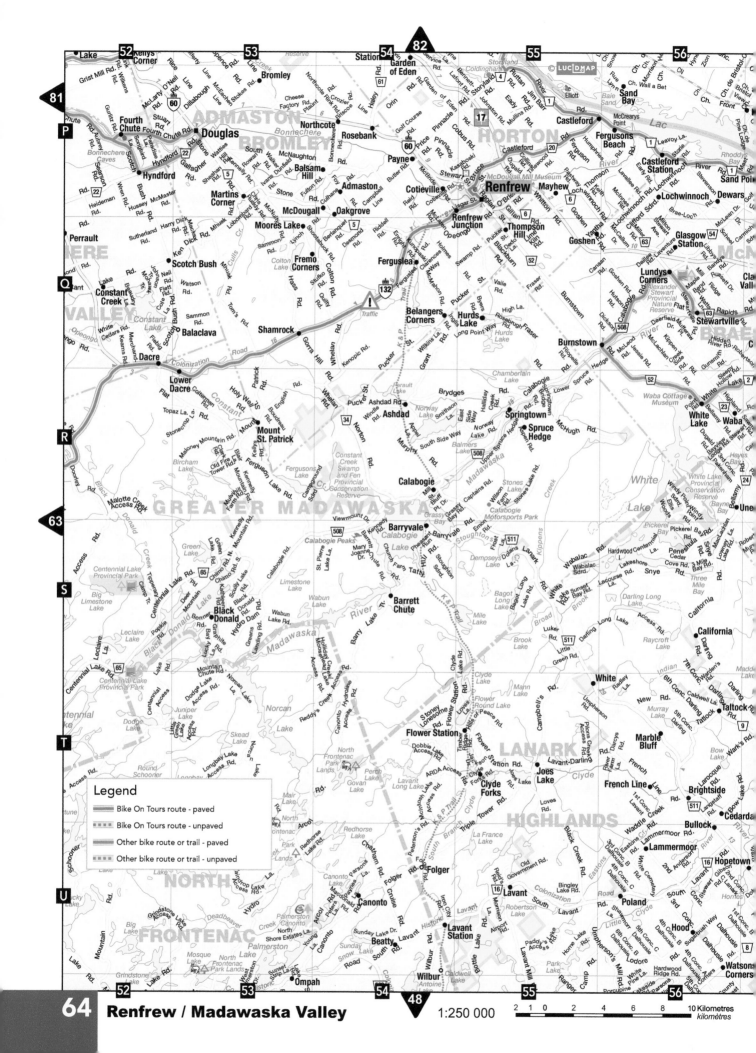

Lake

Grist Mill Rd.

Bromley

Garden of Eden
Station

ADMASTON
BROMLEY

Fourth Chute
Douglas

Northcote
Rosebank

Payne

Renfrew

Mayhew

HORTON

Castleford
Fergusons Beach
Castleford Station
Sand Point
Sand Bay

Hyndford

Balsam Hill

Admaston

Cotieville

Renfrew Junction

Thompson Hill

Goshen

Lochwinnoch
Dewars

Martins Corner
McDougall
Oakgrove

Moores Lake

Glasgow Station

Perrault

Scotch Bush

Fremo Corners

Ferguslea

Lundys Corners

Stewartville

Q

Constant Creek

Balaclava

Shamrock

Belangers Corners
Hurds Lake

Burnstown

White Lake
Waba

Dacre

Lower Dacre

Ashdad

Springtown
Spruce Hedge

R

Mount St. Patrick

Calabogie

63

Black Donald

Barryvale

Barrett Chute

Barryvale

Wabalac

California

S

California

Flower Station

White

Marble Bluff

Taltock

T

Flower Station

Joes Lake

French Line

Brightside

Clyde Forks

LANARK

HIGHLANDS

Bullock

Cedarda

Folger

Lammermoor

Hopetown

North
Frontenac

Canonto

Lavant

Poland

U

Beatty

Lavant Station

Hood

Ompah

Wilbur

Watsons Corners

Legend

- Bike On Tours route - paved
- Bike On Tours route - unpaved
- Other bike route or trail - paved
- Other bike route or trail - unpaved

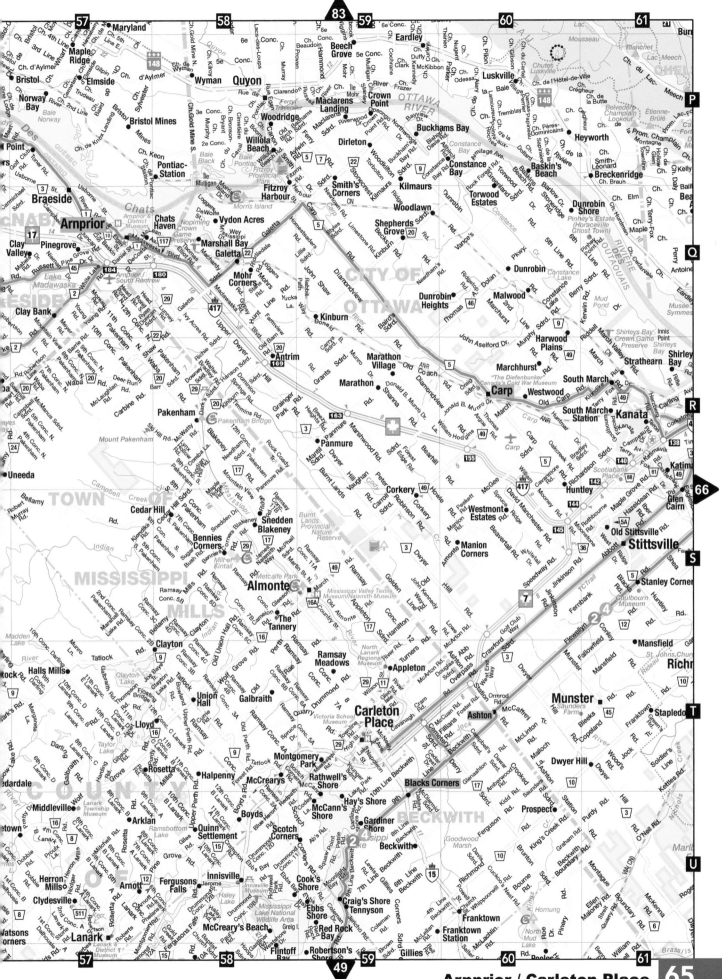

1:250 000

2 1 0 2 4 6 8 10 Kilometres
kilomètres

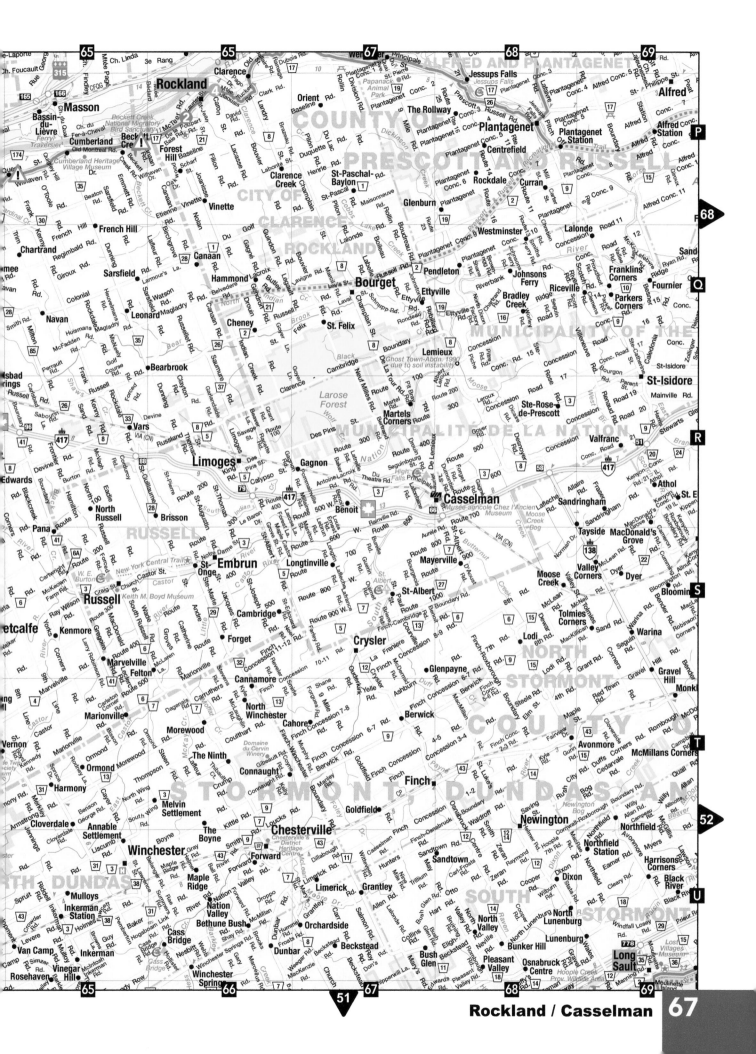

1:250 000

2 1 0 2 4 6 8 10 Kilometres
kilomètres

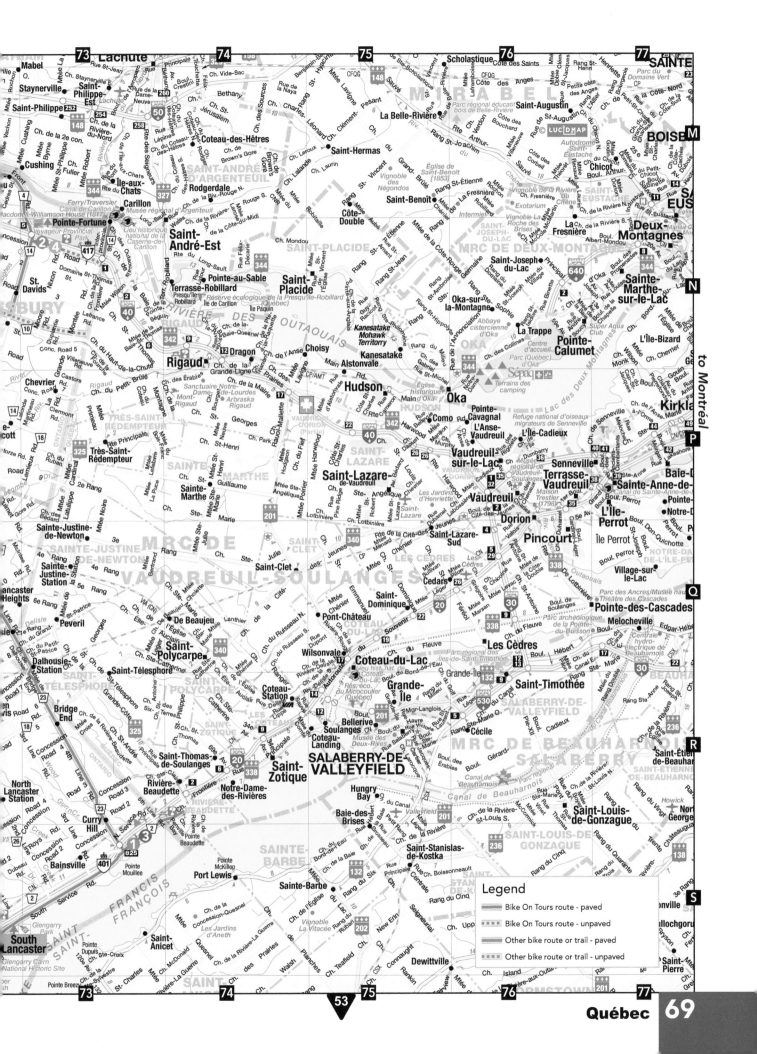

ONTARIO CANADA
MICHIGAN U.S.A.

Glen Cove
Glen Point

DRUMMOND
ISLAND

Thompson Point

Monk Point

Pitman Point

Robb's
Lake

False Detour Channel

Cockburn
Island
First
Nation

14th Conc.

12th   Concession

Tolsma
Bay

Ross
Point

Robinson Bay

Devil's
Horn

Big
Bay

Crescent Island

TOWN OF NORTHEASTERN
MANITOULIN AND THE ISLANDS

Batture
Island

West
Point

Boat Harbour

Vidal Island

Arthur
Point

Harold
Point

Meldrum
Bay

Creasor
Bight

Vidal Bay

COCKBURN

20th Sdrd.
15th Sdrd.
W St.
10th Sideroad
Water St.

Tolsmaville (Cockburn Island)

I St.
L St.

Mississagi Strait

Gravy
Lake

Maggies
Sdrd.

Wasnage
Rd.

Water St.

Meldrum Bay
Net Shed
Museum

Linda
Lake

Pothole
Lake

Maple
Lake

Essing Rd.

Herschell
Island

Little
Kitchener
Island

Kitchener
Island

ISLAND

Wagoose Lake

COCKBURN   ISLAND

McCaigs
Hill
7th-8th Concession

Scotch
Block

Cinder
Point

Totten
Lake

Cemetery Rd.

Joyce Rd.

Mississagi
West
Bass
Lake   Lighthouse

Young
Lake

Rd.

Wickett
Lake

Whitesea Rd.

Burnett
Lake

Kerr Lake
Dump Rd.

540

Hog
Lake

28

Wagoose
Bay

Station
Point

Pulpwood
Point

Hindman Bay

Sand Lake

Sand Rd.

15th Sideroad

Ricketts
Harbour

Sand
Bay

Boom
Point

There is no ferry service
to Cockburn Island.
Visitors must arrange
their own transport.

Mississagi Lighthouse
Heritage Park & Museum
Carter
Lake

Falls
Lake Rd.

Falls
Lake

Lily
Lake Rd.

Lily
Lake

Loon
Lake

Falls

Dawson

Quarry
Bay

Steevens
Island

Greene
Island

Quarry
Point

TOWN OF NORTHEASTERN
MANITOULIN AND THE ISLANDS

Twin
Lakes

West Belanger Bay

East Belanger Bay

Dorny Grant Rd.

Beaver
Meadow
Lakes

The Queen Elizabeth
The Queen
Mother M'Nidoo M'Nissing
Provincial Park

Girouard
Point

Rickley
Point

Burnt Island
Harbour

Burnt
Island

Western
Duck
Island

Blake Point

TOWN OF NORTHEAST
MANITOULIN AND THE IS

Middle
Duck
Island

Bluff Point

Desert P

Horseshoe
Bay

Duck
Island

Grave

ONTARIO
MICHIGAN

CANADA
U.S.A.

© LUCIDMAP

1:250 000

2 1 0   2   4   6   8   10 Kilometres
kilomètres

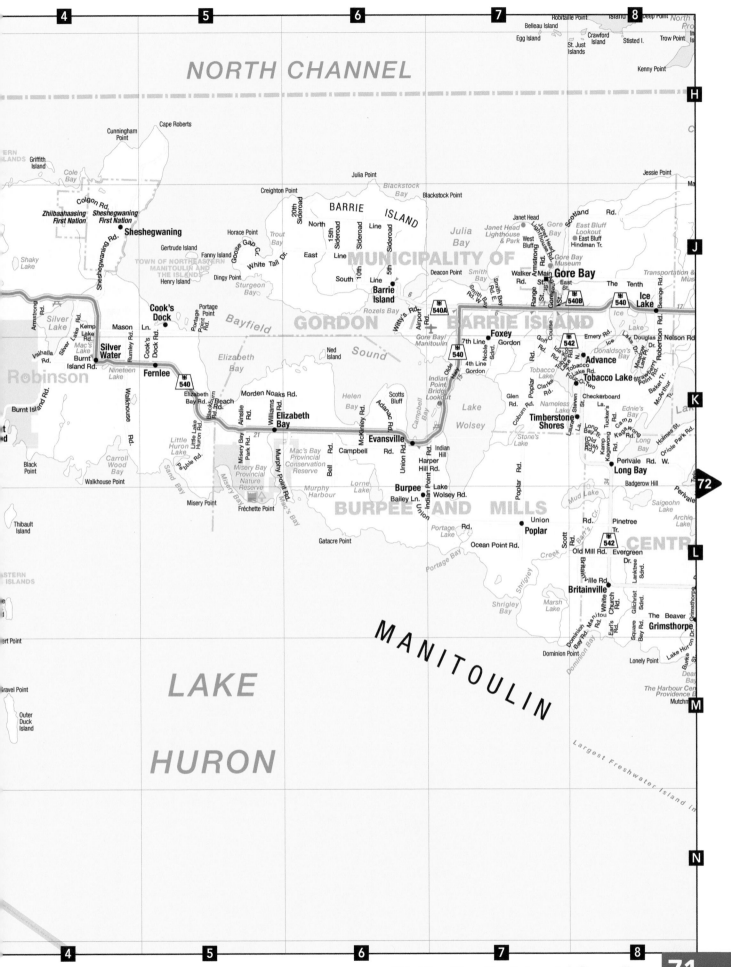

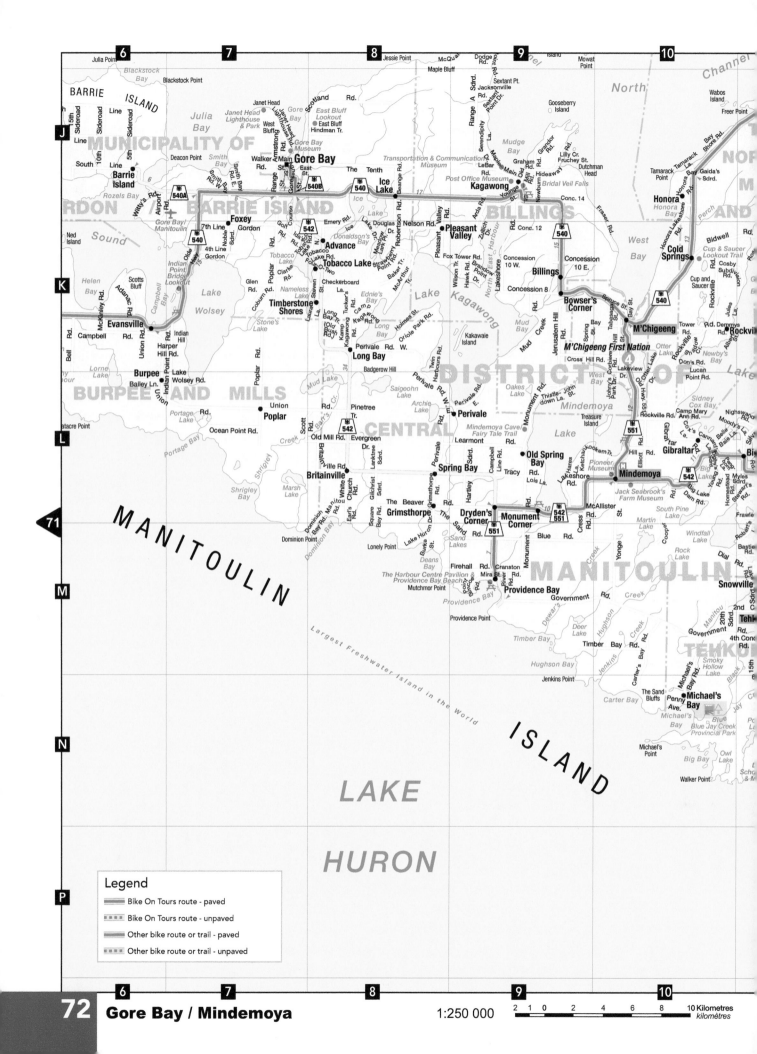

1:250 000

2 1 0 2 4 6 8 10 Kilometres
kilomètres

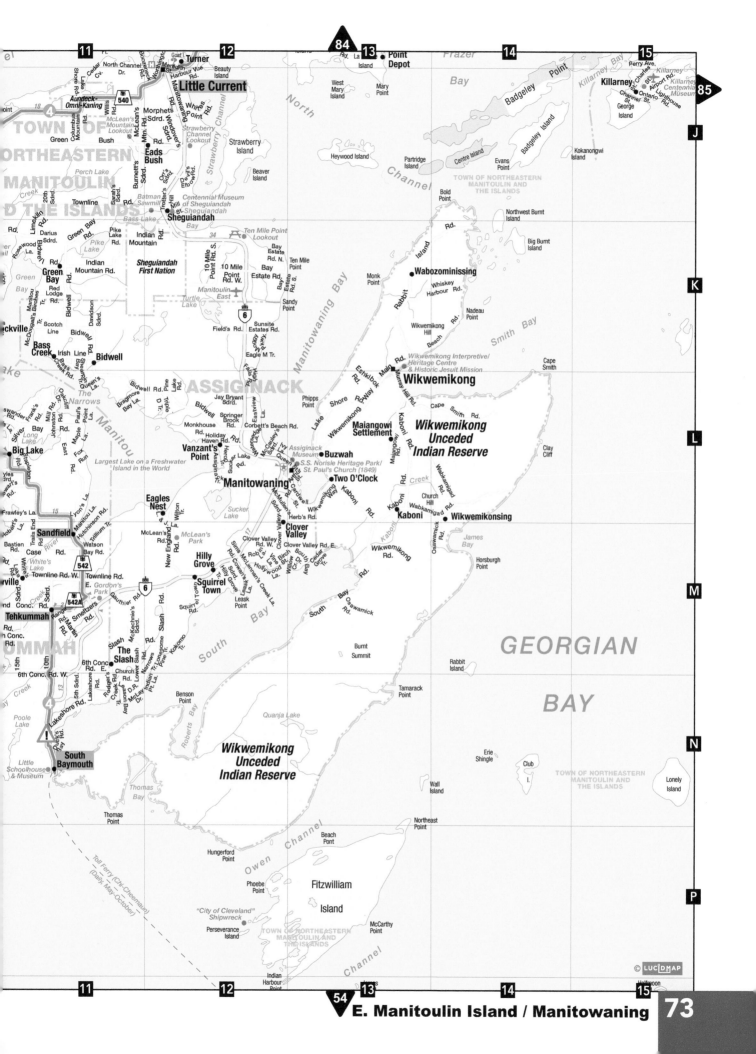

1:250 000

2 1 0 2 4 6 8 10 Kilometres
kilomètres

Legend

Bike On Tours route - paved

Bike On Tours route - unpaved

Other bike route or trail - paved

Other bike route or trail - unpaved

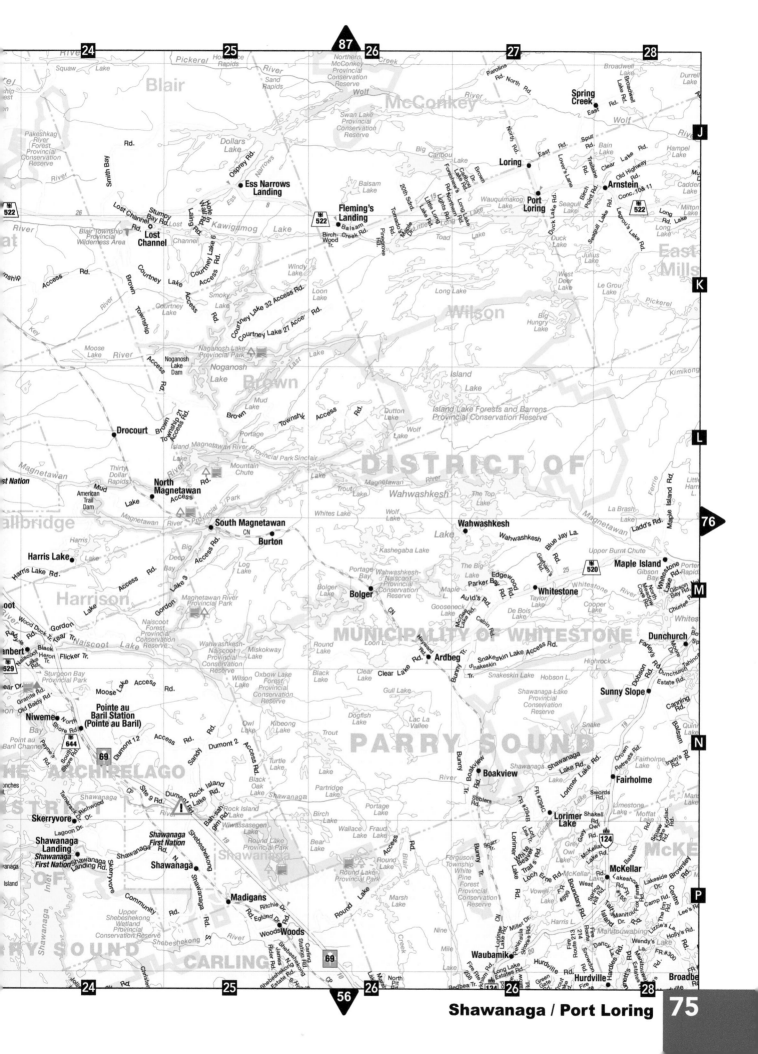

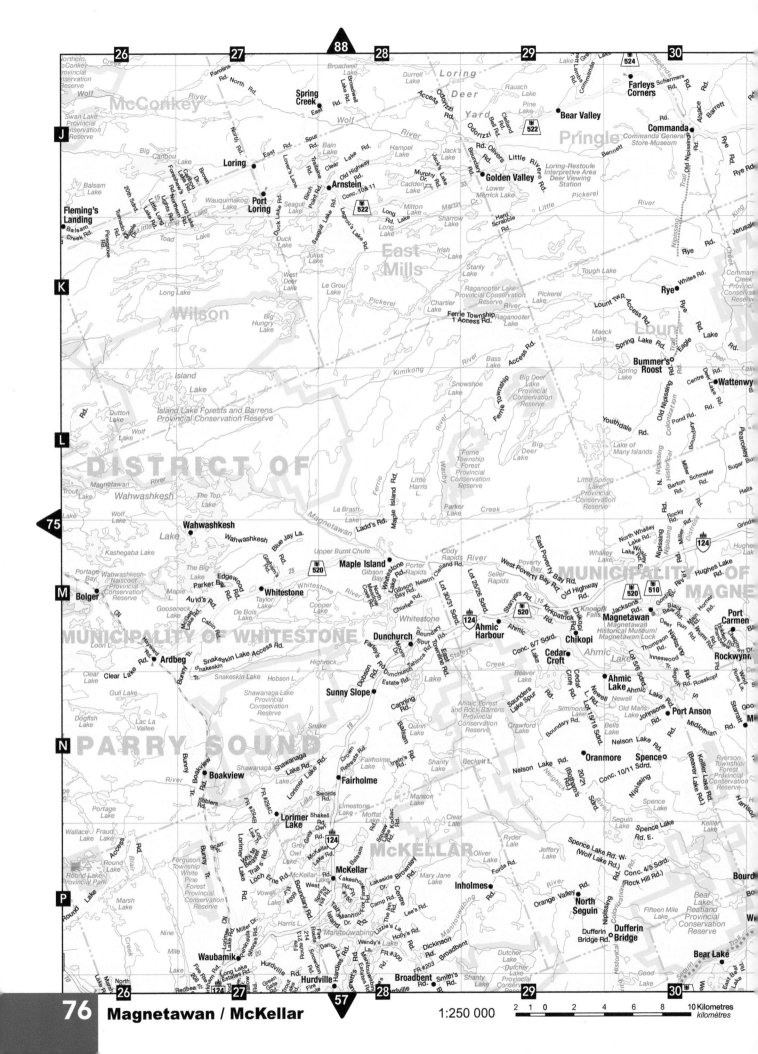

Legend

Bike On Tours route - paved
Bike On Tours route - unpaved
Other bike route or trail - paved
Other bike route or trail - unpaved

34 **35** **36** **90** **37** **38**

J

K

L

77

M

N

P

59 **34** **35** **36** **60** **37** **38**

Lister

Osier

Algonqu

Biggar

Bishop

Devine

Butt

McLaughlin

Hunter

McCraney

Canisbay

Peck

Finlayson

TOWN OF KEARNEY

Ravensworth
Ahola's

Paxton

Lorne Lake

Lost D... Lake

Pipe Lake

Charr Lake

Pishnecka Lake

Craig Creek

Craig Lake

Axton Lake

Mujekiwis Lake

Winifred Lake

Big Bob Lake

Graphite Lake

Kent Mill Access Rd.

Tim Lake Access Rd.

Tim Lake Access Rd.

Forestry Tower Rd.

Tim River

Little Trout Lake

Mubwayake Lake

Queer Lake

Shah Lake

Ralph Bice Lake

Petawawa

Misty Lake

Daisy Lake

Sawyer Lake

Rain Lake

Islet Lake

Brown Lake

Brûlé Lake

Furrow Lake

Potter Lake

Tom Thomson Lake

Little Doe Lake

Tepee Lake

Linda Lake

Owl Lake

Polly Lake

Raven Lake

Joe Lake

Source Lake

Canisbay Lake

Minesing

MacDougall

Mizzy Lake

Canoe Lake

Arowhon Rd.

Frank

Tanamakoon Lake

Little Island Lake

Hilliard Lake

Head Lake

Kenneth Lake

Peck Lake

Algonquin Gallery

Portage Store

Hardwood Lookout

Tea Lake

Smoke Lake

Swan Lake

Ragged Lake

Tea Lake Dam

Westward Lake

Whiskey Rapids

Oxtongue River

Maple Leaf Lake

Minnow Lake

Maggie Lake

West Harry Lake

Pincher Lake

McCraney Lake

Thirty Lake

Morgan's Lake

Bear Creek Provincial Conservation Reserve

Cripple Lake

Cripple Lake

Bridge Lake

Fox Lake

Willie Lake

Cripple Lake 5 Access Rd.

Cripple Lake 15 Access Rd.

Snowshoe Lake

Rain Lake Rd.

Rain Lake Rd.

Bridge Lake Outwash Plain Forest Provincial Conservation Reserve

Tohawanda

Hart Lake

Marion Lake

Nelson Lake Access Rd.

Marion Lake 1 Access Rd.

Dotty Lake Access Rd.

Tasso Lake

North Camp Lake

North Camp Lake Access Rd.

Ralston Rd.

Limberlost

Brooks Lk.

Dotty Lake

Billie Bear Rd.

Bella Stores Rd.

Fieldale

Oxbow Lake

Distress Dam Rd.

Williamsport

East River

Lower Raft Lake

Upper Raft Lake

Cashman

Rain Lake Rd.

Dewfish Lake

Middle Shanty Rd.

Little Patterson Lake

TR 5 Access Rd.

TR 10 Access Rd.

TR 18 Access Rd.

TR 4 Tower Rd.

MD 13 Access Rd.

Tim Lake

Lonely Lake

Longer Lake

Hemlock Lake

Blue Lake

Big Trout Lake

Trout Lake

Dan Lake

Otterslide Lake

Little Otterslide Lake

Alder Lake

Burnt Island Lake

Sunbeam Lake

McIntosh Lake

Timberwolf Lake

Grassy Bay

Burntroot Lake

Redpine Lake

Minnehaha Lake

Coldspring Lake

Kennedy Lake

Loontail Lake

Alder Creek

Shippagew Lake

Devine Lake

Devine Creek

Rosebary Lake

Gibson Lake

Nipissing

Loughrin Lake

Loughrin Creek

Birchcliffe Lake

Biggar Lake

Behan Lake

Whiskyjack Lake

Osler Lake

Nadine Lake

Robinson Lake

Hayes Lake

Perley Lake

Cuckoo Lake

Calume Lake

Sunfish Lake

Luckless Lake

Lynx Lake

Plumb Lake

Narrow Lake

Skuce Lake

Devil Lake

Lantern

Little

La Mur

Joe Lake

Little Joe Lake

Source Lake Rd.

Roger Lake Access Rd.

Luck Lake

Big Porcupine Lake

McGarvey

Bonnechere

Parkside Bay

Heron Lake

Ermine Lake

Traffic

Rain Lake Access Point Permits required

Rain Lake

He Lake

Madawaska

North

Waymog

Access Rd.

Jyne

Access ...

Rain River

Bear Creek

Thirty Lake

Camp... Rd.

Roger ... Tr.

78 **Algonquin Provincial Park** 1:250 000

2 1 0 2 4 6 8 10 Kilometres
kilomètres

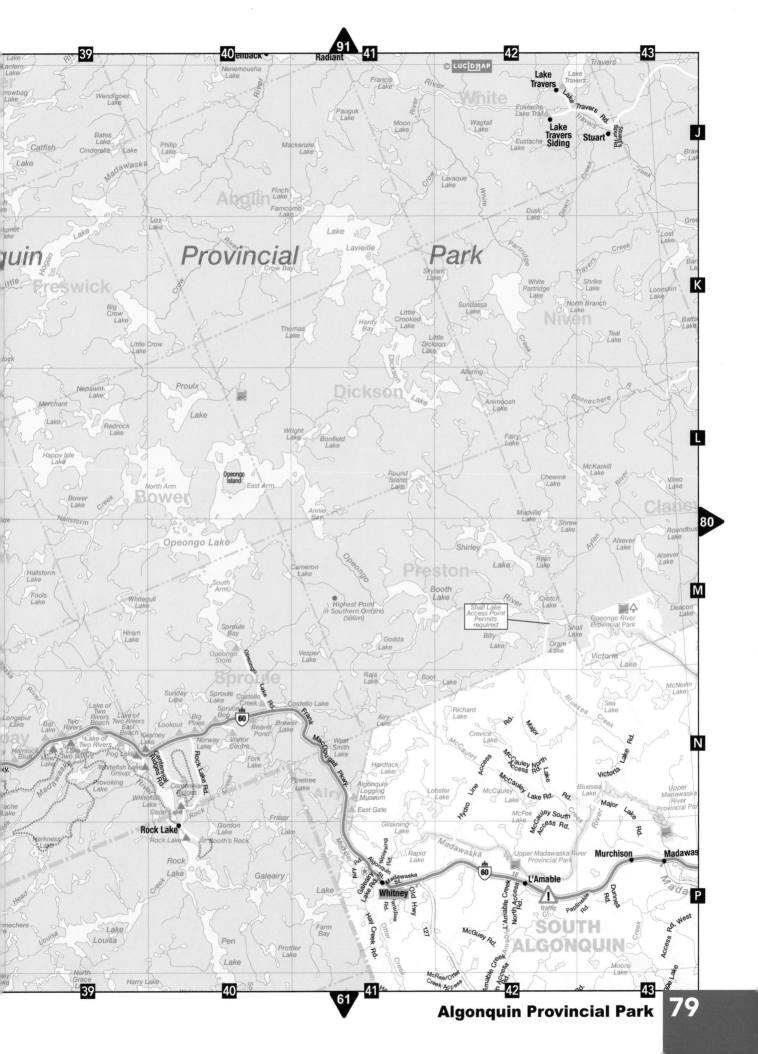

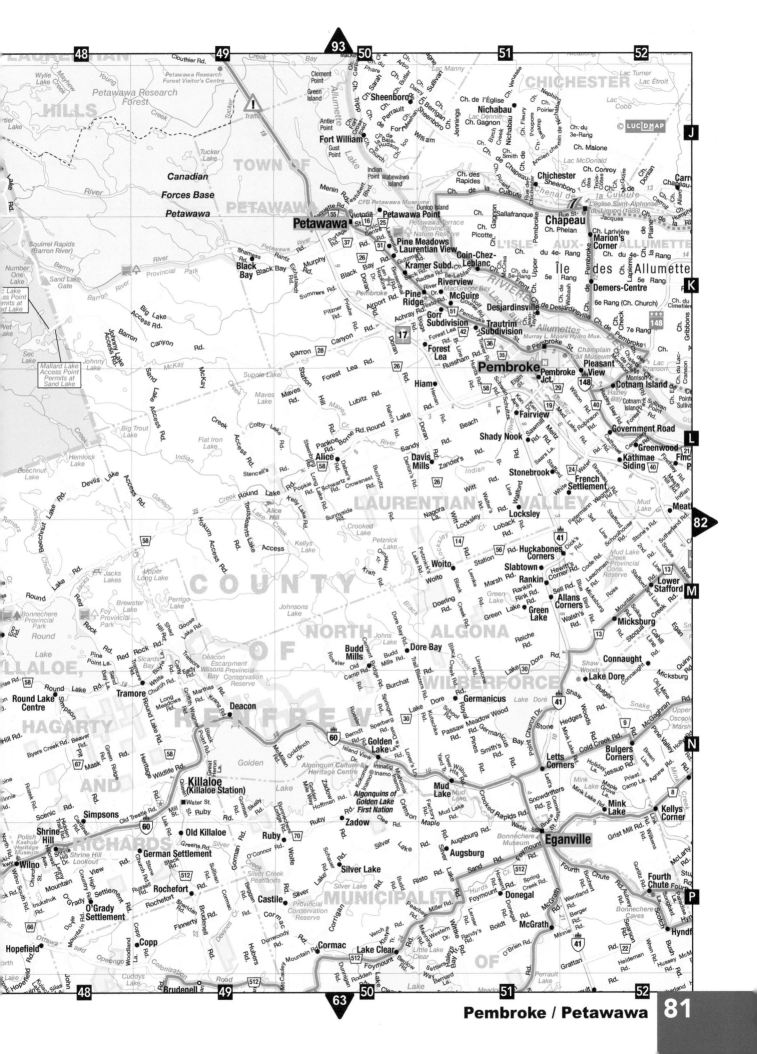

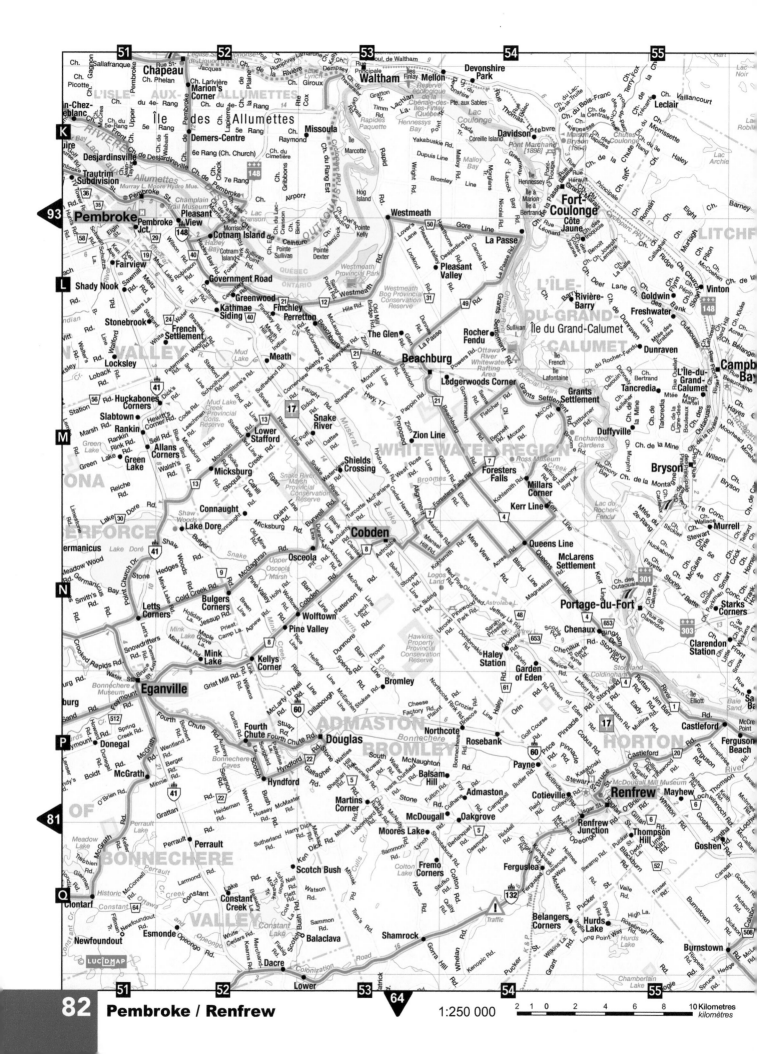

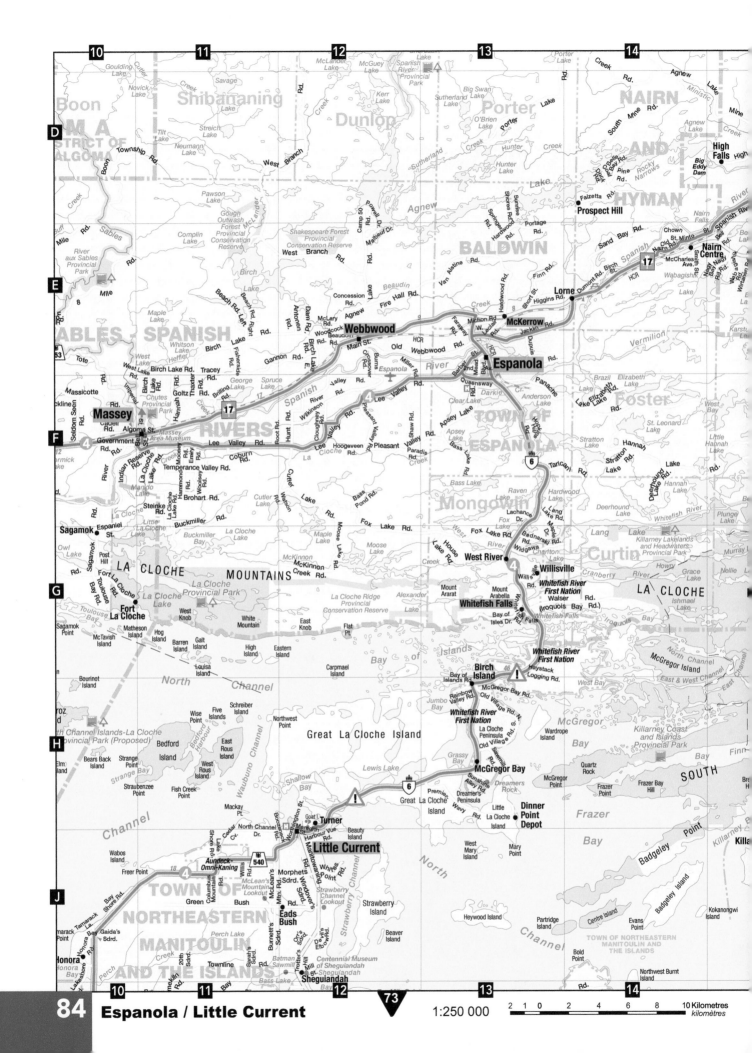

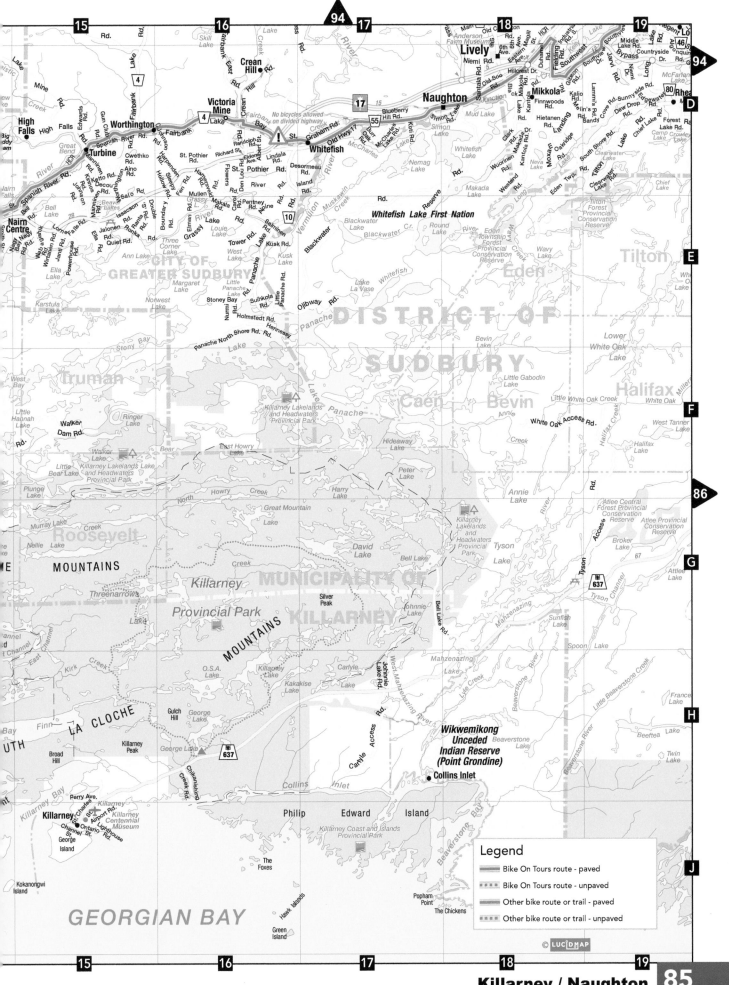

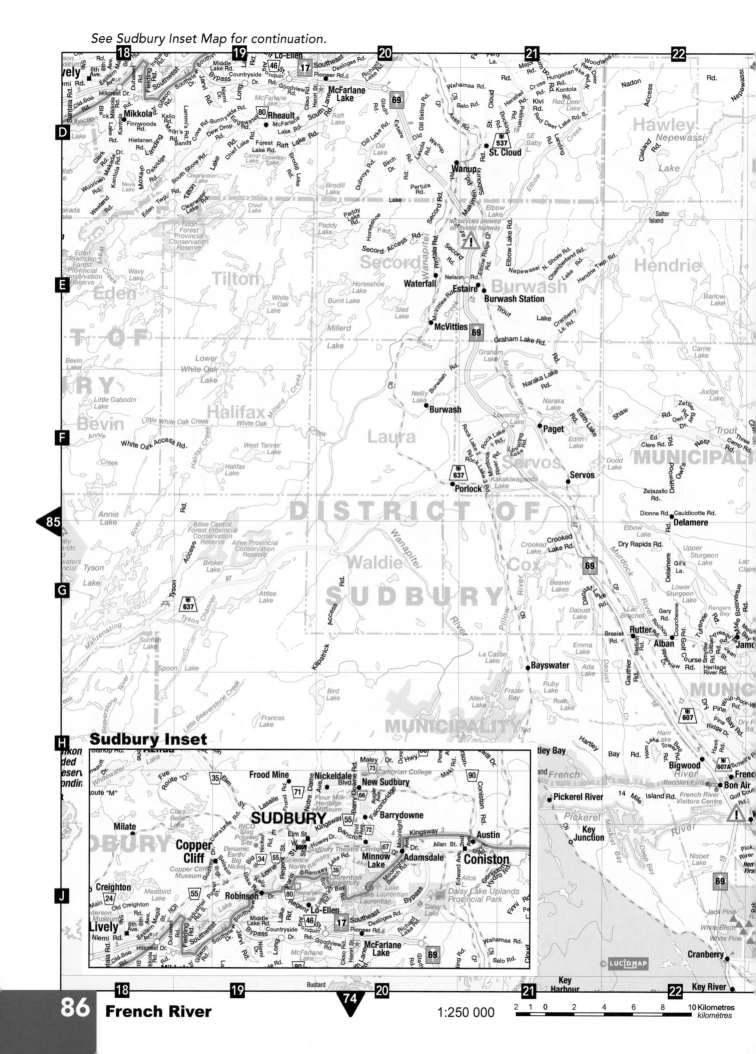

Sudbury Inset

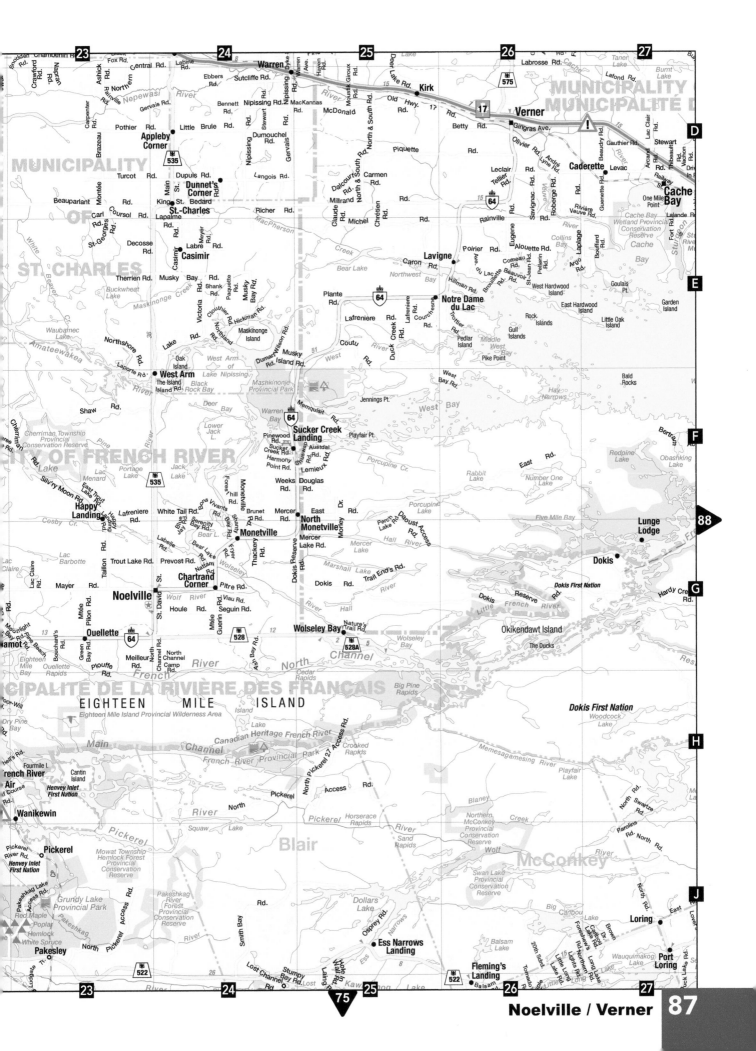

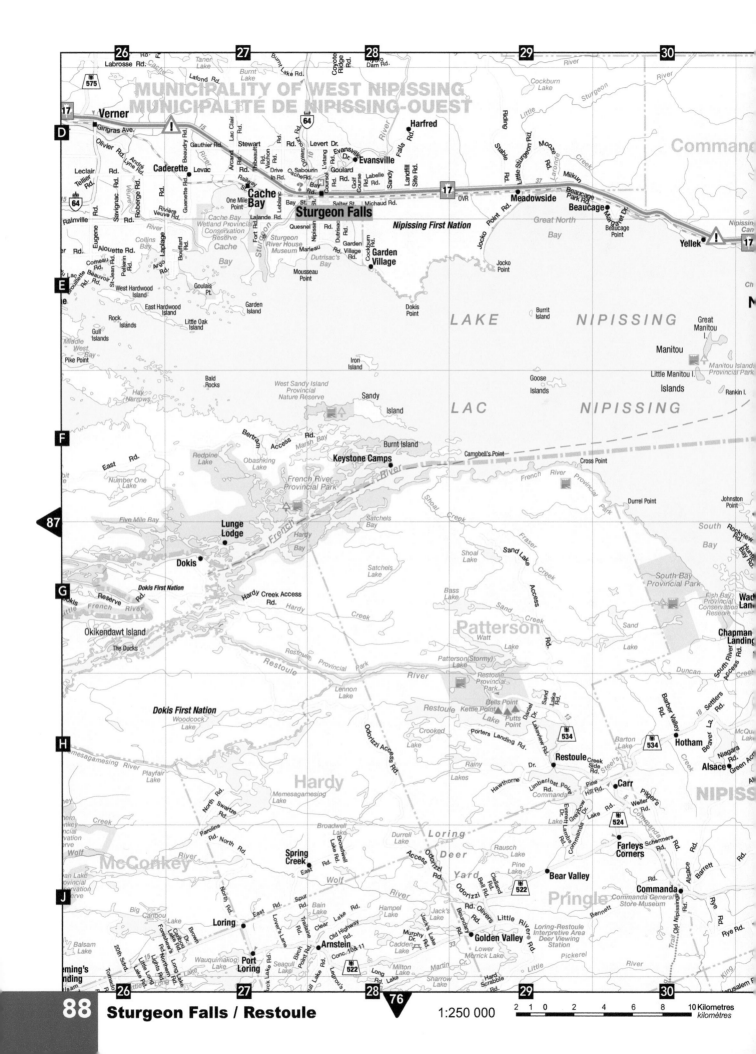

MUNICIPALITY OF WEST NIPISSING
MUNICIPALITÉ DE NIPISSING-OUEST

Comman

575

17   Verner
D

Gingras Ave.

Harfred

Caderette

Evansville

Meadowside

17

Beaucage

Cache
Bay

Sturgeon Falls

Yellek   17

Nipissing First Nation

Garden
Village

Cache Bay
Wetland Provincial
Conservation
Reserve

Sturgeon River House
Museum

E

Dutrisac's
Bay

LAKE   NIPISSING

West Hardwood
Island

Garden
Island

East Hardwood
Island

Little Oak
Island

Great
Manitou
I.

Manitou

Collins
Bay

Rock
Islands

Gull
Islands

Middle
West
Bay

Pike Point

Bald
Rocks

West Sandy Island
Provincial
Nature Reserve

Sandy
Island

Little Manitou I.

Islands

Goose
Islands

LAC   NIPISSING

Manitou Island
Provincial Park

Rankin I.

Iron
Island

F

Bertram

Access   Rd.

Marsh   Rd.

Redpine
Lake

Obashking
Lake

Keystone Camps

Burnt Island

Campbell's Point

Cross Point

French   River

French River
Provincial Park

Durrel Point

Johnston
Point

East   Rd.

Number One
Lake

Shoal   Creek

South
Bay

87

Five Mile Bay

Lunge
Lodge

Hardy
Bay

Satchels
Bay

Shoal
Lake

Sand Lake

Fraser   Creek

Rockview
Bay   Rd.

South Bay
Provincial Park

Dokis

Satchels
Lake

Fish Bay
Provincial
Conservation
Reserve

Wad
Lan

G

Reserve   Rd.

Dokis First Nation

Bass
Lake

Sand

Creek

Access

Sand
Lake

Chapman
Landing

Okikendawt Island

The Ducks

Patterson

Watt
Lake

Duncan

Restoule   Provincial   Park

Patterson(Stormy)
Lake

South River
Access Rd.

Dokis First Nation

Woodcock
Lake

Restoule   River

Restoule
Provincial
Park

Barber Valley
Rd.

Settlers
Rd.

Lennon
Lake

Restoule
Lake

Bells Point

Kettle Point

Putts
Point

Daniel

Dr.

Sand
Lake
Rd.

13

Hotham

McQue
Lake

H

Memesagmesing   River

Playfair
Lake

Crooked
Lake

Porters Landing Rd.

Lakeview Rd.

534

Barton
Lake

534

Niagara
Rd.

Green Acr

Alsace

Rainy
Lakes

Restoule
Dr.

Creek
Side
Rd.

Steel's

Pine
Hill Rd.

Carr

NIPISS

Hardy

Memesagamesing
Lake

Hawthorne

Limberlost Point
Rd.

Commanda

Greybow
Dr.

Everett

Pine

524

Loring

Deer

Rausch
Lake

Weller
Rd.

Farleys
Corners

Schermers   Rd.

North   Rd.

Swartze
Rd.

Broadwell
Lake

Durrell
Lake

Yard

Pine
Lake

Bear Valley

Commanda

McConkey

Parolins

North   Rd.

Spring
Creek

Broadwell
Lake Rd.

Access

Odonzi

Rd.

Odorizzi

Clalland
Bell Rd.

Olivers

522

Commanda General
Store Museum

Pringle

Wolf   River

Creek

J

Big
Caribou
Lake

North   Rd.

Spur

East   Rd.

Bain
Lake

Hampel
Lake

Jack's
Lake

Little   River   Rd.

Golden Valley

Loring-Restoule
Interpretive Area
Deer Viewing
Station

Loring

Balsam
Lake

Port
Loring

Lower's Lane

Seagull
Lake

Clear   Lake

Old Highway

Murphy
Dr.

Cadden
Rd.

Lower
Merrick Lake

Pickerel

20th Sdrd.

Arnstein

Tealane   Rd.

Birch

Conc. 10 & 11

Milton
Lake

Martin

Little

Hard
Scrabble
Rd.

Long
Lake

522

Sharrow
Lake

Trail Old Nipissing
Rd.

River

King

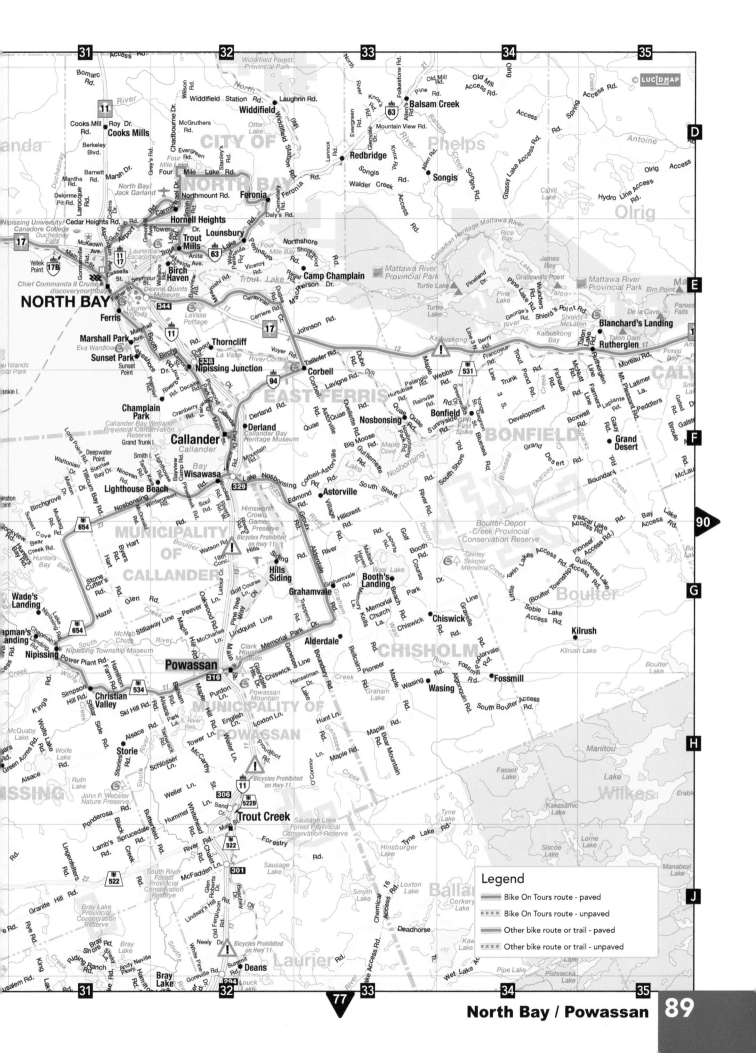

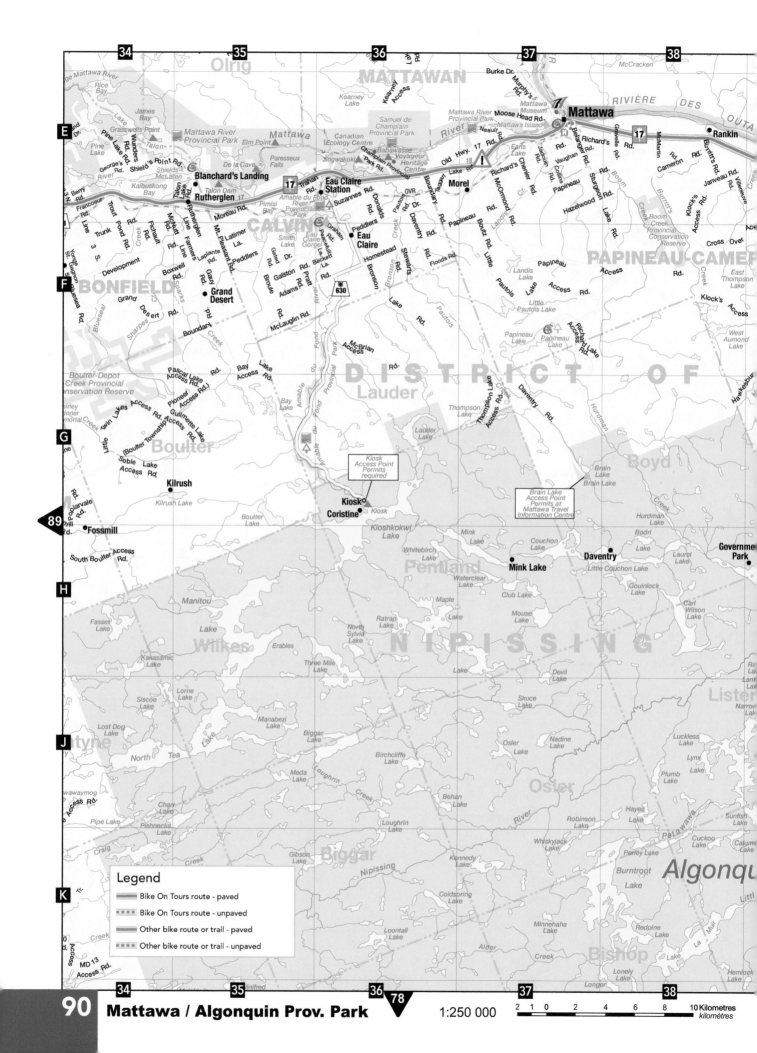

1:250 000

2 1 0 2 4 6 8 10 Kilometres
kilomètres

Legend

Bike On Tours route - paved

Bike On Tours route - unpaved

Other bike route or trail - paved

Other bike route or trail - unpaved

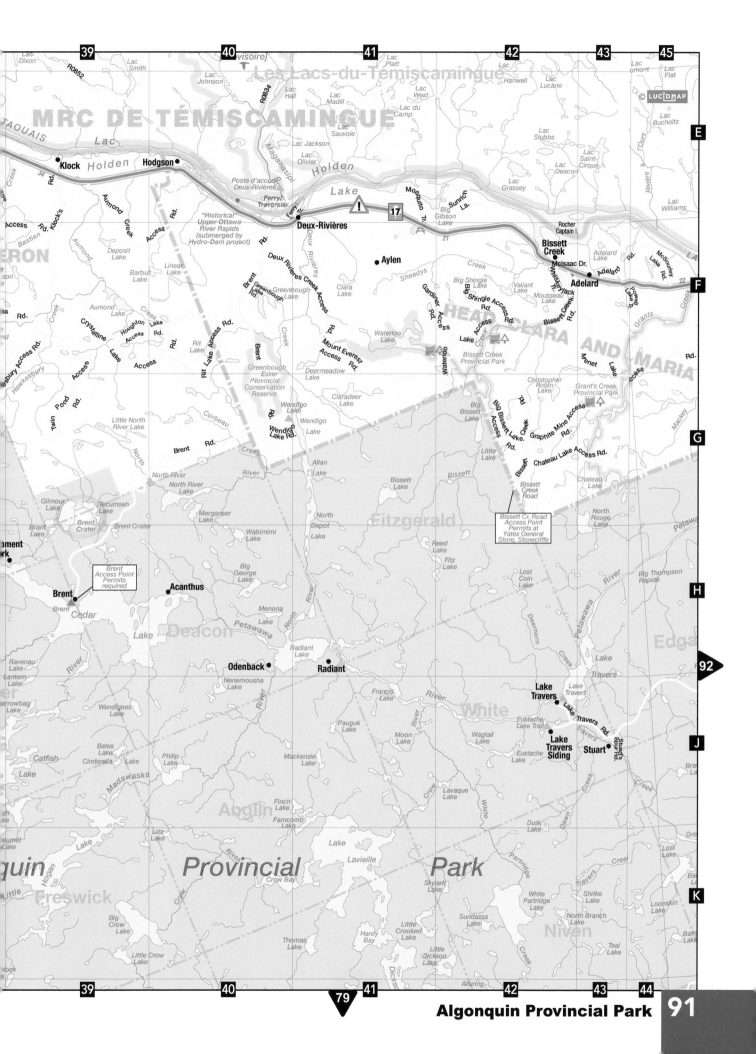

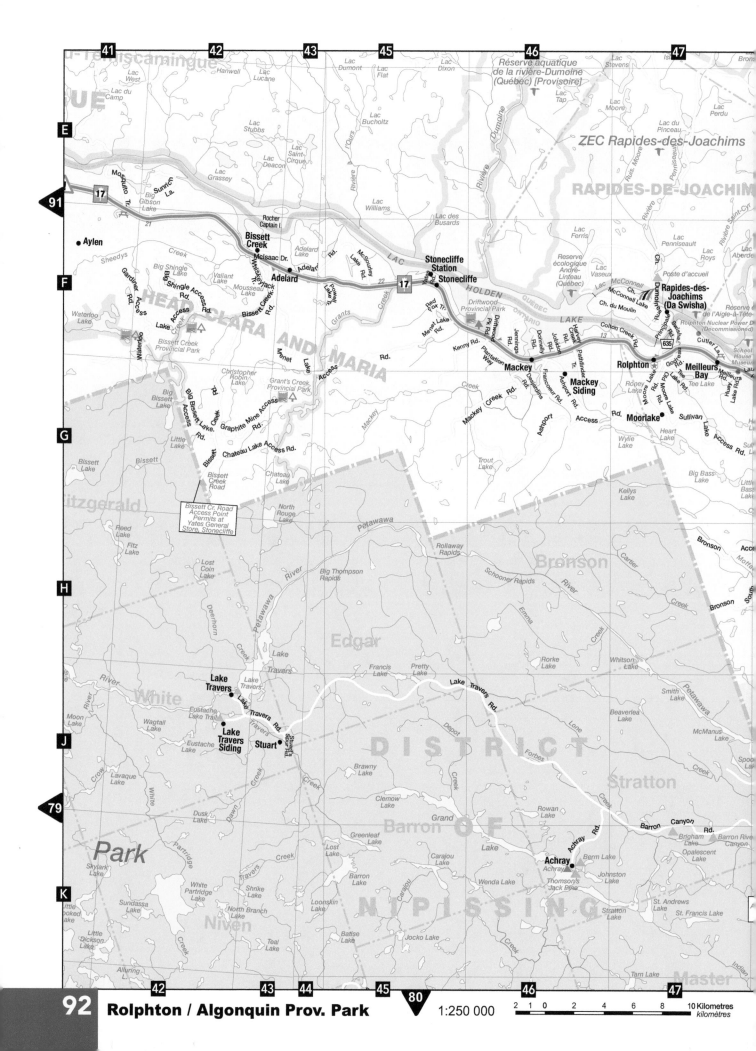

1:250 000

2 1 0 2 4 6 8 10 Kilometres
kilomètres

ZEC Rapides-des-Joachims

RAPIDES-DE-JOACHIM

Réserve aquatique de la rivière-Dumoine (Québec) [Provisoire]

Réserve écologique André-Linteau (Québec)

Poste d'accueil

Rapides-des-Joachims (Da Swisha)

Réserve naturelle de l'Aigle-à-Tête

Rolphton Nuclear Power D (Decommissioned)

Rolphton

Meilleurs Bay

Moorlake

HEAD CLARA AND MARIA

Bissett Creek Provincial Park

Christopher Robin Lake

Grant's Creek Provincial Park

Graphite Mine Access Rd.

Chateau Lake Access Rd.

Bissett Creek Road

Bissett Cr. Road Access Point Permits at Yates General Store, Stonecliffe

Bissett Creek

Adelard

Stonecliffe Station

Stonecliffe

Driftwood Provincial Park

Mackey

Mackey Siding

Fitzgerald

Aylen

Bronson

Edgar

Lake Travers

Lake Travers Siding

Stuart

White

DISTRICT

Stratton

Park

Niven

Barron

Achray

Thomson's Jack Pine

OF

NIPISSING

Master

Canyon

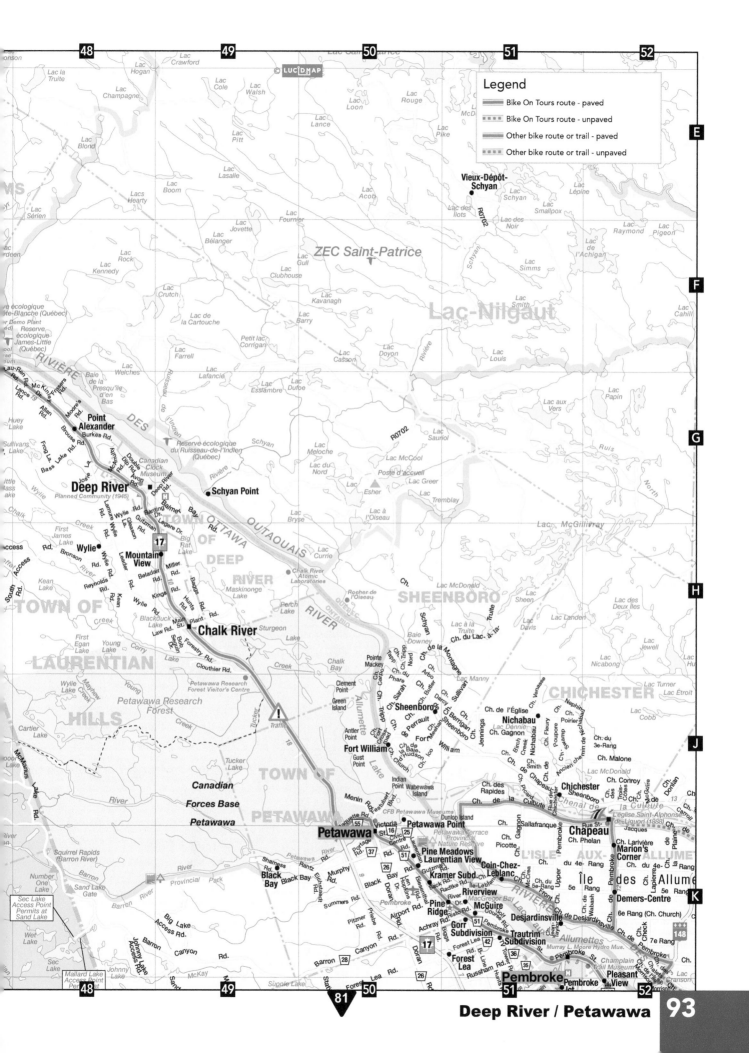

Routes Across Ontario
by Howard Pulver

With the Ontario Bicycle Touring Atlas you have a choice of a number of routes across Ontario. Five of them are described below. Long distance cyclists traveling between the northeastern United States and Michigan or Minnesota have found that bicycling across Ontario eliminates many miles of travel required to go around the Great Lakes.

These routes are described going from west to east, but of course you can follow them in the reverse direction as well, or just tour a section of a route.

Consult the Community Guide in the next section to plan your stops along the way.

1 – WATERFRONT ROUTE

Features: Go right across Southern Ontario following the shore of Lake Erie, Lake Ontario and the St. Lawrence River.

Distance: 1011 km.

Characteristics: All paved; via backroads from Windsor to Hamilton, and the Waterfront Trail from Hamilton to Quebec border.

Description: This is a scenic waterfront route all the way across Ontario from Windsor to the Quebec border east of Cornwall. The route goes close to Lake Erie, then along Lake Ontario and the St. Lawrence River using the Lake Ontario Waterfront Trail.

Major Waypoints: Windsor (Detroit MI) - Leamington/Kingsville (Pelee Island Ferry, Sandusky OH) - Port Dover - Ohsweken – Hamilton – Toronto - Picton - Kingston (Wolfe Island Ferries, Cape Vincent NY) - Cornwall (Massena NY) - Quebec border (continue along Quebec's Route Verte to Montreal)

Consult these atlas pages to track this route on the maps: Marked as ➊

Map 4 B1	Windsor	E4 Kingsville
Map 5 E5	Leamington	D8 Port Alma
Map 6 C9	Dealtown	
Map 7 Y14	Eagle	
Map 8 W17	Port Stanley	
Map 9 X22	Jacksonburg	
Map 10 V25	Port Dover	
Map 17 V28	Nanticoke	
Map 18 U30	Dunnville	Q28 Hamilton
Map 19 T36	Fort Erie	Q33 St Catharines
Map 23 P28	Aldershot	
Map 24 N29	Bronte	L32 Toronto
Map 25 H37	Oshawa	
Map 32 G40	Wesleyville	
Map 33 F44	Colborne	
Map 34 G49	Wellington	
Map 35 G51	Picton	E54 Bath
Map 36 D56	Kingston	D57 Pitts Ferry
Map 37 A62	Butternut Bay	
Map 50 X65	Cardinal	
Map 51 V68	Ingleside	
Map 52 U71	Cornwall	T72 South Lancaster
Map 53 T73	Quebec border	

2 – BACKROADS ROUTE

Features: Across Southern Ontario generally through the Highway 7 corridor.

Distance: 1021 km from Windsor – 917 km from Sarnia

Characteristics: All paved back roads, except for 20 km unpaved route from Fergus to Orton.

Description: Start from the Bluewater International Bridge in Sarnia or from Riverside Drive in Windsor and bicycle this back road route through the scenic countryside and lakelands of Southern Ontario. Route includes the Thames River valley, Stratford - home of the internationally famous Stratford Festival, Ontario's Mennonite Country, Ontario's last remaining covered bridge, the Trent Canal, many small lakes and quiet countryside to no end. The topography is moderate; quite flat for the first 200 kilometers, rolling through the central 600 kilometers and then quite flat again for the final 200 kilometers from Perth to the Quebec border.

Major Waypoints: Windsor (Detroit MI) or Sarnia (Port Huron MI) - Stratford – St. Jacobs – Orangeville – Bradford – Campbellford – Tweed – Perth - Ottawa – Quebec border (Quebec's Route Verte)

Consult these atlas pages to track this route on the maps: Marked as ➋

From Windsor:

Map 4 B1	Windsor	
Map 5 B6	Lighthouse Cove	
Map 6 A9	Chatham	X9 Dawn Mills
Map 7 W10	Shetland	

From Sarnia:

Map 12 T7	Sarnia

These routes meet at:

Map 13 T14	Strathroy

Map 14 R16	Birr	
Map 15 Q18	St. Marys	
Map 21 P27	Stratford	L21 Linwood
Map 22 M22	St. Jacobs	K24 Fergus
Map 23 J25	Orton	
Map 29 H26	Orangeville	F29 Tottenham
Map 30 E31	Bradford	E32 Sharon
Map 31 F36	Purple Hill	
Map 32 E40	Millbrook	
Map 33 C45	Campbellford	
Map 34 C46	Pethericks Corners	
Map 46 A49	Tweed	
Map 47 B53	Enterprise	
Map 36 A54	Verona, Godfrey	
Map 48 Y57	Westport	
Map 49 W58	Perth	U59 Blacks Corners
Map 65 S61	Stanley Corners	
Map 66 Q63	Ottawa	P64 Orleans
Map 67 P68	Jessups Falls	
Map 68 N72	Chute a Blondeau	
Map 69 N73	Pointe Fortune, Carillon ferry, Quebec border	

3 – CENTRAL ONTARIO ROUTE

Features: Across Southern Ontario generally through the area where Highways 401, 402 and 403 are located.

Distance: 936 km

Characteristics: All paved back roads from Windsor or Sarnia to Hamilton; Waterfront Trail from Hamilton to Quebec border.

Description: This is a countryside route from Sarnia or Windsor that goes quite directly east toward Toronto including the Thames River valley, lush scenic farmland, the Native Canadian Six Nations Territory and historic Ancaster. From Hamilton to the east the route uses the Lake Ontario Waterfront Trail, close to Lake Ontario and the St. Lawrence.

Major Waypoints: Windsor (Detroit MI) or Sarnia (Port Huron MI) – London – Ohsweken – Hamilton - – Toronto - Picton - Kingston - Cornwall (Massena NY) - Quebec border (Quebec's Route Verte to Montreal)

Consult these atlas pages to track this route on the maps: Marked as ❸

From Windsor:
Map 4 B1	Windsor	
Map 5 B6	Lighthouse Cove	
Map 6 A9	Chatham	X9 Dawn Mills
Map 7 W10	Shetland	

From Sarnia:
| Map 12 T7 | Sarnia | |

These routes meet at:
Map 13 T14	Strathroy	
Map 14 U16	Lambeth, London	
Map 15 T20	Mount Elgin	
Map 16 S24	Scotland	
Map 17 S26	Ohsweken	Q28 Hamilton
Map 23 P28	Aldershot	
Map 24 N29	Bronte	L32 Toronto
Map 25 H37	Oshawa	
Map 32 G40	Wesleyville	
Map 33 F44	Colborne	
Map 34 G49	Wellington	
Map 35 G51	Picton	E54 Bath
Map 36 D56	Kingston	D57 Pitts Ferry
Map 37 A62	Butternut Bay	
Map 50 X65	Cardinal	
Map 51 V68	Ingleside	
Map 52 U71	Cornwall	T72 South Lancaster
Map 53 T73	Quebec border	

4 – TRANS-CANADA ROUTE

Features: Across Ontario from the Manitoba border to the Quebec border through Southern Ontario.

Distance: 2423 km. from Manitoba border - 1243 km. from Sault Ste. Marie.

Characteristics: All paved. Main roads from Manitoba border to Manitoulin Island. Back roads from Manitoulin Island to Quebec border

Description: Bicycle across Ontario from Manitoba, Quebec and United States border crossings from Minnesota and Michigan, connecting with Quebec's Route Verte and American Cycling Association Routes. Explore the northern edge of Southern Ontario.

Major Waypoints: Kenora – Fort Frances (International Falls MN) - Thunder Bay (Grand Portage MN) – Sault Ste. Marie (Sault Ste. Marie MI) – Manitoulin Island (ferry) – Owen Sound – Collingwood – Bradford – Campbellford – Tweed – Perth – Ottawa – Quebec border (Quebec's Route Verte

Consult these atlas pages to track this route on the maps: Marked as ❹

Map 2	Manitoba border	
	Kenora	Fort Frances
	Thunder Bay	White River
	Sault Ste Marie	Massey

To avoid traffic on the TransCanada Highway
From Sault Ste. Marie:
East on Road 17 (Trunk Road) to Road 638 at Echo

Bay
Left to go East on Road 638 to Gordon Lake Road
Right to go South on Gordon Lake Road to Highway 17 at Portlock
Left to continue East on Highway 17

Alternate Route From Sault Ste Marie
East on Road 17 (Trunk Road) and pass Echo Bay to Bar River Road
Left to go East on Bar River Road to Government Road
Right to go South and East on Government Road to Road 638
Right to go South on Road 638 to Highway 17 at Portlock
Left to continue East on Highway 17

From Bruce Mines:
North on Road 638 pass Bruce Station to Cloudslee Road
Right to go East on Cloudslee Road and continure on Ansonia Road to Little Rapids Road
Right to go South on Little Rapids Road to Road 129
Left to go East on Road 129 to Station Road
Right to go south on Station Road to Highway 17

Map 84 J12	Little Current	
Map 73 J12	Little Current	
Map 72 L10	Mindemoya	
Map 73 N11	South Baymouth (Note: toll ferry crossing to Tobermory)	
Map 54 X18	Wiarton	
Map 39 Z19	Owen Sound	A21 Walters Falls
Map 40 A25	Collingwood	
Map 41 A26	Batteaux	
Map 29 F29	Beeton	
Map 30 E31	Bradford	E32 Sharon
Map 31 F36	Purple Hill	
Map 32 E40	Millbrook	
Map 33 C45	Campbellford	
Map 34 C46	Pethericks Corners	
Map 46 A49	Tweed	
Map 47 B53	Enterprise	
Map 36 A54	Verona, Godfrey	
Map 48 Y57	Westport	
Map 49 W58	Perth	U59 Blacks Corners
Map 65 S61	Stanley Corners	
Map 66 Q63	Ottawa	P64 Orleans
Map 67 P68	Jessups Falls	
Map 68 N72	Chute a Blondeau	
Map 69 N73	Pointe Fortune, Carillon ferry, Quebec border	

Description: Enjoy this waterfront route between Windsor and Tobermorey. Watch the ships on the Detroit River and St. Clair River as you bicycle along. Visit the scenic and historic port towns and lighthouses.

Major Waypoints: Windsor (Detroit MI) or Sarnia (Port Huron MI) – Goderich – Kincardine – Port Elgin – Wiarton – Owen Sound – Tobermory (Manitoulin Island ferry)

Consult these atlas pages to track this route on the maps: Marked as ❺

From Windsor:

Map 4 B1	Windsor	
Map 5 B6	Lighthouse Cove	
Map 6 W6	Sombra	
Map 12 T7	Sarnia	S9 Errol
Map 13 Q13	Corbett	
Map 20 P13	Dashwood	J13 Goderich
Map 26 E13	Kincardine	C38 Inverhuron
Map 38 B16	Port Elgin	X18 Wiarton
Map 39 Z19	Owen Sound	
Map 55 S13	Tobermory [Manitoulin Is. Ferry]	

5 – HURON TRAIL ROUTE

Features: Near the shore of the Detroit River, St. Clair River, Lake St. Clair and Lake Huron.

Distance: 557 kilometers

Characteristics: All Paved Except For 6 kilometers south of Grand Bend.

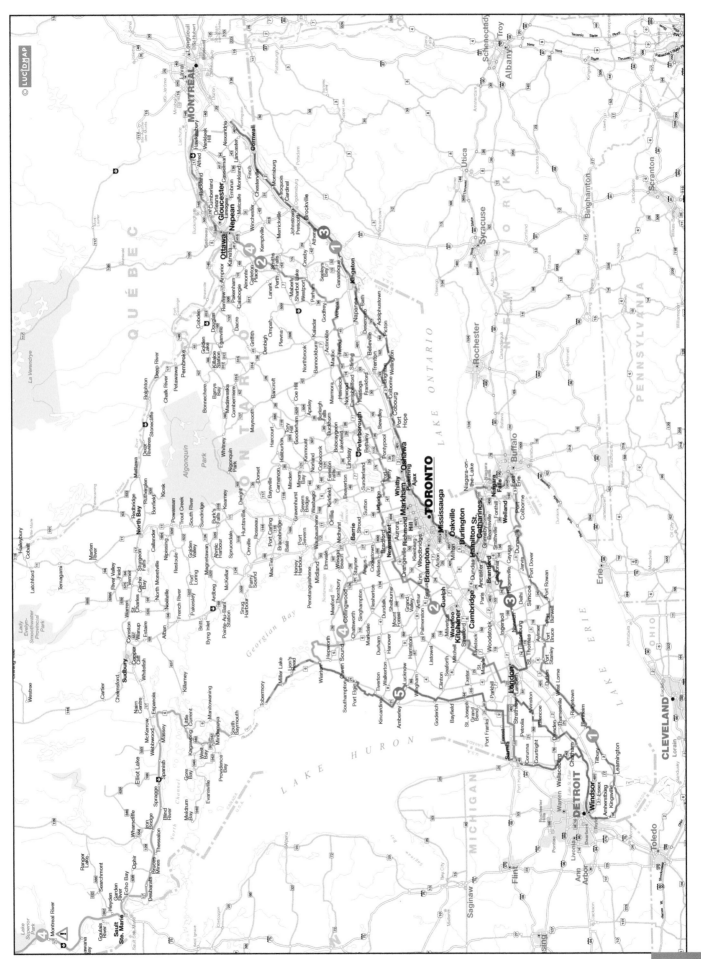

COMMUNITY INDEX
DESTINATIONS

Where To Go, What To See, Where To Stay - Over 400 Places In Ontario Bicycle Touring Atlas

Listings Include Services For Cyclists Including Grocery Store, Restaurant, Accommodation, Camping, Event/Attraction, Winery, Historic Site, Natural Area, Bike Shop, Library, Information, Map Page and Coordinates.

Go to http://www.bicycleontario.ca/destinations.html for this Community Index with live links to related web sites and updated information.

Legend of Symbols

- Conservation/Park/Zoo
- Bike shop
- Grocery Store
- Information
- Restaurant
- Library
- Accommodation
- Camping
- Event/Attraction
- Brewery
- Winery
- Historic Site

Aamjiwnaang First Nation 12 U7
GPS 42.92368,-82.45195
- Annual Pow-Wow in late June
www.aamjiwnaang.ca

Adolphustown 35 F52: Hamlet
GPS 44.06307,-77.00686
- United Empire Loyalist Heritage Centre & Park
54 Adolphustown Park Road
Box 112 RR#1 Bath ON K0H 1G0
www.uel.ca
Tel: (877) 384-1784 (613) 373 2196

Ailsa Craig 14 R14 GPS 43.14693,-81.53308:
Town
- Ailsa Craig Public Library
147 Main Street
Ailsa Craig ON N0M 1A0
www.middlesex.library.on.ca/branch/ailsacraig.asp
Tel: (519) 293-3441

Ajax 25 H35 GPS 43.85075,-79.02109:
City
- Before The Mast B&B
1144 Shoal Point Road
Ajax ON L1S 1E2
www.beforethemast.ca
Tel: (905) 683-4830
- Northern Cycle
889 Westney Road South
Ajax ON L1S 3M4
www.northerncycle.com
Tel. (877) 220-7336 (905) 619-8875

Alderville First Nation 33 D43
GPS 44.18122,-78.06747: Village
- First Nation Pow Wow, June
www.aldervillefirstnation.ca

Algoma Mills 2 GPS 46.18493,-82.81948:
Village

Algonquin 50 Y63 GPS 44.70941,-75.67383:
Hamlet

Alliston 29 E28 GPS 44.15421,-79.86812:
Town
- Alliston Potato Festival in early August
- Alliston Bed & Breakfast
139 Victoria Street West
Alliston ON L9R 1L7
Tel: (705) 434-2253
- Red Pine Motor Inn - Restaurant
497 Victoria Street East
Alliston ON L9R 1T9
www.redpineinn.com
Tel: (800) 328-1404 (705) 435-4381
- Earl Rowe Provincial Park
2 km west, on Highway 89
Tel: (705) 435-4331
Reservations: www.ontarioparks.com
Tel: (888) 668 7275
- 17 Victoria Street
Alliston ON L9R 1V6
www.ntpl.ca
Tel: (705) 435-5651
- MacKenzie's Bike Shop
13 Tupper Street West
Alliston ON L9R 1E4
Tel: (705) 435-5964

Alton 29 H26 GPS 43.85847,-80.06530:
Village
- Alton Mill Arts Centre
1402 Queen Street
Alton ON L7K 0C3
Tel: (519) 941-9300
- Millcroft Inn - Restaurant
55 John Street East
Alton ON L0N 1A0
www.millcroft.com
Tel: (800) 383-3976 (519) 941-8111

Ameliasburg 34 F48 GPS 44.05912,-77.43614:
Village
- Ameliasburg Heritage Village
- Harry Smith Conservation Area and Roblin Lake Beach

Amherstburg 4 D1 GPS 42.10187,-83.10892:
Town
- Erie Shores Package Route
- Amherstburg Navy Yard Park, Fort Malden
- Shores of Erie International Wine Festival in September
- D'Angelo Estate Winery
55141 Concession 5 North RR4 Amherstburg
www.dangelowinery.com
Tel: (519) 736-7959
- Sanson Estate Winery
9238 Walker Road
Amherstburg ON N0R 1J0
www.sansonestatewinery.com
Tel: (519) 726-9609
- Allen's Bed & Breakfast
259 George Street
Amherstburg ON N9V 2G1
Tel: (519) 736-6731

- Bondy House Bed & Breakfast
199 Dalhousie Street
Amherstburg ON N9V 1W5
www.bbcanada.com/bondyhousebnb
Tel: (519) 736-9433
- Ricardo's Italian Restaurant
238 Dalhousie Street
Amherstburg ON N9V 1W4
Tel: (519) 736-4333
- Ducks On The Roof
1430 Front Road
Amherstburg ON N9V 3K1
www.ducksontheroof.com
Tel: (519) 736-0044
- Essex County Library
232 Sandwich Street South
Amherstburg ON N9V 2A4
www.essexcountylibrary.ca
Tel: (519) 736-4632

Ancaster 17 Q27 GPS 43.22502,-79.97737:
Former town in City of Hamilton
- Hamilton Online Cycling Map
www.hamilton.ca/BikeRides
- Hamilton Tourism
www.tourismhamilton.com
- Ancaster Cycle Ltd.
365 Wilson Street East
Ancaster ON
www.ancastercycle.ca
Tel: (905) 648-2288
- Hamilton Public Library Ancaster Branch
300 Wilson Street East
Ancaster ON L9G 2B9
Tel: (905) 648-6911

Angus 29 C28 GPS 44.32145,-79.88728:
Town
- Essa Public Library
8505 County Road 10, Unit 1
Angus ON L0M 1B1
www.essa.library.on.ca/index.htm
Tel: (705) 424-6531

Arkona 13 S12 GPS 43.07436,-81.83414:
Town
- Rock Glen Conservation Area
8680 Rock Glen Road
waterfall, Devonian fossils and Aboriginal artifacts
- Rock Glen Motel
7502 Arkona Road
Arkona ON N0M 1B0
Tel: (519) 828-3838
- Lambton County Library
16 Smith Street
Arkona ON N0M 1B0
Tel: (519) 828-3406

Arnprior 65 Q57 GPS 45.43563,-76.35837:
Town
- Ottawa Valley Tourist Association
- Kirkman House Bed & Breakfast
294 John Street North
Arnprior ON K7S 2P6
www.bbcanada.com/3742.html

Tel: (613) 623-5890

Arnprior Quality Inn
70 Madawaska Boulevard
Arnprior ON K7S 1S5
www.arnpriorqualityinn.com
Tel: (877) 700-5637 (613) 623-7991

Arnprior Public Library
147 Main Street Arnprior ON
Tel: (613) 293-3441

Ashton 65 T60 GPS 45.15710,-76.03225:
Village

Athens 49 Z60 GPS 44.62545,-75.95344:
Town

History of the town, pictured in thirteen murals.

Atikokan 2 GPS 48.75923,-91.59287:
Town

Atikokan Hotel restaurant
400 Front Street Box 1448
Atikokan ON P0T 1C0
www.atikokanhotel.com
Tel: (807) 597-2533

Burns Street B&B
127 Burns Street Box 662
Atikokan ON P0T 1C0
Tel: (807) 597-4353

Quetico Provincial Park - Dawson Trail Campground
40 kilometers east
Reservations: www.ontarioparks.com
Tel: (888) 668-7275 (807) 597-2735

Aurora 30 G31 GPS 43.99973,-79.46746:
City

York Region Cycling Map

Rec Cycle n' Sports
15483 Yonge Street
Aurora ON L4G 1P3
www.recsports.ca
Tel: (905) 841-5757

Aurora Public Library
15145 Yonge Street
Aurora ON L4G 1M1
www.library.aurora.on.ca
Tel: (905) 727-9493

Ayr 16 Q23 GPS 43.28565,-80.45000: Town

The Swan and the Peacock Bed & Breakfast
1140 Swan Street
Ayr ON N0B 1E0
www.theswanandthepeacock.ca
Tel: (519) 632-5058

Region of Waterloo Library
137 Stanley Street
Ayr ON N0B 1E0
www.rwl.library.on.ca
Tel: (519) 632-7298

Bamberg 22 M21 GPS 43.48930,-80.68909:
Hamlet

Bancroft 61 U45 GPS 45.05654,-77.85335:
Town

Bancroft Tourism

Rockhound Gemboree gem and mineral show - early August

Shamrock Hill Bed & Breakfast
59 Monck Street Box 427
Bancroft ON K0L 1C0
www.bbcanada.com/6237.html
Tel: (613) 332-8204 (866) 742-6705

Bancroft Inn & Suites
528 Hastings Street North
RR#1 Bancroft ON K0L 1C0
www.bancroftmotorinn.com
Tel: (888) 219-4900 (613) 332-4900

Sword Inn Bancroft
146 Hastings Street North
Bancroft ON K0L 1C0
www.bestwesternontario.com/hotels/best-western-sword-motor-inn
Tel: (800) 780-7234 (613) 332-2474

Trips and Trails Adventure Outfitting
258 Hastings Street North
RR#2 Bancroft ON K0L 1C0

tripsandtrails.ca
Tel: (613) 332-1969

Bancroft Public Library
14 Flint Street Box 127
Bancroft ON K0L 1C0
www.bancroftpubliclibrary.ca
Tel: (613) 332-3180

Barrie 42 B30 GPS 44.38930,-79.68632:
City

Tourist Information: Tourism Barrie
205 Lakeshore Drive
Barrie ON L4N 7Y9
www.tourismbarrie.com
Tel: (800) 668-9100 (705) 739-9444

Simcoe County Cycling Routes

Kempenfest early August

Richmond Manor Bed & Breakfast
16 Blake Street
Barrie ON L4M 1J6
www.bbcanada.com/1145.html
Tel: (705) 726-7103

Best Western Royal Oak Inn
35 Hart Drive Barrie ON
www.bestwesternontario.com/hotels/best-western-royal-oak-inn
Tel: (800) 780-7234 (705) 721-4848

Comfort Inn Barrie
75 Hart Drive Barrie ON
www.comfortinnbarrie.com
Tel: (877) 424-6423 (705) 722-3600

Bikeland
75 Dyment Road
Barrie ON L4N 3H6
www.bikeland.ca
Tel: (705) 726-7372

Barrie Public Library
60 Worsley Street
Barrie ON L4M 1L6
www.library.barrie.on.ca/main.html
Tel: (705) 728-1010

Barrow Bay 55 V17 GPS 44.96003,-81.22703:
Village

Barry's Bay 80 P47 GPS 45.48819,-77.67849:
Town

Fortune's Madawaska Valley Inn
19854 Hwy. 60
Barry's Bay ON K0J 1B0
www.madawaskavalleyinn.com
Tel: (800) 363-2758 (613) 756-9014

Barry's Bay Public Library
19474 Opeongo Line P.O. Box 970
Barry's Bay ON K0J 1B0
library.barrys-bay.ca/
Tel: (613) 756-2000

Batchawana Bay 96 K13
GPS 46.93948,-84.59061: Village

Pancake Bay Provincial Park
Box 61
Batchawana Bay ON P0S 1A0
Reservations: www.ontarioparks.com
Tel: (888) 668-7275 (705) 882-2209

Bath 36 E54 GPS 44.18304,-76.77526:
Village

Lake Ontario Trent Canal Package Route

Bergeron Estate Winery
9656 Loyalist Parkway
Bath ON K0H 1G0
www.bergeronestatewinery.ca
Tel: (613) 373-0181

33 Vines Winery
9261 Loyalist Parkway
Bath ON K0H 1G0
Tel: (613) 373-1133

Bayshore Bed & Breakfast
34 Bayshore Drive
Bath ON K0H 1G0
www.bbcanada.com/bayshorebb
Tel: (613) 352-5889

Hetherington Hall
338 Main Street
Bath ON K0H 1G0
Tel: (613) 352-0012

Lennox and Addington Public Library -

Layer Cake Hall Museum
197 Davy Street
Bath ON K0H 1G0
www.lennox-addington.on.ca
Tel: (613) 352-5600

Battersea 36 B57 GPS 44.43217,-76.38345:
Village

Bayfield 20 L13 GPS 43.56138,-81.69643:
Historic Village

Huron County Cycling Guide

Bayfield Fall Fair mid August

Folmar Windmill replica mill north of Bayfield just off Road 13

The Little Inn - restaurant
Main Street Box 100
Bayfield ON N0M 1G0
www.littleinn.com
Tel: (800) 565-1832 (519) 565-2611

Albion Hotel - restaurant
1 Main Street Box 114
Bayfield ON N0M 1G0
www.thealbionhotel.com
Tel: (519) 565-2641

The Red Pump - restaurant
21 Main Street Box 40
Bayfield ON N0M 1G0
www.theredpumpinn.com
Tel: (519) 565-2576

Huron County Public Library
18 Main Street
Bayfield ON N0M 1G0
www.huroncounty.ca/library
Tel: (519) 565-2886

Beamsville 18 R31 GPS 43.16583,-79.47634:
Town

Grand Niagara Package Route

Theatre to Theatre Package Route

Silver Birches by the Lake Bed and Breakfast
4902 Mountainview Road
Beamsville ON L0R 1B3
www.silverbirchesbythelake.com
Tel: (905) 563-9479

Grapeview Guesthouse on the Vinyard B&B
4163 Merritt Road
Beamsville ON L0R 1B1
www.bbcanada.com/grapeview
(905) 563-5077

August Restaurant
5204 King Street West
Beamsville ON
www.augustrestaurant.ca
Tel: (905) 563-0200

Peninsula Ridge Estates Winery Restaurant
5600 King Street West Beamsville ON
www.peninsularidge.com
Tel: (905) 563-0900

Mountainview Cycle
4282 Mountainview Road South
Beamsville ON L0R 1B0
www.mountainviewcycle.ca
Tel: (905) 563-8585

Lincoln Library
5020 Serena Drive
Beamsville ON L0R 1B0
www.lincoln.library.on.ca
Tel: (905) 563-7014

Beeton 30 F29 GPS 44.07882,-79.78498:
Town

New Tecumseth Library
42 Main Street West
Beeton ON L0G 1A0
www.ntpl.ca
Tel: (905) 729-3726

Belfountain 23 J27 GPS 43.79388,-80.01394:
Village

Belle River 4 B4 GPS 42.29306,-82.70632:
Town

Essex County Library

447 Renaud Line Road
Belle River ON N0R 1A0
www.essexcountylibrary.ca
Tel: (226) 946-1529

Belleville 34 E49 GPS 44.16105,-77.38190:
City

🛈📧⭐️🛏️🍴🚲🛍
🛈 Bay of Quinte Package Route
🛈 Lake Ontario Trent Canal Package Route
🛈 Bay of Quinte Tourism
🛈 Great Waterway Tourist Region cycling
Itineraries - [Cornwall, Brockville, Gananoque,
Kingston, Belleville]
⭐️ Waterfront Festival and Ethnic Festival mid July
⭐️ Farmers Market at City Hall; Tuesday, Thursday
and Saturday
⭐️ Glanmore National Historic Site Museum
restored Victorian mansion
257 Bridge Street East
www.glanmore.org/glanmoreind.html
Tel: (613) 962-2329
⭐️ Empire Theatre & Centre for the Performing
Arts
321 Front Street
Belleville ON K8N 2Z9
Tel: (613) 969-0099
🛏️ Best Western Belleville
387 North Front Street
Belleville ON K8P 3C8
Tel: (613) 969-1112
🛏️ Holiday Inn Express
291 North Front Street
Belleville ON K8P 3C3
Tel: (613) 962-1200
🛏️ Belle Vie Belleville Bed & Breakfast
194 Lingham Street
Belleville ON K8N 3T4
Tel: (613) 962-2487
🛏️ The Moira Bed & Breakfast
21 Elvins Gardens
Belleville ON K8P 2T2
Tel: (613) 967-7856
🍴 L'Auberge de France
304 Front Street
Belleville ON K8N 2Y6
www.aubergedefrance.ca
Tel: (613) 966-2433
🍴 Capers Restaurant
272 Front Street Belleville ON
Tel: (613) 968-7979
www.capers.ca
🍴 Boathouse Restaurant
32 Front Street
Belleville, ON K8N 2Y3
www.boathouselure.ca
Tel: (613) 969-2211
🚲 Ideal Bike
316 Front Street
Belleville ON K8N 2Z8
www.idealbike.ca
Tel: (613) 779-6979 - rentals
🛍 Belleville Public Library & John M Parrott Art
Gallery
254 Pinnacle Street
Belleville ON K8N 3B1
www.bellevillelibrary.com
Tel: (613) 968-6731

Belmont 9 U18 GPS 42.88064,-81.08735:
Village

🍴🛏️

Benmiller 20 K14 GPS 43.72844,-81.64078:
Resort village

🛏️⛺️
🛏️ Benmiller Inn & Spa restaurant
81175 Benmiller Road RR#4
Goderich ON N7A 3Y1
www.benmillerinnandspa.com
Tel: (800) 265-1711 (519) 524-2191
⛺️ Falls Reserve Conservation Area
Benmiller
Tel: (877) 325-5722 (519) 524-6429

Big Bay 39 X19 GPS 44.79158,-80.94727:
Village

🛍

Big Chute 41 W30 GPS 44.88680,-79.66727:

Village

🛏️🍴⭐️
⭐️ Trent Severn Waterway
Marine Railway Lock 44
Group camping at most lock stations with prior
approval
www.pc.gc.ca/eng/lhn-nhs/on/trentsevern/visit/
visit6.aspx

Birr 14 R16 GPS 43.11903,-81.33316:
Village

🛍

Black River 35 G51 GPS 43.96811,-77.03476:
Village

⭐️ Black River Cheese
913 County Road 13 RR#2
Milford ON K0K 2P0
www.pec.on.ca/blackrivercheese
Tel: (888) 252-5787 (613) 476-2575

Blacks Corners 65 T-U59
GPS 45.11824,-76.11568: Hamlet

🛍

Blenheim 7 B10 GPS 42.33519,-81.99770: Town

🛈📧🍴🛍🛍
🛈 Erie Shores Package Route
🛏️ Silver Motel
398 Chatham Street South
Blenheim ON N0P 1A0
Tel: (519) 676-5156
🍴 Jack's Family Restaurant
67 Talbot Street West
Blenheim ON N0P 1A0
Tel: (519) 676-5050
🛍 Chatham Kent Public Library
16 George Street
Blenheim ON N0P 1A0
 www.chatham-kent.ca/PublicLibraries/Pages/
Home.aspx
Tel: (519) 676-3174

Blessington 35 D50 GPS 44.25553,-77.30186:
Village

🛍

Blind River 2 GPS 46.18769,-82.96038:
Town

🍴🛏️🛈🛏️⛺️🛍
🛈 Regional Tourist Information Centre, Timber
Village Museum
243 Causley Street
Blind River ON P0R 1B0
Tel: (800) 563-8719
🛏️ Auberge Eldo Inn
1 White Road Box 156
Blind River ON P0R 1B0
www.eldoinn.on.ca
Tel: (800) 798-3536 (705) 356-2255
🛏️ Old Mill Motel
Highway 17 and Woodward Avenue
Blind River ON
www.oldmillmotel.ca
Tel: (800) 871-0842 (705) 356-2274
🛏️ A Taste of Home Bed & Breakfast
29 Fullerton Street
Blind River ON P0R 1B0
www.bbcanada.com/989.html
Tel: (705) 356-7165
⛺️ MacIver's Mississauga Motel and Camp
Box 502 Highway 17 West
Blind River ON P0R 1B0
Tel: (877) 573-1078 (705) 356-7411
🛍 Blind River Public Library
8 Woodward Avenue
Blind River ON P0R 1B0
Tel: (705) 356-7616

Bloomfield 35 G50 GPS 43.98549,-77.23418:
Village

🛏️🚲🛍🛏️
🛏️ Angeline's Inn - restaurant
433 Main Street Box 16
Bloomfield ON K0K 1G0
www.angelinesrestaurantinn.com
Tel: (613) 393-3301
🛏️ Renlea House Bed & Breakfast
420 Main Street
Bloomfield ON K0K 1G0
www.bbcanada.com/538.html
Tel: (800) 490-7666 (613) 393-1846
🚲 Bloomfield Cycle - rentals

225 Main Street Bloomfield ON
www.torontocyclist.com/bbc/
Tel: (613) 393-1060
🛍 Prince Edward County Library
300 Main Street Bloomfield ON
www.peclibrary.org
Tel: (613) 393-3400

Bobcaygeon 44 A39 GPS 44.54521, -78.541514:
Town

🍴🛏️🛍
🛏️ Bobcaygeon Inn Restaurant &
Waterfront Patio
31 Main Street
Bobcaygeon ON K0M 1A0
www.bobcaygeoninn.com
Tel: (800) 900-4248 (705) 738-5433
🛍 Kawartha Lakes Public Library
21 Canal Street
Bobcaygeon ON K0M 1A0
www.city.kawarthalakes.on.ca/residents/library-
services/hours-and-locations
Tel: (705) 738-2088

Bowmanville 32 G38 GPS 43.91383,-78.68847:
Town

🛈🛏️🍴🛍⛺️🚲🌿🛍
🛈 Clarington Tourism
181 Liberty Street South
Bowmanville ON L1C 3Z2
www.claringtontourism.net
Tel: (800) 563-1195 (905) 623-4356
🛏️ Holiday Inn Express and Suites
37 Spicer Square
Bowmanville ON L1C 2W4
Tel: (877) 660-8550 (905) 697-8089
⛺️ Darlington Provincial Park
1600 Darlington Beach Road
Bowmanville ON L1C 5M2
Reservations: www.ontarioparks.com
Tel: (888) 668-7275 (905) 436-2036
🚲 Bowmanville Sports Shop
58 King Street West Bowmanville ON
Tel. (905) 623-0322
www.bowmanvillesportshop.com
🌿 Bowmanville/Westside Marshes Conservation
Area
180 West Beach Road Clarington ON
🛍 Clarington Public Library
163 Church Street
Bowmanville ON L1C 1T7
Tel: (905) 623-7322

Bracebridge 59 U5 GPS 45.05558,-79.28863:
Town

🛏️🍴🚲🛏️🛍
🛏️ Century House Bed and Breakfast
155 Dill Street
Bracebridge ON P1L 1E5
www.bbmuskoka.com/centuryhouse
Tel: (705) 645-9903
🛏️ The Monastery B&B
15 Sadler Drive
Bracebridge ON P1L 1K5
www.bbmuskoka.com/themonastery
Tel: (705) 646-0871
🛏️ Quality Inn Bracebridge
300 Ecclestone Drive
Bracebridge ON P1L 1G5
Tel: (705) 645-8775 (800) 461-4474
🛏️ Wellington Motel
265 Wellington Street Bracebridge ON
www.wellingtonmotel.com
Tel: (800) 212-2280 (705) 645-2238
🚲 Ecclestone Cycling Company
230 Ecclestone Drive
Bracebridge ON P1L 1G4
www.ecclestonecycle.com
Tel: (705) 645-1166
🛍 Bracebridge Public Library
94 Manitoba Street
Bracebridge ON P1L 2B5
www.bracebridge.library.on.ca
Tel: (705) 645-4171

Bradford 30 E-F30 GPS 44.11455,-79.56366:
Town

⭐️🍴🛏️🛍
⭐️ Carrot Fest mid August

Brampton 24 K29 GPS 43.68431,-79.75873: City

🛈🚲🛏️🛍🛍
🛈 Peel Trails Map - walking and cycling

Best Western Brampton
30 Clark Boulevard
Brampton ON L6W 1X3
www.bestwesternontario.com/hotels/best-western-brampton
Tel: (800) 780-7234 (905) 454-1300

Comfort Inn
5 Rutherford Road South
Brampton ON L6W 3J3
www.choicehotels.ca/en/brampton-hotel-comfort-ontario-cn256-en
Tel: (877) 424-6423 (905) 452-0600

Residence & Conference Centre Brampton
7897 McLaughlin Road
Brampton ON N6Y 5H9
www.stayrcc.com
Tel: (905) 874-4393 (877) 225-8664

The Cyclepath Brampton
60 Main Street North
Brampton ON L6V 1N6
www.cyclepathbrampton.com
Tel: (905) 457-4481

Brampton Public Library
65 Queen Street East
Brampton ON L6W 3L6
www.bramlib.on.ca
Tel: (905) 793-4636

Brantford 16 R24 GPS 43.14136,-80.26174:
City

Theatre to Theatre Package Route

The Hub of Ontario Trails Map

Brantford Tourism Brantford Visitor & Tourism Centre
399 Wayne Gretzky Parkway
Brantford ON N3R 8B4
www.discoverbrantford.com
Tel: (800) 265-6299 (519) 751-9900

Bell Homestead Museum - Alexander Graham Bell
94 Tutela Heights Road
Brantford ON
www.bellhomestead.ca
Tel: (519) 756-6220

Glenhyrst Art Gallery of Brant
22 Ava Road
www.glenhyrst.ca
Tel: (519) 756-5932

Sanderson Centre for the Performing Arts
88 Dalhousie Street
www.sandersoncentre.ca
Tel: (800) 265-0710 (519) 758-8090

Brantford International Jazz Festival - September

The Canadian Military Heritage Museum and Vintage Motorcycle Museum
347 Greenwich Street
www.cmhmhq.ca
Tel: (519) 759-1313

Kanata reconstructed 1600's Iroquoian village and Her Majesty's Royal Chapel of the Mohawks
291 Mohawk Street
www.mohawkchapel.ca
Tel: (519) 756-0240

Brantford International Villages Cultural Festival early July

Mimi's Bed & Breakfast
103 William Street
Brantford ON N3T 3K9
Tel: (519) 381-6828

Quality Inn & Suites
664 Colborne Street East
Brantford ON N3S 3P8
www.qualityinn.com/hotel-brantford-canada-CN870
Tel: (877) 424-6423 (519) 758-9999

Hampton Inn & Suites
20 Fen Ridge Court
Brantford ON N3V 1G2
hamptoninnbrantford.com
Tel: (519) 720-0084

The Piston Broke Gastro Pub
93 Dalhousie Street
Brantford ON N3T 2J1
Tel: (519) 304-4568

Warmington's Bistro
42 George Street
Brantford ON N3T 2Y1
Tel: (519) 770-4941

The Bicycle Shop
228 Clarence Street

Brantford ON
www.thebicycleshopbrantford.ca
Tel: (519) 752-2414

Brantford Public Library
173 Colborne Street
Brantford ON N3T 2G8
www.brantford.library.on.ca
Tel: (877) 424-6423 (519) 758-9999

Bridgenorth 44 B40 GPS 44.38497,-78.38608:
Village

Brighton 34 F46 GPS 44.04247,-77.73562:
Town

Bay of Quinte Package Route

Bay of Quinte and Northumberland Package Route

Lake Ontario Trent Canal Package Route

Proctor House Museum and Brighton Barn Theatre
96 Young Street Brighton ON K0K 1H0
www.proctorhousemuseum.ca
Tel: (613) 475-2144

Presqu'ile Beach Motel
243 Main Street RR#4
Brighton ON K0K 1H0
www.ruralroutes.com/presquilebeachmotel
Tel: (877) 769-6153 (613) 475-1010

Cider House Bed & Breakfast
74 Prince Edward Street
Box 1138 Brighton ON K0K 1H0
www.ciderhouse.ca
Tel: (613) 475-5087

Brighton Inn
40 Young Street
Brighton ON K0K 1H0
Tel: (888) 895-5807 (613) 475-9706

Presqu'ile Provincial Park
RR#3 Brighton ON K0K 1H0
Reservations: www.ontarioparks.com
Tel: (888) 668-7275 (613) 475-2204

The Gables Restaurant
14 Division Street Brighton ON
www.thegablesrestaurant.net
Tel: (613) 475-5565

Dougalls on the Bay
75 Harbour Street, Box 762
www.ruralroutes.com/dougalls
Tel: (613) 475-4142

Brighton Public Library
35 Alice Street Brighton ON
www.brighton.library.on.ca
Tel: (613) 475-2511

Brockville 50 Z62-63 GPS :44.59039,-75.68301:
City

St. Lawrence and Rideau Canal Package Route

Brockville Railway Tunnel

Fulford Place - 1900 Edwardian Mansion
287 King Street East Brockville ON
www.heritagefdn.on.ca/userfiles/HTML/nts
Tel: (613) 498-3003

Brockville Museum
5 Henry Street
Brockville ON K6V 6M4
Tel: (613) 342-4397

Super 8 Brockville
1843 Road 2
Brockville ON K6V 5T1
Tel: (613) 345-1622

St Lawrence College - Residence Services
2288 Parkedale Avenue
Brockville ON K6V 5X3
www.sl.on.ca/residence/SummerAccomodations.htm
Tel: (613) 345-0660, ext. 3510

St Lawrence Park
Road 2 Brockville ON
Tel: (613) 345-1341

Brockberry Café & Suites
64 King Street East Box 808
Brockville ON K6V SW1
www.brockberry.com
Tel: (613) 498-2692

The Mill Restaurant
123 Water Street Brockville ON
www.themillrestaurant.ca
Tel: (613) 345-7098

Brockville Public Library

23 Buell Street Brockville ON
www.brockvillelibrary.ca
Tel: (613) 342-3936

Bruce Mines 2 GPS 46.30021,-83.79414:
Village

Bruce Mines Museum Simpsons Copper Mine Shaft in town

Bavarian Inn - restaurant
9181 Highway 17
Bruce Mines ON P0R 1C0
www.bavarianinnbrucemines.com
Tel: (705) 785-3447

Bruce Mines Campground
Williams Street
(off Highway 17 at Highway 638)
Bruce Mines ON
Tel: (705) 785-3493

Burford 16 S23 GPS 43.10309,-80.43003:
Town

County of Brant Public Library
24 Park Ave Box 267
Burford ON N0E 1A0
www.brant.library.on.ca
Tel: (519) 449-5371

Burgessville 16 S22 GPS 43.02401,-80.65197:
Town

Oxford County Library – Burgessville
604 Main Street South
Burgessville ON N0J 1C0
Tel: (519) 424-2404

Burlington 18 P29 GPS 43.32618,-79.79854:
City

Tourism Burlington
414 Locust Street
Burlington ON L7S 1T7
www.tourismburlington.com
Tel: (877) 499-9989 (905) 634-5594

Halton Region Cycling Maps

Sound of Music Festival - mid June

Royal Botanical Gardens
680 Plains Road West Burlington ON
Tel: (800) 694-4769 (905) 527-1158

Wilkie House Bed & Breakfast
1211 Sable Drive
Burlington ON L7S 2J7
www.canvisit.com/wilkiehouse
Tel: (866) 233-2632 (905) 637-5553

Waterfront Hotel – Downtown
2020 Lakeshore Road
Burlington ON L7R 4G8
www.thewaterfrontdowntown.com
Tel: (905) 681-5400

Pepperwood Bistro
1455 Lakeshore Road
Burlington ON L7S 2J1
www.pepperwood.on.ca/index2.html
Tel: (905) 333-6999

Spencers at the Waterfront
1340 Lakeshore Road
Burlington ON L7S 1B1
www.spencers.ca
Tel: (905) 633-7494

Brant Cycle
892 Brant Street
Burlington ON L7R 2J5
www.brantcycle.ca
Tel:(905) 637-3737

Burlington Public Library
2331 New Street Burlington ON
www.bpl.on.ca
Tel: (905) 639-3611

Burritts Rapids 50 V62 GPS 44.98345,-75.79860:
Village

Rideau Canal Lock 17, group camping with prior approval
www.pc.gc.ca/lhn-nhs/on/rideau/index.aspx
Tel: (888) 773-8888 (613) 283-5170

Caledon East 29 H28 GPS 43.87526,-79.85994:
Village

Caledonia 17 S28 GPS 43.07356,-79.95072:
Town

🛈🍴🏨⛺🚲

🛈 Haldimand County Cycling Routes
🚲 Haldimand County Library – Caledonia Branch
100 Haddington Street, Unit 2
www.haldimandcounty.on.ca
Tel: (905) 765-2634

Cambridge 22 NP24 GPS 43.36141,-80.31533: City

🛈🍴🏨⭐🚲🚲

🛈 Waterloo Regional Cycling Network
⭐ Cambridge Butterfly Conservatory
2500 Kossuth Road
Cambridge ON N3H 4R7
www.cambridgebutterfly.com
Tel: (519) 653-1234
⭐ Cambridge Farmers Market
Saturday and Wednesday
40 Dickson Street at Ainslie Street
www.cambridgefarmersmarket.ca
⭐ Dunfield Theatre
46 Grand Avenue South Cambridge ON
Tel: (519) 621-8000
🏛 Southworks Outlets & Antiques
64 Grand Avenue South
Cambridge ON N1S 2L8
www.southworks.ca
Tel: (519) 740-0380
🛏 Best Western Cambridge Hotel
730 Hespeler Road
Cambridge ON N3H 5L8
bestwesternontario.com/hotels/best-western-
cambridge-hotel
Tel: (800) 780-7234 (519) 623-4600
🛏 Comfort Inn
220 Holiday Inn Drive Cambridge ON
www.choicehotels.ca/en/cambridge-hotel-
comfort-ontario-CN260-en?cid=1371119
 Tel: (877) 424-6423 (519) 658-1100
🍴 Cambridge Mill
130 Water Street North
Cambridge ON N1R 1P1
www.cambridgemill.ca
Tel: (519) 624-1828
🍴 Blackshop Restaurant
595 Hespeler Road
Cambridge ON N1R 6J3
www.blackshop.ca
Tel: (519) 621-4180
🍴 Melville Café
7 Melville Street
Cambridge ON N1S 2H4
www.melvillecafe.ca
Tel (519) 624-3984
🚲 Hub Bicycle Shop
22 Queen Street West Cambridge ON
www.hubbicycleshop.com
Tel: (519) 249-1473
🚲 Idea Exchange
Queen's Square 1 North Square
Cambridge ON N1S 2K6
www.cambridgelibraries.ca
Tel: (519) 621-0460

Campbellford 34 C45 GPS 44.30921,-77.79749:
Town

🛈🍴🏨⭐🛏🚲

🛈 Bay of Quinte and Northumberland Package
Route
🛈 Lake Ontario Trent Canal Package Route
🛈 Downtown Campbellford
⭐ Westben Arts Festival Theatre
6698 Road 30
www.westben.on.ca
Tel: (887) 883-5777 (705) 653-5508
⭐ World's Finest Chocolate Canada Company
103 Second Street
Campbellford ON L0L 1L0
www.worldsfinest.ca
Tel: (800) 461-1957
⭐ Trent Severn Waterway at Lock 13
⭐ Empire Cheese & Butter Co-op
1120 Road 8
Campbellford ON (5 kilometers east)
www.empirecheese.ca
Tel: (800) 461-6480 (705) 653-3187
🍴 Church Key Pub & Grindhouse

26 Bridge Street West
Campbellford ON K0L 1L0
www.churchkeybrewing.com
Tel: (705) 653-0001
🍴 Capers Restaurant
28 Bridge Street West
Campbellford ON K0L 1L0
Tel: (705) 653-5262
🍴 Apollos Pizzeria
92 Bridge Street East
Campbellford ON K0L 1L0
Tel: (705) 753-1414
🛏 Grand Victoria House B&B
258 Grand Road Box 520
Campbellford ON K0L 1L0
www.bbcanada.com/2769.html
Tel: (877) 592-7282 (705) 632-0587
🛏 King and Knight Bed & Breakfast
188 Queen Street Box 310
Campbellford ON K0L 1L0
www.kingandknightbedandbreakfast.com
Tel: (800) 434-0378 (705) 632-1441
🛏 Campbellford River Inn
352 Front Street
Campbellford ON K0L 1L0
www.riverinn.on.ca/
Tel: (800) 984-6665 (705) 653-1771
🚲 Trent Hills Library
98 Bridge Street East
Campbellford ON K0L 1L0
www.trenthillslibrary.ca/campbellford
Tel: (705) 653-3611

Cardiff 61 V39 GPS 44.99251,-78.09247:
Village

🛈🍴🚲

🚲 Haliburton County Public Library
2778 Monck Road
Cardiff ON K0L 1M0
www.haliburtonlibrary.ca
Tel: (613) 339-2712

Cardinal 50 X65 GPS 44.78731,-75.38481:
Village

🛈🚲

🚲 Cardinal Public Library
618 Kings 2 Highway Cardinal ON
www.edwardsburghcardinal.ca/index.php/city-
hall/departments/cityhall_library-facilities/
Tel: (613) 657-3822

Carp 65 R60 GPS 45.35004,-76.04258: Village

🛈🍴🚲🚲

⭐ Carp Farmers Market
🚲 Ottawa Library – Carp Branch
3911 Carp Road
Carp ON K0A 1L0
www.biblioottawalibrary.ca
Tel: (613) 580-2951
🚩 Diefenbunker, Canada's Cold War Museum
3911 Carp Road
Carp ON K0A 1L0
www.diefenbunker.ca

Castleton 33 E44 GPS 44.09270,-77.93811:
Village

🏛

Cataract 23 J27 GPS 43.82338,-80.02304:
Hamlet

🚩 Forks of the Credit Provincial Park - Cataract
Falls and mill ruins

Cayuga 18 T28: Town

🛈🍴🏨🚲

🛈 Haldimand County Cycling Routes
🛏 Carrousel Bed & Breakfast
51 Winnett Street North
Cayuga ON N0A 1E0
www.carrouselbb.ca
Tel: (905) 772-5348
🛏 Broecheler Inn
4648 Talbot Road West, Highway 3 RR#4
Cayuga ON
www.broechelerinn.com
Tel: (905) 772-5362
🍴 Twisted Lemon Restaurant
3 Norton Street West
Cayuga ON N0A 1E0
www.twistedlemon.ca
Tel: (905) 772-6636
🚲 Haldimand County Library
28 Cayuga Street North

Cayuga ON N0A 1E0
Tel: (289) 674-0400

Cedar Springs 7 C10 GPS 42.28163,-82.03217:
Village

🛈🍴🏛

🛈 Erie Shores Package Route

Centreville 47 B53 GPS 44.40665,-76.90439:
Village

🏛

Chatham 6 A8-9 GPS 42.40444,-82.18958:
City on the Thames River

🍴🏨🛈🛈⭐🚲🚲🚲

🛈 Erie Shores Package Route
🛈 Chatham Kent Tourism
www.cktourism.com
Tel: (800) 561-6125
🛈 Chatham Kent Bicycle Routes
⭐ Chatham Cultural Centre and
Milner Heritage House
75 William Street North Chatham ON
www.theculturalcentre.com
Tel: (866) 807-7770 (519) 354-8338
⭐ St. Clair College Capitol Theatre
238 King Street West Chatham ON
Tel: (866) 807-7770 (519) 354-8338
⭐ RM Classic Car Exhibit
1 Classic Car Drive
Blenheim ON N0P 1A0
Tel: (877) 523-2684 (519) 352-9024
🛏 Chatham Comfort Inn
1100 Richmond Street
Chatham ON N7M 5J5
www.choicehotels.ca/hotels/hotel?hotel=CN262
Tel: (877) 424-6423 (519) 352-5500
🛏 The Duchess of Wellington Bed & Breakfast
320 Wellington Street West
Chatham ON N7M 1K1
www.theduchessofwellington.com
Tel: (519) 351-3126
🛏 Retro Suites & Chilled Cork Restaurant
2 King Street West
Chatham ON N7M 1C6
www.retrosuites.com
Tel: (866) 617-3876 (519) 351-5885
🚲 Smith Cycle
181 Thames Street
Chatham ON N7L 2Z2
Tel: (519) 351-5588
🚲 Chatham Kent Public Library
120 Queen Street
Chatham ON N7M 2G6
www.chatham-kent.ca/community+services/
library/library.htm
Tel: (519) 354-2940

Cheltenham 23 J28 GPS 43.76665,-79.92518:
Village

🏛

Chepstow 27 E17 GPS 44.15438,-81.27425:
Village

🏛

Cherry Valley 35 G50 GPS 43.93585,-77.15443:
Hamlet

Chesley 27 C18 GPS 44.30223,-81.08803:
Town

🍴🏛

Chippawa 19 S35 GPS 43.05000,-79.05000:
Village

🍴🏛

Clarksburg 40 A23 GPS 44.54538,-80.46170:
Village

🍴🏛

Clinton 20 L14 GPS 43.61767,-81.53970: Town

🏛⭐🛏🍴

⭐ Clinton PluckinFest
early July
🛏 The Parker House Motel
77575 London Road RR#5
Clinton ON N0M 1L0
www.parkerhousemotel.com
Tel: (519) 482-3469

Cloyne 47 X50 GPS 44.8161,-77.1856: Village

[icons] **Kingston Frontenac Public Library**
1011 Little Pond Road
Cloyne ON K0H 1K0
Tel: (613) 336-8744

Cobden 82 N53 GPS 45.62707,-76.87998: Town

[icons] **17 West Motel Bar & Grill**
9 Pembroke Street
Cobden ON K0J 1K0
Tel: (613) 646-2091

[icon] **Whitewater Region Library**
P.O. Box 152 Cobden ON K0J 1K0
Tel: (613) 646-7592

Cobourg 33 G42 GPS 43.95961,-78.16778: Town

[icons]
[icon] **Bay of Quinte and Northumberland Package Route**

[icon] **Historic town on Lake Ontario, beach**

[icon] **Waterfront Festival** July 1 weekend

[icon] **Marie Dressler House & Visitor Centre**
212 King Street West Cobourg ON

[icon] **Concert Hall at Victoria Hall**
courtroom, concert hall, art gallery
55 King Street West Cobourg ON

[icon] **Best Western Plus Cobourg Inn**
930 Burnham Street
Cobourg ON K9A 2X9
bestwesternontario.com/cobourg-hotels
Tel: (905) 372-2105

[icon] **The Woodlawn Inn** restaurant
420 Division Street Cobourg ON
www.woodlawninn.com
Tel: (800) 573-5003 (905) 372-2235

[icon] **The King George Inn**
77 Albert Street
Cobourg ON K9A 2L9
thekinggeorgeinn.com
Tel: (905) 373-4610

[icon] **North Side Grill**
92 King Street West
Cobourg ON K9A 2M3
thenorthside.ca
Tel: (905) 377-9709

[icon] **Matterhorn Restaurant**
95 King Street West Cobourg ON
www.matterhorn.ca
Tel: (905) 372-5231

[icon] **Victoria Park Campground**
138 Division Street
Cobourg ON K9A 3P3
www.cobourg.ca/victoria-park-camp-
ground.html
Tel: (905) 373-7321

[icon] **The Bike Shop**
1040 Division Street
Cobourg ON K9A 5Y5
www.tbs-cobourg.ca
Tel: (905) 372-1788

[icon] **Cobourg Public Library**
200 Ontario Street
Cobourg ON K9A 5P4
www.cobourg.library.on.ca
Tel: (905) 372-9271

Colborne 33 F44 GPS 44.00559,-77.88576: Town

[icons]
[icon] **Big Apple - 401 Cider Brewery**
262 Orchard Drive
Colborne ON K0K 1S0
www.visitcramahe.ca/cramahe/
tourism/apple.asp
Tel: (905) 355-2574

[icon] **Colborne Art Gallery**
51 King Street East
Colborne ON K0K 1S0
Tel: (905) 355-1798

[icon] **Loughbreeze Bay B&B**
105 Victoria Beach Road
Colborne ON K0K 1S0
www.loughbreezebay.com
Tel: (905) 355-1487

[icon] **Cramahe Public Library**
6 King Street West Colborne ON
Tel: (905) 355-3722

Colchester 4 F2 GPS 41.98655,-82.92961: Village

[icons]
[icon] **Erie Shores Package Route**

[icon] **1850 John Park Homestead**
915 County Road 50 Kingsville ON
www.erca.org/conservation/area.john_r_park_
homestead.cfm
Tel: (519) 738-2029

Colebrook 36 B54 GPS 44.38571,-76.77109: Village

[icon]

Collingwood 40 A25 GPS 44.49989,-80.21682: Town

[icons]
[icon] **South Georgian Bay Tourism**
www.visitsouthgeorgianbay.com
Tel: (888) 227-8667 (705) 445-7722

[icon] **Harbourview Park** - beach on Georgian Bay

[icon] **Collingwood Elvis Festival** late July

[icon] **Holiday Inn Express**
4 Balsam Street
Collingwood ON L9Y 3J4
www.hiexpress.com
Tel: (877) 660-8550 (705) 444-2144

[icon] **The Findlay House Bed & Breakfast**
29 Findlay Drive
Collingwood ON L9Y 3J4
Tel: (705) 441-2235

[icon] **Azzurra**
100 Pine Street Collingwood ON
azzurra.ca
Tel: (705) 445-7771

[icon] **Tesoro Restaurant**
18 School House Lane Collingwood ON
Tel: (705) 444-9230

[icon] **Little Ed's Ski and Bike Shop**
15 Balsam Street Collingwood ON
www.littleeds.com
Tel: (705) 444-5488

[icon] **Kamikaze Bikes** - rentals
100 Second Street Collingwood ON
Tel: (705) 446-1243

[icon] **Collingwood Public Library**
100 Second Street
Collingwood ON L9Y 1E5
www.collingwoodpubliclibrary.ca
Tel: (705) 445-1571

Collins Bay 36 D55: Part of Kingston
[icons]

Conestogo 22 M23 GPS 44.23954,-76.61453: Village
[icons]

Consecon 34 G47 GPS 43.99142,-77.52149: Village
[icons]
[icon] **Prince Edward County Library**
211 Road 29 Consecon ON
www.peclibrary.org
Tel: (613) 392-1106

Copenhagen 9 W19 GPS 42.67436,-80.98434: Hamlet
[icon]

Corbett 13 Q13 GPS 43.24720,-81.68884: Village
[icon]

Cornwall 52 U70 GPS 45.02844,-74.73569: City
[icons]
[icon] **Ontario Travel**
Seaway International Bridge
903 Brookdale Avenue
Cornwall ON K6J 4P3
www.ontariotravel.net
Tel: (613) 933-2420 (800) 668-2746

[icon] **Tourist Information** - Cornwall & The Counties
www.visit.cornwall.on.ca
Tel: (800) 937-4748 (613) 938-4748

[icon] **Great Waterway Tourist Region Cycling Itineraries** - Cornwall, Brockville, Gananoque, Kingston, Belleville

[icon] **Cornwall Community Museum**
160 Water Street West
Cornwall ON K6J 1A3
Tel: (613) 936-0280

[icon] **Lighthouse Landing Bed & Breakfast**

18177 Road 2 RR#1
Cornwall ON K6H 5R5
www.lighthouse-landing.com
Tel: (877) 501-2508 (613) 931-2508

[icon] **Best Western Parkway Inn**
1515 Vincent Massey Drive
Cornwall, ON K6H 5R6
www.bestwesterncornwall.com
Tel: (613) 932-0451

[icon] **St. Lawrence College – Residence Services**
2 St Lawrence Drive
Cornwall ON K6H 4Z1
www.sl.on.ca/residence/
SummerAccomodations.htm
Tel: (613) 933-6080 ext. 2106

[icon] **Eight Zero Zero Fine Dining**
903 Brookdale Avenue Cornwall ON
Tel: (613) 936-0322

[icon] **Table 21**
157 Pitt Street Cornwall ON
Tel: (613) 933-9117

[icon] **Bicycle World**
150 Pitt Street
Cornwall ON N6J 3P4
www.bicycleworld.com
Tel: (866) 216-6668 (613) 932-2750

[icon] **Cornwall Public Library**
45 Second Street East
Cornwall ON K6H 5V1
www.library.cornwall.on.ca
Tel: (613) 932-4796

Corunna 12 U7 GPS 42.88552,-82.42561: Village
[icons]
[icon] **1862 St. Joseph's Roman Catholic Church**

Courtland 10 V22 GPS 42.840407,-80.632582: Village
[icons]

Courtright 12 V6 GPS 42.81656,-82.47093: Hamlet
[icons]

Craigleith 40 A24 GPS 44.56112,-80.44739: Hamlet
[icons]
[icon] **Blue Mountain Resort Restaurant**
108 Jozo Weider Boulevard
Blue Mountains ON L9Y 3Z2

[icon] **Craigleith Provincial Park**
209403 Highway 26
Collingwood ON L9Y 0T6
Tel: (705) 445-4467

Creemore 29 C26 GPS 44.33044,-80.10857: Village
[icons]
[icon] **Creemore Springs Brewery**
139 Mill Street
Creemore ON L0M 1G0
www.creemoresprings.com/live
Tel: (800) 267-2240 (705) 466-2240

[icon] **Blacksmith House Bed & Breakfast**
7 Caroline Street West Box 130
Creemore ON L0M 1G0
www.blacksmithhouse.ca
Tel: (705) 466-3373

[icon] **Angel House Bed & Breakfast**
3 Nelson Street
Creemore ON L0M 1G0
www.angelhouse.ca
Tel: (705) 466-6505 (877) 842-4438

[icon] **Clearview Public Library**
165 Library Street
Creemore ON L0M 1G0
Tel: (705) 466-3011

Crofton 34 F49 GPS 44.06736,-77.31697: Hamlet
[icon]

Crosshill 22 M21 GPS 43.55651,-80.61390: Village
[icon]

Crystal Beach 19 U35 GPS 42.86363,-79.03427: Town
[icons]

Crystal Beach Motel
122 Ridgeway Road Box 1261
Crystal Beach ON L0S 1B0
www.crystalbeachmotel.com
Tel: (905) 894-1750
Fort Erie Public Library
89 Ridge Road South Ridgeway ON
Tel: (905) 894-1281

Damascus 28 H23 GPS 43.91471,-80.48172:
Hamlet
Pritty Place Bed & Breakfast
8924 Road 16 Damascus RR#4
Kenilworth ON N0G 2E0
www.bbcanada.com/3092.html
Tel: (519) 848-3598

Dashwood 20 P13 GPS 43.34607,-81.63452:
Village

Dealtown 6 C9 GPS 42.26461,-82.04796: Village

Delta 49 Z59 GPS 44.60935,-76.12289:
Village

Demorestville 35 F50 GPS 44.09253,-77.20802:
Hamlet
Demorestville Dam Conservation Area

Denbigh 63 T50 GPS 45.14279,-77.26554:
Village

Desbarats 2 GPS 46.34407,-83.92423:
Village

Deseronto 35 D51 GPS 44.19458,-77.04929:
Town
**Bay of Quinte and Northumberland Package
Route**
Bay of Quinte Package Route
**Tyendinaga First Nation Mohawks of the Bay of
Quinte** - historic landing, native arts and crafts
Town's Edge Bed & Breakfast
73 Main Street
Deseronto ON K0K 1X0
www.bbcanada.com/townsedgebb
Tel: (613) 396-6389
Deseronto Public Library
358 Main Street Box 302
Deseronto ON K0K 1X0
www.deserontopubliclibrary.ca
Tel: (613) 396-2744

Dorchester 9 T18 GPS 42.98908,-81.04889:
Town
Dorchester Public Library
2123 Dorchester Road
Dorchester ON N0L 1G2
Tel: (519) 268-3451

Dorset 60 S36 GPS 42.98908,-81.04889:
Village
The Nordic Inn Restaurant
Highway 35
Dorset ON P0A 1E0
Tel: (705) 766-2343
The Moose B & B
1029 West Harvey Avenue
Dorset ON P0A 1E0
Tel: (705) 766 -0900
Haliburton Public Library
1051 Main Street
Dorchester ON P0A 1E0
Tel: (705) 766-9969

Dresden 6 X9 GPS 42.58951,-82.17964:
Town
Uncle Tom's Cabin historic home of Rev. Josiah
Henson
www.uncletomscabin.org
Tel: (519) 683-2978

Chatham Kent Public Library
187 Brown Street
Dresden ON N0P 1M0
www.chatham-kent.ca/community+ services/
library/library.htm
Tel: (519) 683-4922

Drumbo 16 Q23 GPS 43.23675,-80.55288:
Town

Dunnville 18 U30 GPS 42.90436,-79.61987:
Town
Grand Niagara Package Route
Haldimand County Cycling Routes
Mudcat Festival early June
Riverview Motel
642 Main St West
Dunnville ON N1A 1W7
Tel: (844) 774-5788 (905) 774-5634
Lalor Estate Inn B&B
241 Broad Street West
Dunnville ON N1A 1S8
www.bbcanada.com/lalorestateinn
Tel: (905) 774-5438
Port Maitland Bed & Breakfast
8 Lighthouse Drive
Dunnville ON N1A 2W6
Tel: (905) 774-6026
Byng Island Conservation Area
4969 Road 20
Dunnville ON N1A 2W3
Reservations: www.grandriver.ca
Tel: (877) 558-4722
Rock Point Provincial Park
215 Niece Road
Dunnville ON N1A 2X5
Tel: (905) 774-6642
Reservations: www.ontarioparks.com
Tel: (888) 668-7275
Haldimand County Public Library
317 Chestnut Street
Dunnville ON N1A 2H4
www.haldimandcounty.on.ca/residents.aspx?id=258
&ekmensel=c580fa7b_32_524_btnlink
Tel: (289) 674-0400

Dutton 8 W15 GPS 42.66620,-81.49950:
Town
Dutton Public Library
236 Shackleton Street
Dutton ON N0L 1J0
www.library.elgin-county.on.ca
Tel: (519) 762-2780

Eagle 8 Y14 GPS 42.56775,-81.56250: Hamlet

Echo Bay 2 GPS 46.48493,-84.07005: Village

Eganville 81 P51 GPS 45.53329,-77.11235:
Village
Pine Tree Motel
Highway 41 and 60 RR#6
Eganville ON K0J 1T0
www.pinetreemotel.ca
Tel: (800) 517-9382 (613) 628-2832
Bonnechere Union Public Library
74A Maple Street Box #39
Eganville ON K0J 1T0
Tel: (613) 628-2400

Elmira 22 L22 GPS 43.59865,-80.55872: Town
Region of Waterloo Public Library
65 Arthur Street South
Elmira ON N3B 2M6
www.rwl.library.on.ca
Tel: (519) 669-5477

Elora 22 K23 GPS 43.68158,-80.42975:
Town
Elora Festival, music mid-July to early August
www.elorafestival.com
Tel: (888) 747-7550 (519) 846-0331
The Flying Leap B&B
249 Geddes Street
Elora ON N0B 1S0
Tel: (226) 369-0376

The Village Inn Elora
66 Wellington Road 7
Elora ON N0B 1S0
Tel: (519) 846-5910
Elora Gorge Conservation Area scenic river
valley, trails
7400 Road 21 Box 356
Elora ON N0B 1S0
Tel: (519) 846-9742
Reservations: www.grandriver.ca
Tel: (877) 558-4722
Cork Restaurant
146 Metcalf Street
Elora ON N0B 1S0
www.eloracork.com
Tel: (519) 846-8880
Mill Street Bistro & Smokehouse
15 East Mill Street
Elora ON N0B 1S0
Tel: (226) 384-2277
Salem Cyclery
115 Geddes Street
Elora ON
www.salemcycleryelora.com
Tel: (519) 846-8446
Wellington County Public Library
144 Geddes Street Box 280
Elora ON N0B 1S0
www.county.wellington.on.ca
Tel: (519) 846 0190

Embro 15 R20 GPS 43.15611,-80.90123:
Town
Embro Highland Games July 1
Oxford County Library
135 Huron Street Box 193
Embro ON N0J 1J0
Tel: (519) 475-4172

Emeryville 4 B4: Village

Emo 2 GPS 48.63254,-93.83885: Town
Emo Inn restaurant
Highway 11 Box 598
Emo ON P0W 1C0
www.emoinn.com
Tel: (807) 482-2272

Empire Corners 18 S29
GPS 43.02398,-79.89189: Village

Enterprise 47 B53 GPS 44.46257,-76.87797:
Village

Espanola 84 E13 GPS 46.25677,-81.76423:
Town
Harvie House B&B
2-109 Sheppard Street
Espanola ON P5E 1A1
Tel: (705) 583-2326
Pinewood Motor Inn
378 Centre Street Box 1578
Espanola ON P5E 1G3
Tel: (705) 869-3460
Espanola Public Library
245 Avery Drive
Espanola ON P5E 1S4
Tel: (705) 869-2940

Eugenia 28 C23 GPS 44.31230,-80.52567:
Village

Everett 29 E27 GPS 44.19123,-79.93888:
Village

Fairground 10 X22 GPS 42.63497,-80.65956:
Village

Fenwick 19 S32 GPS 43.02616,-79.35745:
Town

Fergus 22 K24 GPS 43.70544,-80.37814:
Town

⬛🛏♣✦🔧

★ **Fergus Scottish Festival and Highland Games,**
early August
Belwood Lake Conservation Area
8282 Wellington County Road 18 RR#4
Fergus ON N1M 2W5

🛏 **Breadalbane Inn** restaurant
487 St. Andrew Street West Fergus ON
www.breadalbaneinn.com
Tel: (519) 843-4770 (888) 842-2825

🛏 **Stonehurst Bed & Breakfast**
265 St. David Street South
Fergus ON N1M 2L6
www.stonehurstbb.com
Tel: (519) 843-8800

🛏 **Best Western Plus Fergus**
830 St. David Street North
Fergus ON N1M 2L2
Tel: (519) 843-2100

📖 **Wellington County Public Library**
181 St. Andrew Street East
Fergus ON N1M 1P9
www.county.wellington.on.ca
Tel: (519) 843-1180

Fingal 8 W16 GPS 42.71325,-81.31187: Village
🛏

Flesherton 28 D22 GPS 44.26123,-80.54986: Town
🛏🍴🛏ℹ📖

🛏 **Munshaw Village Inn** restaurant
1 Toronto Street
Flesherton ON N0C 1E0
www.bbcanada.com/4058.html
Tel: (888) 209-6222 (519) 924-2282

📖 **Grey Highlands Public Library**
101 Highland Drive
Flesherton ON N0C 1E0
www.greyhighlandspubliclibrary.com
Tel: (519) 924-2241

Floradale 22 L22 GPS 43.63489,-80.58008: Village
🛏

Fonthill 19 S33 GPS 43.04409,-79.28182: Town
🛏🍴📖

📖 **Pelham Library**
43 Pelham Town Square
Pelham ON L3C 1E0
Tel: (905) 892-6443

Forest 13 S10 GPS 43.09797,-81.99934: Town
★🛏🛏ℹ🔧🛏📖

★ **Forest Lambton Museum**
8 Main Street North Forest ON
www.lambtononline.com/forest_lambton
Tel: (519) 786-3239

★ **Western Ontario Steam Threshers Reunion**
Forest Fair Grounds, mid August
www.steamthresher.com

★ **Forest Fall Fair,** late September
www.forestfair.ca

🛏 **Forest Golf & Country Hotel** Restaurant
102 Main Street South
Forest ON N0N 1J0
www.golfforest.com
Tel: (800) 265-0214 (519) 786-2397

🛏 **Through Windows Past Bed & Breakfast**
64 King Street West Forest ON
www.throughwindowspast.ca
Tel: (519) 786-5070

📖 **Lambton County Library**
61 King Street West
Forest ON N0N 1J0
www.lclmg.org
Tel: (519) 786 5152

Formosa 27 F17 GPS 44.06701,-81.21409: Village
1870 Formosa Springs Brewery operated by
Brick Brewing tours, retail outlet
🛏🍴

Fort Erie 19 T36 GPS 42.90197,-78.97420: City
🍴ℹ🔧🛏🛏🅰🚲📖

ℹ **Bike Peace Bridge Fort Erie to Buffalo USA**
100 Queen Street
Fort Erie ON L2A 3S6
1 Peace Bridge Plaza
Buffalo NY 14213

ℹ **Grand Niagara Package Route**

ℹ **Niagara Cycling Tourism Centre**

ℹ **Niagara Region Bicycling Map**

★ **Historical Railroad Museum**
400 Central Avenue Fort Erie ON
www.museum.forterie.ca/railroad.html
Tel: (905) 871-1412

🛏 **Friendship Trail Bed & Breakfast**
328 Kraft Road
Fort Erie ON L2A 4M5
www.friendshiptrailbandb.ca
Tel: (905) 871-1424

🛏 **Clarion Hotel and Conference Centre**
restaurant
1485 Garrison Road
Fort Erie ON L2A 1P8
www.clarionhotel.com/hotel-fort_erie-canada-CN965
Tel: (877) 424-6423 (905) 871-8333

🛏 **Comfort Inn**
1 Hospitality Drive
Fort Erie ON L2A 6G1
www.choicehotels.com
Tel: (877) 424-6423 (905) 871-8500

🅰 **Windmill Point Park**
2409 Dominion Road
Ridgeway ON L0S 1N0
www.windmillpointpark.com
Tel: (888) 977-8888 (905) 894-2809

🚲 **Steve's Place Bicycles & Repair** bicycle rental
181 Niagara Boulevard Fort Erie ON
www.cycleman.com
Tel: (905) 871-7517

📖 **Fort Erie Public Library**
136 Gilmore Road
Fort Erie ON L2A 2M1
www.forterie.library.on.ca
Tel: (905) 871-2546

Fort Frances 2 GPS 48.61001,-93.39111:
Town bridge to International Falls, Minnesota USA
🛏🍴ℹ🔧🛏📖

🛏 **La Place Rendez-Vous** restaurant
1201 Idylwild Drive East Fort Frances ON
www.rendezvoushotel.com
Tel: (800) 544-9435 (807) 274-9811

🛏 **Super 8 Motel**
810 King's Hwy, Highway 11 West
Fort Frances ON P9A 2X4
www.super8.com
Tel: (800) 800-8000 (807) 274-4945

📖 **Fort Francis Public Library**
363 Church Street
Fort Frances ON P9A 1C9
library.fort-frances.com
Tel: (807) 274-9879

Foxboro 34 D48 GPS 44.25125,-77.43913:
Former village now part of Belleville
🛏🍴

Frankford 34 D47 GPS 44.20112,-77.59635:
Town
ℹ🛏🍴🛏★

ℹ **Bay of Quinte Package Route**

🛏 **Frankford Bed & Breakfast**
86 Mill Street Box 111
Frankford ON K0K 2C0
Tel: (613) 210-0658

★ **Trent Canal Lock 6**
camping for organized cycling groups at most
locks if approved in advance

Frankville 49 Y60 GPS 44.72096,-75.96107:
Village
🛏

Gananoque 37 C59 GPS 44.32848,-76.16426:
Town, Thousand Islands area
🛏🛏🍴ℹ🔧🛏🚲📖

ℹ **Tourist Information:** 1000 Islands Gananoque
Chamber of Commerce
10 King Street East
Gananoque ON
www.1000islandsgananoque.com
Tel: (800) 561-1595 (613) 382-3250

ℹ **St. Lawrence and Rideau Canal Package Route**

ℹ **Great Waterway Tourist Region Cycling**
Itineraries - Cornwall, Brockville, Gananoque,
Kingston, Belleville

★ **Thousand Islands Playhouse**
185 South Street Gananoque ON
www.1000islandsplayhouse.com

Tel: (866) 382-7020 (613) 382-7020

★ **Gananoque Boat Lines**
6 Water Street Gananoque ON
Tel: (888) 717-4837

🛏 **Sleepy Hollow Bed & Breakfast**
95 King Street West
Gananoque ON K7G 2G2
www.sleepyhollowbb.ca
Tel: (866) 426-7422 (613) 382-4377

🛏 **Beaver Hall Bed & Breakfast**
75 King Street West
Gananoque ON K7G 2G2
www.beaverhallbedandbreakfast.com
Tel: (613) 382-4590

🛏 **Gananoque Inn** restaurant
550 Stone Street South
Gananoque ON K7G 2A8
www.gananoqueinn.com
Tel: (888) 565-3101 (613) 382-2165

🚲 **TI Cycle** rentals
711 King Street East, Unit 7
Gananoque ON K7G 1H4
www.ti-cycle.com
Tel: (613) 382-5144

📖 **Gananoque Public Library**
100 Park Street
Gananoque ON K7G 2Y5
Tel: (613) 382-2436

Garden Hill 32 F40 GPS 44.05762,-78.40256: Village
🔧🛏

🔧 **1869 Dorothy's Historic House Museum**
Road 9 west of Road 10 in Garden Hill
www.porthopehistorical.ca/museum.htm

🛏 **Woodland Gardens Bed & Breakfast**
8250 Woodland Avenue Box 7
Garden Hill ON
www.bbcanada.com/woodlandgardens
Tel: (905) 797-2799

Garden River First Nation 32 F40
GPS 46.55206,-84.18150: Village

Georgetown 23 L28 GPS 43.65001,-79.89888: Town
🛏ℹ★🛏🍴🚲📖

ℹ **Halton Region Cycling Maps**

★ **Downtown Farmers Market**
Saturday mornings on Main Street south of
Guelph Street
www.downtowngeorgetown.com/directory/
farmers-market-co-georgetown-bia

🛏 **Best Western Inn On the Hill**
365 Guelph Street
Georgetown ON L7G 4B6
www.bestwesternontario.com/georgetown-hotels
Tel: (800) 780-7234 (905) 877-6986

🛏 **Main Street Inn Bed & Breakfast**
126 Main Street South
Georgetown ON L7G 3E6
www.bbcanada.com/9452.html
Tel: (905) 702-5411

🚲 **Ollie's Cycle & Ski**
30 Main Street South
Georgetown ON
www.olliescycle.com
Tel: (905) 873-2441

📖 **Halton Hills Public Library**
9 Church Street
Georgetown ON L7G 2A3
www.library.hhpl.on.ca
Tel: (905) 873-2681

Glencoe 7 W13 GPS 42.74855,-81.71080: Town
🛏🍴📖

📖 **Middlesex County Library** – Glencoe Branch
178 McKellar Street
Glencoe ON N0L 1M0
www.middlesex.library.on.ca/branch/glencoe.asp
Tel: (519) 287-2735

Glen Morris 16 Q24 17 Q25
GPS 43.27594,-80.34362: Village
🛏

Glen Ross 34 D47 GPS 44.26475,-77.59695:
Hamlet
🛏★

Trent Canal Lock 7
camping for organized cycling groups at most locks if approved in advance

Glen Williams 23 K28 GPS 43.68447,-79.93013: Village

Glencairn 29 C27 GPS 44.30072,-80.01719: Village

Glenora 35 F51 GPS 44.04071,-77.05811: Hamlet

Glenora - Adolphustown Ferry - free continuous half hour service

Goderich 20 K13 GPS 43.74264,-81.70776: Town: lighthouse, beach

Huron County Cycling Guide
Celtic Roots Festival - early August
Lions Harbour Park, West Street
Huron County Museum
110 North Street Goderich ON
Historic Gaol
181 Victoria Street North Goderich ON
Colborne Bed & Breakfast
72 Colborne Street Goderich ON
www.colbornebandb.com
Tel: (800) 390-4612
Twin Porches B&B
55 Nelson Street East
Goderich ON N7A 1R7
Tel: (519) 524-5505
Samuel's Hotel
34031 Saltford Road RR#4
Goderich ON N7A 3Y1
Tel: (877) 524-1371 (519) 524-1371
Point Farms Provincial Park
82491 Bluewater Highway RR#3
Goderich ON N7A 3X9
Tel: (519) 524-7124
Reservations: www.ontarioparks.com
Tel: (888) 668-7275
Goderich Cyclery - rentals
622 Pentland Avenue Goderich ON
Tel: (519) 524-4720
Huron County Library
52 Montreal Street Goderich ON
www.huroncounty.ca/library/index.php
Tel: (519) 524-9261

Godfrey 36 A55 GPS 44.54311,-76.67906: Village

Gooderham 60 V40 GPS 44.906384,-78.379801: Village

Haliburton Public Library
1032 Gooderham Street Gooderham ON
Tel: (705) 447-3163

Gore Bay 71 J7 GPS 45.91657,-82.46608:

The Queen's Inn
19 Water Street Box 677
Gore Bay ON P0P 1H0
www.thequeensinn.ca
Tel: (705) 282-0665
Gore Bay Union Public Library
15 Water Street, P.O. Box 225
Gore Bay ON P0P 1H0
www.gorebay.ca
Tel: (705) 282 2221

Gores Landing 33 E42
GPS 44.11920,-78.23249: Village

Bay of Quinte & Northumberland Package Route
Lake Ontario Trent Canal Package Route
Rice Lake Tourist Information
The Victoria Inn restaurant
Gores Landing ON K0K 2E0
www.thevictoriainn.ca

Tel: (905) 342-3261
Aye Lighthouse Bed & Breakfast
5303B Traill Road North RR#1
Gores Landing ON K0K 2E0
www.ayelighthouse.info
Tel: (905) 342-5570

Grafton 33 G43 GPS 43.99238,-78.02431: Village

Shelter Valley Folk Festival early September
Vernonville Road north of Highway 2
www.sheltervalley.com
Grafton Village Inn restaurant
10830 Road 2
Grafton ON K0K 2G0
www.graftonvillageinn.ca
Tel: (905) 349-3024 (Restaurant)
Tel: (905) 376-9130 (Accommodation)

Grand Bend 20 P12-13 GPS 43.31247,-81.75653: Town

Huron Country Playhouse
RR#1 Grand Bend 3 kilometers east
Highway 81 at Stephen B Line
www.draytonentertainment.com
Tel: (855) 372-9866 (519) 238-6000
Rotary Trail to Pinery Provincial Park
Pine Dale Motor Inn
107 Ontario Street South Box 191
Grand Bend ON N0M 4T0
www.pinedale.on.ca
Tel: (888) 838-7463 (519) 238-2231
Pinery Provincial Park
9526 Lakeshore Road RR#2
Grand Bend ON N0M 1T0
Tel: (519) 243-2220
Reservations: www.ontarioparks.com
Tel: (888) 668-7275
FINE A Restaurant
42 Ontario Street South Grand Bend ON
www.finearestaurant.com
Tel: (519) 238-6224
Schoolhouse Restaurant
19-81 Crescent Street Grand Bend ON
www.schoolhouserestaurant.ca
Tel: (519) 238-5515
Lambton County Library
15 Gill Street
Grand Bend ON N0M 1T0
www.lclmg.org
Tel: (519) 238-2067

Grande Pointe 6 A7 GPS 42.44145,-82.35558: Village

Gravenhurst 58 V32 GPS 44.92084,-79.37370: Town

Muskoka Tourism Information Centres:
Kilworthy - Highway 11 North of Severn Bridge
Port Severn - Highway 400
www.discovermuskoka.ca
Tel: (800) 267-9700
Blaincroft Bed & Breakfast
180 Hughson Street
Gravenhurst ON P1P 1H2
www.bbmuskoka.com/blaincroft
Tel: (705) 684-8994
The Inn on the Bay Bed & Breakfast
291 Bay Street
Gravenhurst ON P1P 1H1
www.innonbay.com
Tel: (800) 493-0235 (705) 681-0258
Howard Johnson Inn
1165 Muskoka Road South
Gravenhurst ON P1P 1K6
www.hojo.com
Tel: (800) 406-1411 (705) 687-7707
Gravenhurst Public Library
180 Sharpe Street West
Gravenhurst ON P1P 1J1
www.surenet.net/~glib
Tel: (705) 687-3382

Grimsby 18 Q31 GPS 43.19902,-79.58552: Town

Grand Niagara Package Route
Theatre to Theatre Package Route
Gateway Niagara Visitor Centre

QEW at Casablanca Boulevard and South Service Road
Niagara Cycling Tourism Centre
Niagara Region Bicycling Map
Doran House Bed & Breakfast
470 Main Street West Grimsby ON
www3.sympatico.ca/doranhouse
Tel: (905) 309-1312
Vinifera Inn Bed & Breakfast
245 Main Street East Grimsby ON
www.viniferainn.ca
Tel: (905) 309-8873
Casablanca Winery Inn restaurant
4 Windward Drive Grimsby ON
www.casablancawineryinn.com
Tel: (877) 446-5746 (905) 309-7171
Grimsby Public Library
18 Carnegie Lane
www.town.grimsby.on.ca/Library
Tel: (905) 945-5142

Guelph 23 M25 GPS 43.54730,-80.24414: City

Guelph and Wellington County Tourism Services
1 Carden Street
Guelph ON N1H 3A1
www.visitguelphwellington.ca
Tel: (800) 334-4519
Guelph Cycling Map
Guelph Jazz Festival - early September
Downtown Guelph
London House B&B
80 London Road West
Guelph ON N1H 2B7
www.londonhouse.ca
Tel: (877) 836-6874 (519) 824-6874
Lyon's Den Bed & Breakfast
18 University Avenue East
Guelph ON N1G 1M9
www.bbcanada.com/3260.html
Tel: (519) 821-2556
Best Western Royal Brock Hotel & Conference Centre
716 Gordon Street Guelph ON
www.bestwesternontario.com/hotels/best-western-royal-brock-hotel-and-conference-centre
Tel: (800) 780-7234 (519) 836-1240
Artisanale Cafe & Bistro
37 Quebec Street
Guelph ON N1H 2T1
artisanale.ca
Tel: (519) 821-3359
Diana's Downtown
141 Wyndham Street North Guelph ON
www.dianadowntown.com
Tel: (519) 836-3460
Speed River Bicycle
135 Wyndham Street North
Guelph ON N1H 4E9
Tel: (519) 824-9371
Guelph Public Library
100 Norfolk Street
Guelph ON N1H 4J6
www.library.guelph.on.ca
Tel: (519) 824-6220

Haliburton 60 U39 GPS 45.04670,-78.50880: Town

Haliburton Tourism Association
PO Box 485
Haliburton ON K0M 1S0
www.haliburton-tourism.com
Haliburton Cycling Map
Country Charm Bed and Breakfast
152 Mountain Street
Haliburton ON K0M 1S0
www.countrycharmbb.ca/index.htm
Tel: (705) 457-8821 (866) 457-8821
Heritage House Bed & Breakfast
33-35 Pine Street PO Box 1076
Haliburton ON K0M 1S0
www.bbcanada.com/10967.html
Tel: (705) 312-8800
Haliburton County Public Library
78 Maple Avenue Haliburton ON
www.haliburton.canlib.ca
Tel: (705) 457-2241

Hamilton 17 Q28 GPS 43.26099,-79.88845: City

🏕️🍴🚻📷⭐🚌🚲🚶

ℹ️ Hamilton Online Cycling Map
http://www.hamilton.ca/streets-transportation/
biking-cyclists/cycling-routes-maps

ℹ️ Hamilton Tourism
www.tourismhamilton.com

🪖 **Reenactment of Battle of Stoney Creek**
Battlefield House and Park - early June
77 King Street West Stoney Creek ON

🪖 **Dundurn National Historic Site**
castle and military museum
610 York Boulevard Hamilton ON
www.hamilton.ca/CultureandRecreation/
Arts_Culture_And_Museums/
HamiltonCivicMuseums/Dundurn/
Tel: (905) 546-2872

🪖 **HMCS Haida -**
WW II and the Korean War warship
658 Catherine Street North Pier 9
Hamilton ON
www.pc.gc.ca/eng/lhn-nhs/on/haida/index.aspx
Tel: (905) 526 0911

🪖 **Whitehern Historic House & Garden**
41 Jackson Street West Hamilton ON
www.whitehern.ca
Tel: (905) 546-2018

⭐ **Its Your Festival** - mid July

⭐ **Dundas Cactus Festival** - mid August

⭐ **Art Gallery of Hamilton**
123 King Street West Hamilton ON
www.artgalleryofhamilton.com
Tel: (905) 527-6610

⭐ **Hamilton Farmers Market**
Tuesday, Thursday, Friday, Saturday
35 York Boulevard Hamilton ON
www.hamilton.ca/CultureandRecreation/
Arts_Culture_And_Museums/
HamiltonFarmersMarket

🛏️ **Four Oaks B&B**
149 Dundurn Street North
Hamilton ON L9C 1K2
Tel: (905) 537-1451

🛏️ **Admiral Inn**
2 Westcliffe Avenue
Hamilton ON L8R 3M1
www.admiralinn.com
Tel: (866) 236-4662 (905) 529-2311

🛏️ **Visitors Inn**
649 Main Street West
Hamilton ON L8S 1A2
www.visitorsinn.com
Tel: (800) 387-4620 (905) 529-6979

🚲 **Bike Locke** - rentals
246 Locke South
Hamilton ON L8P 4B9
Tel: (905) 769-4320

🚲 **All the Right Gears**
442 Millen Road Unit 16
Stoney Creek ON L8E 6H2
Tel: (905) 662-2453

🚶 **Hamilton Public Library**
55 York Boulevard
Hamilton ON L8N 4E4
www.myhamilton.ca/public-library
Tel: (905) 546-3200

Hanover 27 E19 GPS 44.15237,-81.02582:
Town

ℹ️🛏️🍴🚻🚲🚶

ℹ️ **Bruce Peninsula Package Route**

🛏️ **Travellers Inn Hanover**
244 7th Avenue
Hanover ON N4N 2H1
www.tih.ca
Tel: (800) 801-8398 (519) 364-1911

🛏️ **Moms Bed & Breakfast**
540 10th Avenue
Hanover ON N4N 2P4
Tel: (519) 364-0466 (877) 868-8883

🍴 **Queen's Bush Pub**
451 10th Street Hanover ON
www.queensbushpub.com
Tel: (519) 364-6666

🍴 **The Grey Rose Restaurant and Suites**
319 10th Street Hanover ON
www.greyrose.ca
Tel: (877) 473-9767 (519)-364 2600

🚲 **Wheelfast The Bicycle Shoppe**
292 10th Street
Hanover ON N4N 1P2
www.wheelfast.ca
Tel: 519 372-7022

🚶 **Hanover Public Library**
451 10th Avenue
Hanover ON N4N 2P1
Tel: (519) 364-1420

Harcourt 81 T42 GPS 45.08575,-78.15122:
Village

🍴 **The Olde Ridge Authentic Barbeque**
4167 Loop Road Harcourt ON
Tel: (705) 448-3676

Harrow 4 E2 GPS 42.03552,-82.91791: Town

⭐🛒🍴🍇

⭐ **Canadian Transportation Museum and**
Heritage Village
Road 23 6155 Arner Townline Box 221
Harrow ON N0R 1G0
www.ctmhv.com
Tel: (519) 776-6909

🍇 **Colio Winery**
1 Colio Drive PO Box 372
Harrow ON N0R 1G0
www.coliowines.com
Tel: (800) 265-1322 (519) 738-2241

🍇 **Muscedere Vinyards**
7457 County Road 18 RR#4
Harrow ON N0R 1G0
muscederevineyards.com
Tel: (519) 965-1075

Harrowsmith 36 B55 GPS 44.40499,-76.66557:
Village

🛒🍴

Harwood 33 E42 GPS 4.13751,-78.18044: Village

🛒🍴⛺🚤

⛺ **Golden Beach Resort**
7100 County Road 18, RR#2
Roseneath ON K0K 2X0
www.goldenbeachresort.com
Tel: (800) 263-7781 (905) 342-5366

Hastings 33 C44 GPS 44.51915,-77.78066:
Town

ℹ️⭐🛏️🍴🛒🚶

ℹ️ **Lang Hastings TransCanada Trail**

⭐ **Lock 18 on Trent Severn Waterway**
Tel: (705) 696-2864

🛏️ **Hastings House Bed & Breakfast**
109 Front St WestBox 425
Hastings ON K0L 1Y0
www.bbcanada.com/11411.html
Tel: (705) 696-2045

🚶 **Trent Hills Library**
6 Albert Street East Hastings ON
www.trenthillslibrary.ca/hastings/index.html
Tel: (705) 696-2111

Hawkesbury 68 N71 GPS 45.60790,-74.61414:
Town

🛒🍴ℹ️⛺🚶

ℹ️ **Ontario Travel Information Centre**
777 Highway 417 RR#1
Chute a Blondeau K0B 1B0
www.ontariotravel.net
Tel: (613) 674-2000 (800) 668-2746

🛏️ **Quality Inn & Suites**
1575 Tupper Street
Hawkesbury ON K6A 3T5
Tel: (877) 424-6423 (613) 632-5941

🛏️ **Netheldale Bed & Breakfast**
577 Green Lane Road East
Hawkesbury ON K6A 2R2
www.netherdale.com
Tel: (613) 632-8881

⛺ **Camping Domaine Chartrand**
2775 Chartrand Road
Lefaivre ON K0B 1J0
www.campingdomainechartrand.com
Tel: (613) 679-2687

🚶 **Hawkesbury Public Library**
550 Higginson Street
Hawkesbury ON K6A 1H1
www.bibliotheque.hawkesbury.on.ca
Tel: (613) 632-0106

Hensall 20 N15 GPS 43.43417,-81.50208:
Town

🛒🍴🚶

🚶 **Huron County Library**
108 King Street Hensall ON
www.huroncounty.ca/library

Tel: (519) 262-2445

Highgate 7 Y12 GPS 42.49947,-81.81441: Village
🛒

Hillier 34 G48 GPS 43.97436,-77.45596: Hamlet
🍇🍴

🍇 **Hillier Creek Estates Winery**
46 Stapleton Road
Hillier ON K0K 2J0
Tel: (613) 399-5081

🍇 **Stanners Vineyard**
76 Station Road
Hillier ON K0K 2J0
Tel: (613) 661-3361

Hoards 34 C46 GPS 44.29510,-77.66441:
Village
🛒🍴

Hockley 29 F27 GPS 44.03750,-79.94682:
Village
🛒

Holland Landing 30 F31 GPS 44.10463,-79.49236:
Village
🛒🍴

Holmesville 20 L14 GPS 43.64576,-81.60370:
Village
🛒

Holt 30 E32 GPS 44.12367,-79.34395:
Village
🛒

Hope Bay 39 W18 GPS 44.90598,-81.16699:
Hamlet

⛺ **Hope Bay Campground**
2 Hope Bay Road
South Bruce Peninsula ON N0H 2T0
www.hopebaycampground.com
Tel: (519) 534-1208

Howe Island 37 D58 GPS 44.28896,-76.23688:
Cottages and farms only

ℹ️ **Frontenac County Ferry**
Service Road 22
Joyceville Road
Tel: (613) 542-4959 (613) 548-9400

ℹ️ **Frontenac Islands Township Ferry Service**
Service Road 22
Tel: (613) 542-0550

Huntsville 59 R33 GPS 45.32657,-79.21800:
Town

ℹ️🛒🍴🛏️🚲🚶

ℹ️ **Town of Huntsville**

ℹ️ **Bike Muskoka**

🛏️ **Algonquin Retreat B&B**
7 Forestview Drive
Huntsville ON P1H 1G2
bbcanada.com/aretreat
Tel: (705) 789-4115

🛏️ **Comfort Inn**
86 King William Street Huntsville ON
www.choicehotels.ca/en/huntsville-hotel-
comfort-ontario-CN269-en?cid=1782632
Tel: (877) 424-6423 (705) 789-1701

🛏️ **King William Inn**
23 King William Street
Huntsville ON P1H 1G4
www.kingwilliaminn.com
Tel: (888) 995-9169 (705) 789-9661

🍴 **Spencer's Tall Trees Restaurant**
87 Main Street West
Huntsville ON P1H 1X1
www.spencerstalltrees.com
Tel: (705) 789-9769

🍴 **That Little Place by the Lights**
76 Main Street Huntsville ON
Tel: (705) 789-2536

🚲 **Muskoka Bicycle Pro Shop** - rental
63 Main Street East
Huntsville ON P1H 2B8
www.mbps.ca
Tel: (705) 789-8344

🚶 **Huntsville Public Library**
7 Minerva Street East
Huntsville ON P1H 1W4
Tel: (705) 789-5232

Ingleside 51 V68 GPS 44.99579,-74.98685:
Village

🚌🍴🛏️⛺

🛏️ **Nightingale House B&B**
1 Maxwell Avenue
Ingleside ON K0C 1M0
Tel: (613) 537-4427
⛺ **Farran Park**
14704 County Road 2 Ingleside ON
www.southstormont.ca/tourism/farrans.html
Tel: (800) 437-2233 (613) 543-4328

Ingersoll 15 S20 GPS 43.03811,-80.88385: Town

ℹ️🚌🍴🛏️🛏️📚

ℹ️ **Ports of Lake Erie Package Route**
🛏️ **Comfort Inn & Suites**
20 Samnah Cres Ingersoll ON
www.choicehotels.com
Tel: (877) 424-6423 (519) 425-1100
🛏️ **Elm Hurst Inn & Country Spa** - restaurant
415 Harris Street
Ingersoll ON N5C 3K1
www.elmhurstinn.com
Tel: (800) 561-5321 (519) 485-5321
📚 **Oxford County Library**
The Town Centre
130 Oxford Street
Ingersoll ON N5C 2V5
www.ocl.net/locations/ingersoll
Tel: (519) 485-2505

Inglewood 23 J27-28 GPS 43.80455,-79.93584:
Village

🚌🛒🚲

🚲 **Caledon Hills Cycling**
15640 McLaughlin Road
Inglewood ON L0N 1K0
www.caledonhillscycling.com
Tel: (866) 838-1698 (905) 838-1698

Innerkip 16 Q21 GPS 43.20964,-80.69666: Village
🚌🍴

Inverhuron 26 C14 GPS 44.27765,-81.57349:
Village

⭐🍴⛺🛏️

⭐ **The Philosopher's Wool Company** - wool yarn
and garments on
Albert Road just north of Inverhuron
www.philosopherswool.com
Tel: (519) 368-5354
⛺ **Inverhuron Provincial Park**
19 Jordon Road RR#2
Tiverton ON N0G 2T0
Tel: (519) 368-1959
Reservations: www.ontarioparks.com
Tel: (888) 668-7275

Ipperwash Beach 13 Q11
GPS 43.21393,-81.96144: Resort area, public
beach

🚌🍴🛏️⛺

🛏️🍴 **The Village Inn Motel & Diner**
7424 Lakeshore Road, Highway 21
Ravenswood ON
Tel: (519) 243-3535
⛺ **Carolinian Forest Campground**
9589 Ipperwash Road RR#2
Forest ON N0N 1J0
Tel: (519) 243-2258

Iron Bridge 2 GPS 46.27860,-83.21959:
Village

🚌🍴🛒🛏️⛺

🛒 **Iron Bridge Historical Museum**
1 James Street Box 460
Iron Bridge ON P0R 1H0
🛏️ **Red Top Motor Inn & Restaurant**
114 Highway 17 East Box 427
Iron Bridge ON P0R 1H0
www.redtopmotorinn.com
Tel: (877) 843-2100 (705) 843-2100
⛺ **Viking Tent and Trailer Park**
21715 Highway 17
Iron Bridge ON P0R 1H0
Tel: (705) 843-2834

Iroquois 51 W-X66 GPS 44.85172,-75.31518:
Village

🚌🍴

Ivy Lea 37 C60 GPS 44.36816,-75.99003: Village
ℹ️ Thousand Islands International Bridge, Bicycles
prohibited on Highway 137 between the bridge
and the Thousand Islands Parkway. Use the
Wolfe Island ferries Cape Vincent New York to
Kingston Ontario as an alternative
⛺ **Ivy Lea Campsite**
649 Thousand Islands Parkway
Lansdowne ON K0E 1L0
www.stlawrenceparks.com
Tel: (613) 659-3057 (800) 437-2233

Jasper 49 X61 GPS 44.83273,-75.93421:
Village

🛏️

Johnstown 50 Y64-65 GPS 44.74698,-75.46165:
Village

🚌ℹ️🛏️⛺

ℹ️ Bicycles and pedestrians are prohibited on the
Ogdensburg-Prescott International Bridge. Use
Seaway International Bridge, Cornwall
⛺ **Grenville Park**
2323 County Road 2
Johnstown ON K0E 1T1
Tel: (613) 925-2000

Jones Falls 37 A58 GPS 44.55244,-76.23928:
Hamlet

ℹ️⭐🪝

ℹ️ **St. Lawrence and Rideau Canal Package Route**
⭐ **Rideau Canal Locks 39-42**
Cyclist camping permitted
🪝 **Walking Tour of Jones Falls Lock Station**
Defensible Lockmasters House and Blacksmith
Shop

Jordan 18 R32 GPS 43.14133,-79.37210:
Village

ℹ️🍷🍷🪝🛏️⛺🍴

ℹ️ **Grand Niagara Package Route**
🍷 **Cave Spring Cellars** winery
836 Main Street Jordon ON
www.cavespringcellars.com
Tel: (888) 806-9910 (905) 562-3581
🍷 **Creekside EstateWinery**
2170 4th Avenue Jordon ON
www.creeksidewine.com
Tel: (905) 562-0035 (877) 262-9463
🪝 **Balls Falls Conservation Area**
waterfall, 1806 grist mill
3292 Sixth Avenue
Jordan ON L0R 1S0
www.npca.ca/
Tel: (905) 562-5235
🛏️ **Inn On The Twenty Restaurant & Wine Bar**
3836 Main Street
Jordan ON L0R 1S0
www.innonthetwenty.com
Tel: (800) 701-8074 (905) 562-5336
Restaurant Tel: (905) 562-7313
🛏️ **Martin House B&B**
2437 North Service Road
Jordan Station ON L0R 1S0
www.bbcanada.com/themartinhouse
Tel: (905) 984-9972
🛏️ **Ramada Jordan Beacon Harbourside Hotel &**
Suites
2793 Beacon Boulevard (at North Service Road)
PO Box 70
Jordan ON L0R 1S0
Tel: (888) 823-2266 (905) 562-4155
⛺ **Big Valley Campground**
2211 King Street RR#1
St. Catharines ON L2R 6P7
Tel: (905) 562-5616

Kashabowie 2 GPS 48.64918,-90.43403:
Village

🍴

Keady 39 A18-19 GPS 44.46491,-81.03996:
Village

ℹ️⭐

ℹ️ **Bruce Peninsula Package Route**
⭐ **Keady Farmer's Market**
large regional market Tuesdays
RR#4 Tara ON N0H 2N0
www.keadylivestock.com/farmers_q.html
Tel: (519) 934-2339

Keene 33 D42 GPS 44.24014,-78.16321:
Village

🚌🍴🛏️⛺

🛏️ **Elmhirst's Resort** restaurant
1045 Settlers Line
Keene ON K0L 2G0
www.elmhirst.com
Tel: (800) 461-1940 (705) 295-4591

Kemptville 50 V63 GPS 45.01592,-75.64561:
Town

ℹ️🚌🍴🛏️⛺📚

ℹ️ **St. Lawrence and Rideau Canal Package Route**
🛏️ **Knights Inn Kemptville**
4022 County Road 43
Kemptville ON K0G 1J0
Tel: (613) 258-5939
🛏️ **Kemptville Suites**
103 Clothier Street East
Kemptville ON K0G 1J0
Tel: (613) 702-5000
🛏️ **Nestle Down**
4101 Highway 43 RR#3
Kemptville ON K0G 1J0
www.bbcanada.com/6126.html
Tel: (613) 258 7778
⛺ **Rideau River Provincial Park**
2680 Donnelly Drive
Kemptville ON N0G 1J0
Tel: (613) 258-2740
Reservations; www.ontarioparks.com
Tel: (888) 668-7275
📚 **North Grenville Public Library**
1 Water Street
Kemptville ON K0G 1J0
www.ngpl.ca
Tel: (613) 258-4711

Kenora 2 GPS 49.77066,-94.48930:
City

🚌🍴ℹ️🛏️⭐📚

ℹ️ **Townscape Murals** - Nineteen murals depict
Kenora history
⭐ **Harbourfest** - first weekend in August
www.harbourfest.ca
🛏️ **Kendall House Bed & Breakfast**
127 5th Avenue South
Kenora ON P9N 2A3
www.bbcanada.com/3568.html
Tel: (807) 468-4645
🛏️ **Super 8 Kenora**
240 Lakeview Drive
Kenora ON P9N 3W7
www.super8.com
Tel: (800) 800-8000 (807) 468-8016
🛏️ **Timberline Urban Lodge**
Highway 17 West Box 640
Keewatin ON P9N 1S7
Tel: (807) 547-2471
📚 **Kenora Public Library**
24 Main Street South
Kenora ON K0G 1J0
Tel: (807) 467-2081

Kent Bridge 7 Y10 GPS 42.51506,-82.07304:
Village

🛏️

Kettleby 30 G31 GPS 44.01026,-79.55904:
Village

🛏️

Kettle Point First Nation 13 R10
GPS 43.18040,-81.98959: Village

🚌🍴⭐

⭐ **Chippewas of Kettle and Stony Point First**
Nation Annual Pow Wow - early July

Killaloe 81 N49 GPS 45.56453,-77.41961:
Town

🚌🍴📚

📚 **Killaloe Public Library**
1 John Street
Killaloe ON K0J 2A0
Tel: (613) 757-2211

Kilmarnock 49 W61 44.88677,-75.92686: Hamlet
⭐ **Rideau Canal Lock 24**
group camping with prior approval
www.pc.gc.ca/lhn-nhs/on/rideau/index.aspx
Tel: (888) 773-8888 (613) 283-5170

Kimberley 40 B23 GPS 44.39136,-80.53672:

Village

Kincardine 26 E14 GPS 44.18162,-81.63173:
Town

Bruce Peninsula Package Route

⭐ Scottish Festival and Highland Games - early
July

⭐ Kincardine Scottish Pipe Band - Saturday nights
8 PM march through town

⭐ Piper at Lighthouse - sunset July and August
most nights except Saturday

⭐ Bluewater Summer Playhouse
707A Queen Street
Kincardine ON N2Z 1Z9
www.bluewatersp.on.ca
Tel: (877) 396-5722 (519) 396-5722

Summerplace Bed & Breakfast
78 Boiler Beach Road
Kincardine ON N2Z 2X3
Tel: (519) 396-6070

Best Western Governors Inn restaurant
791 Durham Street
Kincardine ON N2Z 1M4
www.bestwesternontario.com/kincardine-hotels
Tel: (800) 780-7234 (519) 396-8242

Holiday Inn Express
2 Millenium Way
Kincardine ON N2Z 0B5
www.hiexpress.com
Tel: (519) 395-3545

Harbour Street Brasserie
217 Harbour Street Kincardine ON
www.harbourstreetbrasserie.com
Tel: (519) 396-6000

Tramonto
765 Queen Street
Kincardine ON N2Z 2Y2
Tel: (519) 396-8466

Kincardine Home Hardware
Highway 21 North Kincardine ON
Tel: (519) 396-2032

Bruce County Library
727 Queen Street Kincardine ON
library.brucecounty.on.ca/kilib
Tel: (519) 396-3289

Kingston 36 D56 GPS 44.23154,-76.47933:
City

Lake Ontario Trent Canal Package Route

Cape Vincent New York crossing via Wolfe
Island Ferry - Ontario Street and Barrack Street
www.mto.gov.on.ca/english/traveller/ferry
Tel: (613) 548-7227

Tourism Kingston
209 Ontario Street
Kingston ON K7L 2Z1
tourism.kingstoncanada.com/en
Tel: (888) 855-4555 (613) 548-4415

Great Waterway Tourist Region Cycling
Itineraries - Cornwall, Brockville, Gananoque,
Kingston, Belleville

⭐ Fort Henry & Sunset Ceremonies
1 Fort Henry Drive Kingston ON

⭐ Kingston Sheep Dog Trials Grass Creek Park
2991 Highway 2 Kingston ON

Rosemount Inn & Spa
46 Sydenham Street South Kingston ON
www.rosemountinn.com
Tel: (888) 871-8844 (613) 531-8844

Econo Lodge City Centre
840 Princess Street
Kingston ON K7L 1G3
Tel: (613) 549-4546

Four Points by Sheraton Kingston
285 King Street East
Kingston ON K7L 3B1
www.starwoodhotels.com/fourpoints
Tel: (800) 368-7764 (613) 544-4434

St. Lawrence College – Residence Services
23 Country Club Drive
Kingston ON K7M 9A4
www.sl.on.ca/residence/SummerAccomodations.
htm
Tel: (613) 544-6600 ext. 4999

Aquaterra
1 Johnson Street
Kingston ON K7L 5H7
www.aquaterrabyclark.com
Tel: (613) 549-6243

Grecos Grill & Wine Bar
167 Princess Street
Kingston ON K7L 1A9
www.chezpiggy.com
Tel: (613) 542-2229

Le Chien Noir
69 Brock Street
Kingston ON K7L 1R8
Tel: (613) 549-5635

Rideau Canal Locks 46 to 49 - at Kingston Mills
group camping with prior approval
www.pc.gc.ca/lhn-nhs/on/rideau/index.aspx
Tel: (888) 773 8888 (613) 283 5170

The Cyclepath Kingston - rentals
471 Princess Street
Kingston ON K7L 1C3
www.cyclepathkingston.com
Tel: (613) 542-3616

Kingston Frontenac Public Library
130 Johnson Street
Kingston ON K7L 1X8
www.kfpl.ca
Tel: (613) 549-8888

Kingsville 4 E4 GPS 42.03789,-82.74031:
Town

Erie Shores Package Route

Kingsville to Sandusky Ohio - crossing via Pelee
Island Ferry Ferry service from Kingsville and
Leamington to Pelee Island and Sandusky Ohio
USA. March to December
www.ontarioferries.com/jii/english/index.html
Tel: (800) 265-3163

⭐ Jack Miner Migratory Bird Foundation
360 Road 3 West
Kingsville ON N9Y 2E5
www.jackminer.com
Tel: (519) 733-4034

⭐ Colasanti's Tropical Gardens - restaurant, zoo,
greenhouses
1550 Road 3 East
Kingsville ON N9Y 2E5
www.colasanti.com
Tel: (519) 326-3287

Mastronardi Estate Winery
1193 Concession 3
Kingsville ON N9Y 2E5
www.mastronardiwines.com
Tel: (519) 733-9463

Pelee Island Winery
455 Seacliff Drive
Kingsville ON N9Y 2K5
www.peleeisland.com
Tel: (800) 597-3533 (519) 733-6551

Bessie's Bed & Breakfast
333 Millbrook Drive
Kingsville ON N9Y 4A5
www.bbcanada.com/bessies
Tel: (519) 733-9403

The Old Farmhouse B&B
1389 Seacliff Drive
Kingsville ON N9Y 2M4
www.oldfarmhouse.com
Tel: (519) 733-9660

Adams Golden Acres Motel
438 Main Street West
Kingsville ON N9Y 2K2
www.adamsgoldenacres.com
Tel: (519) 733-6531 (888) 234-6018

Jack's Gastropub & Inn
31 Division Street South Kingsville ON
Tel: (519) 733-6900

Mettawas Italian Mediterranean Grill
169 Landsdowne Avenue
Kingsville ON N9Y 1S4
Tel: (519) 733-2459

Kinmount 44 X38 GPS 44.03860,-79.60528:
Village

⭐ Kinmount Farmers Market - Saturdays 9AM to
2 PM
Austin Sawmill Heritage Park
Tel: (705) 488-2612

Kinmount Railway Station

Kinmount House Bed & Breakfast
PO Box 33
Kinmount ON K0M 2A0
Tel: (705) 488-2421 (800) 511-0211

Kinmount Public Library
3980 County Road 121
Kinmount ON K0M 2A0

Tel: (705) 488-3199

Komoka 8 T15 GPS 42.94566,-81.43055:
Village

⭐ The Komoka Railway Museum
133 Queen Street
Komoka ON N0L 1R0
Tel: (705) 488-3199

Lake on the Mountain 35 F51
GPS 44.03726,-77.06291
Glenora Ferry viewpoint

Bay of Quinte Package Route

Lansdowne 37 B60 GPS 44.40574,-76.01893:
Village

Charleston Lake Provincial Park
148 Woodvale Road
Lansdowne ON K0E 1L0
Reservations: www.ontarioparks.com
Tel: (613) 659-2065

Lakefield 44 B41 GPS 44.42251,-78.27278:
Town

Trent Canal Lock 26
Group camping permitted with prior approval
www.pc.gc.ca/eng/lhn-nhs/on/trentsevern/visit/
visit6.aspx
Tel: (888) 773-8888 (705) 750-4900

Harbourne By The Lake B&B
4365 County Road 29 Box 1094
Lakefield ON K0L 2H0
www.harbournebythelake.com
Tel: (888) 441-3686 (705) 652-0882

The Village Inn - restaurant
39 Queen Street
Lakefield ON K0L 2H0
www.villageinn.ca
Tel: (800) 827-5678 (705) 652-1910

Adventure Outfitters
1828 8th Line
Lakefield ON K0L 2H0
www.adventureoutfitters.ca
Tel: (705) 652-7986

Selwyn Public Library
8 Queen Street
Lakefield ON K0L 2H0
www.mypubliclibrary.ca
Tel: (705) 652-8623

Latta 34 C49 GPS 44.29486,-77.34375: Village

Leamington 5 E5 GPS 42.05416,-82.59971:
Town

Erie Shores Package Route

Pelee Island Ferry - Leamington via Pelee Island
- Sandusky, Ohio USA - Bicycle Crossing

Ferry service from Leamington and Kingsville
to Pelee Island and Sandusky Ohio USA -
March to December
www.ontarioferries.com/jii/english/index.html
Tel: (800) 265-3163

⭐ Leamington Arts Centre, Heinz and Henry
Collection
72 Talbot Street West
Leamington ON N8H 1M4
www.leamingtonartscentre.com
Tel: (519) 326-2711

⭐ Leamington Tomato Festival Seacliff Park - mid
August
www.leamingtontomatofestival.com
Tel: (519) 326-2878

⭐ Point Pelee National Park - southernmost point
in Canada; beaches, bird watching
1118 Point Pelee Drive
Leamington ON N8H 3V4
www.pc.gc.ca/eng/pn-np/on/pelee/index.aspx
Tel: (519) 322-2365 (888) 773-8888

⭐ Hillman Marsh Conservation Area
canoeing, bird watching and beach - Road 37 at
2nd Concession Road
www.erca.org
Tel: (888) 487-4760 (519) 776-5209

Comfort Inn

279 Erie Street South
Leamington ON N8H 3C4
www.choicehotels.ca
Tel: (800) 424-6423 (519) 326-9071

🛏 Best Western Plus Leamington Hotel &
Conference Centre
566 Bevel Line Road RR#1
Leamington ON N8H 3V4
Tel: (800) 780-7234 (519) 326-8646

🛏 Quercus Cottage
168 Seacliffe Drive West
Leamington ON N8H 3Y5
www.bbcanada.com/quercuscottage
Tel: (519) 324-0243

🛏 Days Inn Leamington
201 Erie Street North
Leamington N8H 3A5
Tel: (800) 225-3297 (519) 325-0260

🍴 Gallery Restaurant
11 Queens Avenue
Leamington ON N8H 3G5

🍴 Lakeside Bakery Cafe Deli
286 Erie Street South Leamington ON
www.lakesidebakery.com
Tel: (519) 326-2626

⛺ Sturgeon Woods Campground
1129 Mersea Road C, RR#1 Point Pelee
Leamington ON N8H 3V4
www.sturgeonwoods.com
Tel: (877) 521-4990 (519) 326-1156

📖 Essex County Library
1 John Street
Leamington ON N8H 1H1
Tel: (519) 326-3441

Lighthouse Cove 5 B7 GPS 42.31388,-82.45239:
Village
🍴📖
📖 1818 lighthouse at mouth of Thames River
🍴 Lighthouse Inn
19500 Lakeside Drive
Lighthouse Cove ON N0P 2L0
www.thelighthouseinn.ca
Tel: (519) 682-0600

Lindsay 32 C37 GPS 44.35428,-78.74007:
Town
ℹ⭐🛏⛺🚲📖
ℹ Kawarthas Northumberland TransCanada Trail
⭐ Academy Theatre
2 Lindsay Street South
Lindsay ON K9V 2L6
www.academytheatre.ca
Tel: (877) 888-0038 (705) 324-9111
⛺ Trent Severn Waterway Lock 33
Group camping with prior approval
www.pc.gc.ca/eng/lhn-nhs/on/trentsevern/visit/
visit6.aspx
Tel: (888) 773-8888 (705) 750-4900
🛏 Melton's Light House B&B
17 Murdoch Court
Lindsay ON K9V 6L4
www.bbcanada.com/8664.html
Tel: (705) 878-3426
🛏 Days Inn & Suites Lindsay
134 Angeline Street South
Lindsay ON K9V 5S2
Tel: (800) 329-7466 (705) 328-0100
🚲 Down To Earth Adventure Outfitters
82 Kent Street West Lindsay ON
Tel: (705) 328-0230
📖 Kawartha Lakes Public Library
190 Kent Street West
Lakefield ON K9V 2Y6
Tel: (705) 324-5632

Linwood 22 L21 GPS 43.58146,-80.72828:
Town
🛏📖
📖 Region of Waterloo Library
5279 Ament Line
Linwood ON N0B 2A0
www.rwl.library.on.ca
Tel: (519) 698-2700

Lions Head 55 V17 GPS 44.98658,-81.25420:
Village
🛏🍴📖
🛏 Cat's Pajamas Bed & Breakfast
64 Main Street Box 321

Lion's Head ON N0H 1W0
www.bbcanada.com/8946.html
Tel: (519) 793-6700
🛏 Lionheart Guest House B&B
89 Main Street Box 167
Lion's Head ON N0H 1W0
Tel: (519) 793-3325
📖 Bruce County Library
90 Main Street
Lion's Head ON N0H 1W0
www.library.brucecounty.on.ca
Tel: (519) 793-3844

Little Current 84 J12 GPS 45.97939,-81.92538:
Town
📖ℹ🍴📖🍴📖
ℹ Manitoulin Island Cycling Maps
ℹ Manitoulin Tourism
100 Meredith Street East
Little Current ON P0P 1K0
Tel: (705) 368-3021
🛏 Hawberry Motel
36 Meredith Street Box 123
Little Current ON P0P 1K0
www.hawberrymotel.com
Tel: (800) 769-7963 (705) 368-3388
🛏 The Shaftesbury Inn - restaurant
19 Robinson Street
Little Current ON P0P 1K0
www.rockgardenresort.on.ca
Tel: (705) 368-1945
📖 Town of Nemi Library
50 Meredith Street West Box 790
Little Current ON P0P 1K0
www.townofnemi.on.ca/library-0
Tel: (705) 368-2444

London 8 T17 GPS 44.04047,-77.82303: City
📖ℹ⭐🛏⛺🚲📖
ℹ Ports of Lake Erie Package Route
ℹ London Tourism
www.londontourism.ca
Tel: (800) 265-2602 (519) 661-5000
ℹ Middlesex County Tourism
www.middlesextourism.ca
Tel: (866) 205-1188 (519) 641-6100
ℹ Online Cycling Map
www.london.ca/d.aspx?s=/Transportation/
bikepage.htm
⭐ Fanshawe Pioneer Village
2609 Fanshawe Park Road East
London ON N5X 4A1
Tel: (519) 457-1296
⭐ SunFest World Music Festival - Victoria Park
early July
www.sunfest.on.ca
⭐ Home Country Music and Art Festival -
Victoria Park mid July
www.homecounty.ca
Tel: (519) 432-4310
⭐ Western Fair - early September
900 King Street
London ON N5W 2X6
Tel: (800) 619-4629 (519) 438-7203
🛏 Best Western Stoneridge Inn - restaurant
6675 Burtwistle Lane
London ON N6L 1H5
www.stoneridgeinn.com
Tel: (888) 471-2378 (519) 652-6022
🛏 Best Western London Airport Inn & Suites
2230 Dundas Street East at Airport Road
London ON N5V 1R5
www.airportinnandsuites.ca
Tel: (519) 457-1200 (877) 464-1200
🛏 Country Inn & Suites
774 Base Line Road East
London ON N6C 4T8
Tel: (800) 830-5222 (519) 430-1150
🛏 The Edwardian Lady B&B
71 Becher Street
London ON N6C 1A6
Tel: (519) 433-7930
⛺ Fanshawe Conservation Area
1424 Clarke Road
London ON N5V 5B9
www.thamesriver.on.ca
Tel: (866) 668-2267
🍴 Marienbad Restaurant
122 Carling Street London ON
www.marienbad.ca
Tel: (519) 679-9940
🍴 Michaels on the Thames
1 York Street London ON

www.michaelsonthethames.com
Tel: (519) 672-0111
🚲 To Wheels
134 Dundas Street London ON
Tel: (519) 434-4301
📖 London Public Library
251 Dundas Street
London ON N6A 6H9
www.londonpubliclibrary.ca
Tel: (519) 661-4600

Long Sault 52 U69 GPS 45.02998,-74.89832:
Village
🛏🛏⛺
🛏 Lion Motel
15965 County Road 2
Long Sault ON K0C 1P0
Tel: (866) 510-8916 (613) 534-2119
⛺ Long Sault Parkway - McLaren Campground
Between Ingleside and Long Sault off County
Road 2
www.stlawrenceparks.com
Tel: (800) 437-2233 (613) 543-4328

L'Orignal 68 N71 GPS 45.62028,-74.69604:
Town
🛏🍴

Lowbanks 18 U32 GPS 42.87495,-79.45297:
Hamlet
⛺ Long Beach Conservation Area
12965 Lakeshore Road Wainfleet ON
www.npca.ca
Tel: (905) 899-3462

Lucknow 26 G15 GPS 43.96130,-81.51607:
Town
ℹ⭐🛏📖🛏📖
ℹ Bruce Peninsula Package Route
⭐ Strawberry Summerfest - early June
www.strawberrysummerfest.com
⭐ Music in the Fields - August
901 Havelock Street North
Lucknow ON N0G 2H0
www.musicinthefields.ca
🛏 Sommerville Court
287 Ross Street (Huron Road 1)
Lucknow ON N0G 2H0
Tel: (866) 863-2557 (519) 357-7067
🛏 Grey Ox Meadows
875 Grey Ox Line RR#5 Lucknow ON
www.greyoxmeadows.com/bedbreakfast.html
Tel: (866) 433-0533 (519) 395-5007
📖 Bruce County Library
526 Campbell Street Lucknow ON
library.brucecounty.on.ca
Tel: (519) 528-3011

Lyndhurst 37 A59 GPS 44.55081,-76.12365:
Village
🛏

Mabee's Corners 9 V21
GPS 42.77882, -80.680757: Village
🛏

Maitland 50 Z63 GPS 44.63637,-75.61140:
Village
🛏

Malden Centre 4 E1 GPS 41.98527,-82.92686:
Village
ℹ🛏🍴🍴⛺
ℹ Erie Shores Package Route
🍷 Colchester Ridge Estate Winery
108 County Road 50 East Harrow ON
www.colchesterridge.com
Tel: (519) 738-9800
🍷 Erie Shore Vineyard
1410 Road 50 West
Harrow, ON N0R 1G0
www.erieshore.ca
Tel: (519) 738-9858
🍷 Sprucewood Shores Winery
7258 Road 50 West
Harrow ON N0R 1G0
www.sprucewoodshores.com
Tel: (866) 938-9253 (519) 738-9253
🍷 Viewpointe Estate Winery
151 County Road 50 East
Harrow ON N0R 1G0
www.viewpointewinery.com
Tel: (866) 372-8439 (519) 738-0690
⛺ Holiday Beach Conservation Area

www.erca.org
6952 County Road 50
Camping reservations: essexcamping.ca/en
Tel: (888) 487-4760 (519) 736-3772

Manotick 66 E63 GPS 45.22739,-75.68430: Village

1860's Watson's Mill
Chilver's Bed & Breakfast
5220 McLean Crescent
Manotick ON K4M 1G2
www.bbcanada.com/1059.html
Tel: (613) 692-3731
Wright on the River Bed & Breakfast
5224 McLean Crescent
Manotick ON K4M 1G2
www.bbcanada.com/11028.html
Tel: (613) 692-3781

Marathon 2 GPS 48.71993,-86.37570: Town

Lakeview Manor B&B
24 Drake Street
Marathon ON P0T 2E0
Tel: (807) 229-2248
Airport Motor Inn
Hwy #17 & Peninsula Road Box 700
Marathon ON P0T 2E0
Tel: (807) 229-1213
Marathon Public Library
22 Peninsula Road PO Box 400
Marathon ON P0T 2E0
Tel: (807) 229-0740

Markdale 28 C22 GPS 44.31913,-80.64889: Town

Barrhead Pub & Grill
735198 West Back Line RR# 6
Markdale ON N0C 1H0
Tel: (519) 986 3333
Danby House Inc. Bed & Breakfast
46 Main Street East
Markdale ON N0C 1H0
Tel: (519) 900-0399
Grey Highlands Public Library
75 Walker Street
Markdale ON N0C 1H0
www.greyhighlandspubliclibrary.com
Tel: (519) 986-3436

Marlbank 47 B51 GPS 44.43494,-77.09292: Village

Massey 84 F10 GPS 46.21264,-82.07622: Village

Massey Motel
295 Sable Street West
Massey ON P0P 1P0
Tel: (866) 590-2500 (705) 865-2500
Chutes Provincial Park
660 Imperial Street North Box 37
Massey ON P0P 1P0
Tel: (705) 865-2021
Massey Public Library
185 Grove Street Massey ON
www.masseylibrary.com
Tel: (705) 865-2641

Mattawa 90 E37 GPS 46.31748,-78.70219: Town

Mattawa Museum
285 1st Street
Mattawa ON P0H 1V0
Tel: (705) 744-5495
Le Voyageur Inn - restaurant
351 Main Street
Mattawa ON P0H 1V0
Tel: (705) 744-2370
Mattawa Public Library
370 Pine Street
Mattawa ON P0H 1V0
Tel: (705) 744-5550

M'Chigeeng First Nation 72 K10
GPS 45.82354,-82.16125

Meaford 40 Z22 GPS 44.60666,-80.59285: Town

Hilltop Motel

300 Sykes Street South Meaford ON
Tel: (519) 538-1700
Millhollow Bed & Breakfast
212 Miller Street
Meaford ON N4L 1G9
www.millhollow.ca
Tel: (519) 538-0941
Backstreet Cafe
27 Nelson Street West Meaford ON
Tel: (519) 538-4455
Ride On Bikes - rentals
14 Trowbridge Street East Meaford ON
Tel: (519) 538-5030
Meaford Public Library
15 Trowbridge Street West
Meaford ON N4L 1V4
www.meafordlibrary.on.ca
Tel: (519) 538-1060 x1123

Meldrum Bay 70 J2 GPS 45.92150,-83.11570: Village

Mississagi Lighthouse - 1873 Lighthouse, Heritage Park & Campground
Mississagi Lighthouse Road 7 kilometers west of Meldrum Bay
Meldrum Bay Inn - restaurant
25959 Hwy 540
Meldrum Bay ON P0P 1R0
www.meldrumbayinn.com
Tel: (877) 557-1645 (705) 283-3190

Merlin 5 C8 GPS 42.24221,-82.23281: Town

Merrickville 50 W61 GPS 44.91574,-75.83684: Town

St. Lawrence and Rideau Canal Package Route
Rideau Canal Lock 21-23
group camping with prior approval
www.pc.gc.ca/lhn-nhs/on/rideau/index.aspx
Tel: (888) 773-8888 (613) 283-5170
Blockhouse Museum
1840 Guest House
23 Main Street West Box 452
Merrickville ON K0G 1N0
Tel: (613) 269-3025
Merrickville Guest Suites
159 St. Lawrence Street
Merrickville ON K0G 1N0
Tel: (613) 355-0736
Millisle Bed & Breakfast
205 Mill Street Box 341
Merrickville ON K0G 1N0
www.bbcanada.com/millislebb
Tel: (613) 269-3627
Merrickville Public Library
446 Main Street West
Merrickville ON K0G 1N0
www.village.merrickville-wolford.on.ca/mpl/library.htm
Tel: (613) 269-3326

Midland 41 X28 GPS 44.74990,-79.88851: Town

Southern Georgian Bay Tourism
208 King Street
Midland ON L4R 3L9
Tel: (705) 526-7884
Sainte-Marie Among the Hurons
16164 Highway 12 East
Midland ON L4R 4K8
www.saintemarieamongthehurons.on.ca
Tel: (705) 526-7838
The Martyrs' Shrine
16163 Highway 12 West
Midland ON L4R 4K6
www.martyrs-shrine.com
Tel: (705) 526-3788
The Victorian Inn B&B
670 Hugel Avenue
Midland ON L4R 1W9
Tel: (877) 450-7660 (705) 526-4441
1875 A Charters Inn
290 Second Street
Midland ON L4R 3R1
Tel: (800) 724-2979 (705) 527-1572
Best Western Highland Inn & Conference
Centre - restaurant
924 King Street Box 515
Midland ON L4R 4L3
www.bestwesternmidland.com

Tel: (800) 461-4265 (705) 526-9307
Total Sports – The Bike Shop
542 Bay Street
Midland ON L4R 1L3
www.totalsportsmidland.com
Tel: (705) 528-0957
Midland Public Library
320 King Street
Midland ON L4R 3M6
www.midlandlibrary.com
Tel: (705) 526-4216

Mildmay 27 F18 GPS 44.04200,-81.11934: Town

Bruce Peninsula Package Route
Whispering Brook Bed & Breakfast
7 Jane Street Box 127
Mildmay ON N0G 2J0
www.bbcanada.com/1049.html
Tel: (519) 367-2565
Sandy's Family Restaurant
96 Elora Street
Mildmay ON N0G 2J0
Tel: (519) 367-5898
Harley's Pub and Perk
87 Elora Street
Mildmay ON N0G 2J0
www.harleyspubandperk.com
Tel: (519) 367-2683
Liesemer's Home Hardware Cycle & Sports
98 Elora Street
Mildmay ON N0G 2J0
Tel: (519) 367-5314
Bruce County Library
51 Elora Street
Mildmay ON N0G 2J0
Tel: (519) 367-2814

Milford 35 G51 GPS 43.93475,-77.09156: Village

Milford Mill Pond Conservation Area
Milford Bistro
3048 County Road 10 Milford ON
milfordbistro.com
Tel: (613) 476-0004

Millbrook 32 E40 GPS 44.15065,-78.44804: Town

4th Line Theatre
4 Tupper Street
Millbrook ON L0A 1G0
www.4thlinetheatre.on.ca
Tel: (705) 932-4445 (800) 814-0055

Miller Lake 54 T15 GPS 45.10257,-81.44311: Village

Mindemoya 72 L10 GPS 45.74194,-82.14144: Village

Pioneer Museum and Welcome Centre
Highway 551
Manitoulin Inn
Highway 551 Box 59
Mindemoya ON P0P 1S0
www.manitoulininn.ca
Tel: (877) 270-0551 (705) 377-5500
Mindemoya Motel
6375 Highway 542
Mindemoya ON P0P 1S0
Tel: (877) 404-4779 (705) 377-4779

Minden 60 V37 GPS 44.92717,-78.72537: Village

Haliburton Public Library
176 Bobcaygeon Road Minden ON
Tel: (705) 286-2491

Mine Centre 2 GPS 48.76096,-92.64060: Village

Mississauga 24 L-M30 GPS 43.58828,-79.64372: City, includes Port Credit

Peel Trails Map - waking and cycling

Monte Carlo Inn
1886 Dundas Street East
Mississauga ON L4X 1L9
www.montecarloinns.com/torontowest.html
Tel: (800) 363-6400   (905) 273-9500

Waterside Inn - restaurant
15 Stavebank Road South
Mississauga ON L5G 2T2
Tel: (877) 264-7770   (905) 891-7770

Carassauga - Mississauga's Festival of Cultures
May 24 weekend
Highway 401 and Highway 410
Hershey Centre
5500 Rose Cherry Place
Mississauga ON L4Z 4B6

Mississauga Waterfront Festival - mid June
Memorial Park Port Credit
Mississauga ON

Muslim Fest - early September
Mississauga Celebration Square
300 City Centre Drive
Mississauga ON L5B 3Y3

Gears Bike Shop
176 Lakeshore Road West
Mississauga ON L5H 1G4
gearsbikeshop.com
Tel: (905) 271-2400

Port Credit Branch Library
20 Lakeshore Road East
www.mississauga.ca/portal/residents/
branchlibraries
Tel: (905) 615-4835

Mitchells Bay 6 A7 GPS 42.47438,-82.40639:
Village

Mitchell's Bay Marine Park Limited
3 Allen Road
Mitchell's Bay ON N0P 1L0
Tel: (519) 354-8423

Montreal River 96 J13 GPS 47.24195,-84.64142:
Village

Mooretown 12 U6 GPS 42.83985,-82.46576:
Village

Moore Museum
94 Moore Line
Mooretown ON N0N 1M0
www.twp.stclair.on.ca/mooretown_museum.htm
Tel: (519) 867-2020

Morpeth 7 A12 GPS 42.39336,-81.84348:
Village

Greenview Aviaries & Zoo
12752 Talbot Trail Morpeth ON
www.greenviewaviariesparkandzoo.com
Tel: (519) 674-3025

Rondeau Provincial Park
18050 Rondeau Park Road
Morpeth ON N0P 1X0
Tel: (519) 674-1750
Reservations: www.ontarioparks.com
Tel: (888) 668-7275

Morrisburg 51 W76 GPS 44.89983,-75.18717:
Village

Upper Canada Village Museum - village, many
buildings from the St. Lawrence Seaway
13740 County Road 2
Morrisburg ON K0C 1X0
Tel: (800) 437-2233   (613) 543-4328

McIntosh Country Inn
County Road 2 Box 1140
Morrisburg ON K0C 1XO
www.mcintoshcountryinn.com
Tel: (888) 229-2850   (613) 543-3788

Russell Manor Bed & Breakfast
36 First Street Box 219
Morrisburg ON K0C 1X0
www.russellmanorbb.com
Tel: (866) 401-7472   (613) 543-3871

Riverside-Cedar Park
www.stlawrenceparks.com
Tel: (800) 437-2233   (613) 543-3287

S D & G County Library

28 Ottawa Street
Morrisburg ON
www.sdglibrary.ca
Tel: (613) 543-3384

Moscow 36 B53 GPS 44.42888,-76.80679:
Hamlet

Mount Albert 1 E33 GPS 44.13579,-79.30934:
Town

Mount Elgin 9 T20-21 GPS 42.96019,-80.79071:
Village

Mount Pleasant 16-17 S24
GPS 43.07792,-80.31349: Town

Nanticoke 11 V27 GPS 42.81074,-80.07198:
Hamlet

Selkirk Provincial Park
151 Wheeler's Sideroad RR#1
Selkirk ON N0A 1P0
Tel: (905) 776-2600
Reservations: www.ontarioparks.com
Tel: (888) 668-7275

Haldimand Conservation Area
645 South Coast Drive RR#1
Nanticoke ON N0A 1L0
www.lprca.on.ca
Tel: (877) 990-9938   (905) 776-2700

Napanee 35 D52 GPS 44.24832,-76.95158: Town

Lennox and Addington Museum & Archives
97 Thomas Street East
Napanee ON K7R 4B9
www.lennox-addington.on.ca/must-see/l-a-
museum-archives.html
Tel: (613) 354-3027

1826 MacPherson House
180 Elizabeth Street Napanee ON
macphersonhouse.ca

Hampton Inn
40 McPherson Drive
Napanee ON K7R 3L1
www.hamptoninnnapanee.com
Tel: (800) 560-7809   (613) 354-5554

Fox Motor Inn
297 Dundas Street West
Napanee ON K7R 2B3
Tel: (613) 354-3855

Lennox & Addington Library
25 River Road
Napanee ON K7R 3S6
www.lennox-addington.on.ca/library/location-
and-hours.html
Tel: (613) 354-2525

Nestor Falls 2 GPS 49.19676,-93.94612:
Town

Arrowhead Resort & Motel
Box 66
Nestor Falls ON P0X 1N0
www.arrowheadresortmotel.com
Tel: (807) 484-2132

Caliper Lake Provincial Park
Box 188
Nestor Falls ON P0X 1K0
Tel: (807) 484-2181 or (807) 468-2669
Reservations: www.ontarioparks.com
Tel: (888) 668-7275

Neustadt 27 F19 GPS 44.07730,-81.00298:
Village

Bruce Peninsula Package Route

**Canadian Royal Heritage Museum Diefenbaker
Birthplace** - Prime Minister 1957 to 1963
144 Barbara Street   Neustadt ON

Neustadt Springs Brewery - established in 1859
456 Jacob Street Neustadt ON
www.neustadtsprings.com
Tel: (519) 799-5790

Noah's Inn Restaurant
527 Mill Street
Neustadt ON N0G 2M0
www.noahsinn.ca

Tel: (519) 799-5383

Newbury 7 W12 GPS 42.68479,-81.80002: Town

New Hamburg 22 P21 GPS 43.37826,-80.71132:
Village

Oak Grove Cheese
29 Bleams Road East
New Hamburg ON N3A 1G6
www.oakgrovecheese.ca
Tel: (519) 662-1212

New Hamburg Mennonite Relief Sale - last
weekend in May
275 Jacob Street
New Hamburg ON N3A 1C6
www.nhmrs.com

Puddicombe House B&B restaurant
145 Peel Street
New Hamburg ON N3A 1E7
www.puddicombehouse.com
Tel: (519) 662-2111

The Waterlot Restaurant & Inn
17 Huron Street
New Hamburg ON N3A 1K1
www.waterlot.com
Tel: (519) 662-2020

Region of Waterloo Library
145 Huron Street
New Hamburg ON N3A 1K1
www.rwl.library.on.ca
Tel: (519) 662-1112

Newboro 48 Z57 GPS 44.65170,-76.31784:
Town

Rideau Canal Lock 36 - group camping with
prior approval
Tel: (888) 773-8888   (613) 283-5170

General store - Kinborns on the Rideau
10 Drummond Street Newboro ON
Tel: (613) 272-0114

Stagecoach Inn
10 Drummond Street Newboro ON
Tel: (613) 272-2900

Rideau Lakes Public Library
10 Brock Street
Newboro ON K0G 1P0
www.rideaulakeslibrary.ca
Tel: (613) 272-0241

Newcastle 32 G39 GPS 43.91822,-78.58920:
Town

Lilac Cottage Bed & Breakfast
601 Mill Street South
Newcastle ON L1B 1C1
www.bbcanada.com/8602.html
Tel: (905) 987-1123

Niagara Falls 19 R34-35 GPS 43.10663,-79.06424:
City at the falls

Ontario Travel Information Centre -
Rainbow Bridge
5355 Stanley Avenue
Niagara Falls ON L2E 7C2
www.ontariotravel.net
Tel: (905) 358-3221   (800) 668-2746

Niagara Tourism
www.tourismniagara.com
Tel: (800) 263-2988

Niagara Cycling Tourism Centre
www.cyclinginniagara.bike

Niagara Region Bicycling Map

GO Transit Toronto to Niagara Falls - summer
rail service for cyclists and bicycles
4223 Bridge Street Niagara Falls to Union
Station 65 Front Street Toronto
Tel: (888) 438-6646   (416) 869-3200

Falls illuminated nightly

Casino Niagara and other tourist attractions are
located on Clifton Hill

Villa Gardenia Bed & Breakfast
4741 Zimmerman Avenue
Niagara Falls ON L2E 3M8
www.VillaGardeniaBB.com
Tel: (905) 358-1723

Danner House Bed & Breakfast
12549 Niagara River Parkway
Niagara Falls ON L2E 6S6
www.dannerhouse.com

Tel: (866) 295-1805 (905) 295-1805

Old Stone Inn
5425 Robinson Street
Niagara Falls ON L2G 7L6
www.oldstoneinn.on.ca
Tel: (800) 263-6208 (905) 357-1234

Country Inn & Suites
5525 Victoria Avenue
Niagara Falls ON L2G 2L3
www.countryinns.com/niagara-falls-hotel-on-l2g3l3/onniafal
Tel: (800) 596-2375 (905) 374-6040

Secret Garden Restaurant
5827 River Road
Niagara Falls ON L2G 3K9
www.secretgardenrestaurant.net
Tel: (905) 358-4588

Elements on the Falls
6650 Niagara River Parkway
Niagara Falls ON
www.niagaraparks.com/dining/elementsonthefalls.php
Tel: (905) 354-3631

Pedlar Bicycle Shop
4547 Queen Street
Niagara Falls ON
www.pedlarbicycle.com
Tel: (905) 357-1273

Niagara Falls Library
4848 Victoria Avenue
Niagara Falls ON L2E 4C5
www.nflibrary.ca
Tel: (905) 356-8080

Niagara on the Lake 19 Q34-35
GPS 43.25540,-79.07212: historic town

Grand Niagara Package Route

Niagara Cycling Tourism Centre
www.rnbc.info

Niagara Region Bicycling Map

Shaw Festival Theatre
10 Queen's Parade
Niagara-on-the-Lake ON L0S 1J0
www.shawfest.com
Tel: (800) 511-7429 (905) 468-2172

Fort George on the Niagara Parkway - restored to the War of 1812
www.friendsoffortgeorge.ca

Niagara Apothecary - drug store museum
5 Queen Street
Niagara on the Lake ON
www.niagaraapothecary.ca

Chateau des Charmes Wines
1025 York Road
Niagara on the Lake ON
www.chateaudescharmes.com
Tel: (905) 262-4219

Inniskillen Wines
1499 Line 3 at Niagara Parkway
Niagara on the Lake ON L0S 1J0
www.inniskillin.com
Tel: (888) 466-4754

Konzelmann Estate Winery
1096 Lakeshore Road RR#3
Niagara on the Lake ON L0S 1J0
www.konzelmannwines.com
Tel: (905) 935-2866

Lailey Winery
15940 Niagara Parkway
Niagara on the Lake ON
www.laileyvineyard.com
Tel: (905) 468-0503

Palatine Hills Estate Winery
911 Lakeshore Road
Niagara on the Lake ON
www.palatinehillsestatewinery.com
Tel: (905) 646-9617

Reif Estate Winery
15608 Niagara Parkway
Niagara on the Lake ON L0S 1J0
www.reifwinery.com
Tel: (905) 468-7738

Small Talk Vineyards
1242 Irvine Road at Lakeshore Road
Niagara on the Lake ON L0S 1J0
Tel: (905) 935-3535

Strewn Winery
winery and cooking school
1339 Lakeshore Road
Niagara on the Lake ON L0S 1J0
www.strewnwinery.com
Tel: (905) 468-1229

Sunnybrook Wine Company
1425 Lakeshore Road
Niagara on the Lake ON L0S 1J0
www.sunnybrookfarmwinery.com
Tel: (905) 468-1122

Williams Gate Bed & Breakfast
413 Gate Street
Niagara on the Lake ON L0S 1J0
www.williamsgate.com
Tel: (905) 468-3086

The King's Way Bed & Breakfast
308 Nassau Street
Niagara on the Lake ON
www.bbcanada.com/123.html
Tel: (905) 468-5478

Best Western Colonel Butler Inn
278 Mary Street Box 642
Niagara on the Lake ON L0S 1J0
www.bestwesternontario.com/niagara-on-the-lake-hotels
Tel: (866) 556-8882 (905) 468-3251

Moffat Inn & Restaurant
60 Picton Street Box 578
Niagara on the Lake ON L0S 1J0
www.vintage-hotels.com/moffat/default.htm
Tel: (888) 669-5566 (905) 468-4116

Oban Inn - restaurant
160 Front Street Box 94
Niagara-on-the-Lake ON L0S 1J0
www.obaninn.ca
Tel: (866) 359-6226 (905) 468-4116

The Bike Shop
996 Lakeshore Road
Niagara on the Lake ON
Tel: (905) 934-3815

Zoom Leisure - rentals
431 Mississauga Street
Niagara-on-the-Lake ON L0S 1J0
www.zoomleisure.com
Tel: (866) 811-6993 (905) 468-2366

Niagara on the Lake Public Library
10 Anderson Lane
Niagara on the Lake ON
www.notlpubliclibrary.org
Tel: (905) 468-2023

Nipigon 2 GPS 49.01375,-88.26249: Town

Scandia House Bed & Breakfast
17 Second Street
Nipigon ON P0T 2J0
www.bbcanada.com/10834.html
Tel: (807) 887-3133

Northland Motel
Highway 17 Box 1736
Nipigon ON P0T 2J0
www.northland-motel.com
Tel: (807) 887-2032

Nipigon Public Library
25 Third Street Box 728
Nipigon ON P0T 2J0
www.nipigon.net/content/Nipigon_Public_Library
Tel: (807) 887-3142

Normandale 10 W25 GPS 42.71076,-80.31143: Village

Normandale Century Inn and Restaurant
2326 Front Road
Normandale ON N0E 1W0
www.bbcanada.com/normandaleinn
Tel: (519) 426-8345

North Bay 5 8B GPS 46.30911,-79.46082: City

Visiting North Bay
1375 Seymour Street
North Bay ON P1B 9V6
Tel: (800) 465-1882 (705) 474-0400

Discovery Routes Bicycle Routes
1375 Seymour Street
North Bay ON P1B 9V6
Tel: (800) 465-1882 (705) 474-0400

Super 8 North Bay
570 Lakeshore Drive
North Bay ON P1A 2E6
Tel: (888) 828-4551 (705) 495-4551

Sunset Inn B&B
641 Lakeshore Drive
North Bay ON P1A 2E9
Tel: (800) 463-8370 (705) 472-8370

Travelodge North Bay Lakeshore
718 Lakeshore Drive
North Bay ON P1A 2G4
Tel: (800) 578-7878 (705) 472-7171

North Buxton 5 8B GPS 42.30868,-82.22418: Hamlet

Buxton National Historic Site and Museum - celebrating the underground railroad and black settlements in Canada
21975 A. D. Shadd Road
North Buxton ON
Tel: (519) 352-4799
www.buxtonmuseum.com

Norwich 10 T22 GPS 42.98768,-80.59694: Town

Carriage House Bed & Breakfast
55 Stover Street North
Norwich ON
www.bbcanada.com/carriagehousebb
Tel: (877) 351-9831 (519) 863-5918

Oxford County Library
10 Tidey Street Highway 59
Norwich ON N0J 1P0
www.ocl.net/locations/Norwich
Tel: (519) 863-3307

Norwood 45 B44 GPS 44.3823-77.979913: Town

Asphodel Norwood Public Library
2363 County Road 45
Norwood ON K0L 2V0
Tel: (705) 639-2228

Oakland 16 S24 GPS 43.03171,-80.33153: Village

Oakville 24 N30 GPS 43.46617,-79.68958: City

Halton Cycling Maps

Walnut House B&B
134-136 Forsythe Street
Oakville ON L6K 3K2
www.bbcanada.com/6842.html
Tel: (905) 844-7687

Beccofino
263 Lakeshore Road East
Oakville ON
www.beccofino.ca
Tel: (905) 842-2263

Buca Di Bacco Ristorante Italiano
130 Thomas Street
Oakville ON L6J 3B1
Tel: (905) 845-7396

Racer Sportif
151 Robinson Street Unit 1
Oakville ON L6J 7N3
www.racersportif.com
Tel: (905) 815-2100

Oakville Public Library
120 Navy Street
Oakville ON
www.opl.on.ca
Tel: (905) 815-2042

Odessa 36 D54 GPS 44.27697,-76.71892: Town

Lennox & Addington Library
102 Main Street
Odessa ON K0H 2H0
www.lennox-addington.on.ca/library/location-and-hours.html
Tel: (613) 386-3981

Ohsweken 17 S26 GPS 43.06914,-80.11797: Central town for Six Nations Territory

Theatre to Theatre Package Route

Six Nations Tourism
www.sixnationstourism.ca
Tel: (866) 393-3001 (519)758-5444

⭐ **Grand River Champion of Champions Pow Wow**
late July
Tel: (519) 445-4061

🛏 **The Bear's Inn**
1979 4th Line Road Box 187
Ohsweken ON N0A 1M0
www.thebearsinn.com
Tel: (519) 445-4133

🏕 **Chiefswood Tent and Trailer Park**
Ohsweken Road at Road 54
www.sixnations.ca/prChiefswoodPark.htm
Tel: (519) 752-3969

🏛 **Chiefswood National Historic Site**
1037 Road 54
Ohsweken ON N0A 1M0
www.chiefswood.com
Tel: (519) 752-5005

Omemee 32 C39 GPS 44.298884, -78.559769:
Town

🛏🍴⭐🚲

⭐ **Youngtown Rock & Roll Museum** - tribute to Neil
Young who lived in Omemee as a boy
45 King Street East
Omemee ON K0L 2W0
Tel: (705) 799-2903

🚲 **Kawartha Lakes Public Library**
1 King Street West Box 520
Omemee ON K0L 2W0
Tel: (705) 799-5711
www.city.kawarthalakes.on.ca/residents/library-
services/hours-and-locations/omemee-library

Orangeville 29 H26 GPS 43.92012,-80.09349:
Town

🛏🍴🛏⭐🚲

⭐ **Theatre Orangeville** -
1875 Town Hall Opera House
87 Broadway Avenue
Orangeville ON L9W 1K1
www.theatreorangeville.ca
Tel: (800) 424-1295 (519) 942-3423

⭐ **Farmers Market** - Saturday morning
Second Street
www.thehillsofheadwaters.com/
orangevillefarmersmarket

⭐ **Orangeville Blues and Jazz Festival** -
Downtown early June

🛏 **Best Western Orangeville Inn and Suites**
7 Buena Vista Drive
Orangeville ON L9W 0A2
www.bestwesternorangeville.com
Tel: (800) 780-7234 (519) 941-3311

🛏 **At Pam's Place Bed and Breakfast**
160 Church Street
Orangeville ON L9W 1P4
Tel: (519) 941-2549

🍴 **Rustik Restaurant**
199 Broadway
Orangeville ON
Tel: (519) 940 3108

🍴 **Bluebird Cafe**
102 Broadway
Orangeville ON
www.bluebirdcafeandgrill.com
Tel: (519) 941-3101

🚲 **Orangeville Library**
275 Alder Street
Orangeville ON L9W 5H6
www.orangeville.library.on.ca
Tel: (519) 941-0610

Orillia 42 Z32 GPS 44.60659,-79.41823:
Town

ℹ🛏🍴🛏🚲

ℹ **Simcoe County Cycling Routes**

🛏 **Anne's Cranberry House B&B**
25 Dalton Crescent South
Orillia ON L3V 5J7
www.bbcanada.com/cranberryhousebb
Tel: (866) 876-5885 (705) 326-6871

🛏 **Casa Dizon B&B**
9 Tecunseh Street
Orillia ON L3V 1X7
www.bbcanada.com/7918.html
Tel: (866) 833 2272 (705) 326 2841

🛏 **Best Western Plus** - restaurant
440 Couchiching Point Road
Orillia ON L3V 6P8

www.bestwesternorillia.com
Tel: (888) 869-2306 (705) 325-6505

🛏 **Comfort Inn Orillia**
75 Progress Drive
Orillia ON L3V 6H1
www.choicehotels.ca/hotels/hotel?hotel=CN284
Tel: (800) 424-6423 (705) 327-7744

🛏 **Stone Gate Inn**
437 Laclie Street
Orillia ON L3V 4P7
www.stonegateinn.com
Tel: (705) 674-5542 (705) 329-2535

🍴 **Era 67 Restaurant**
64 Mississauga Street West
Orillia ON L3V 3A8
Tel: (705) 259-1867

🍴 **Theo's Eatery**
214 Memorial Avenue
Orillia ON L3V 5X6
Tel: (705) 329-4444

🚲 **Velocity Bike and Multisport**
161 Mississaga Street East
Orillia ON L3V 1V8
www.velocitybicycle.com
Tel: (705) 329-0367

🚲 **Orillia Public Library**
36 Mississauga Street West
Orillia ON L3V 3A6
Tel: (705) 325-2338

Orton 23 J25 GPS 43.78141,-80.22877:
Village

🛏

Oshawa 32 H37 GPS 43.88868,-78.85950:
City

⭐🛏🛏🍴🛏🚲🏕🚲

⭐ **Parkwood The McLaughlin Estate National
Historic Site**
270 Simcoe Street North
Oshawa ON
Tel: (905) 433-4311

⭐ **Peony Festival** - Oshawa Valley Botanical
Gardens - mid June
155 Arena Street
Oshawa ON

🛏 **Best Western Durham Hotel**
550 Bloor Steeet West
Oshawa ON L1J 5Y6
www.bestwesternontario.com/oshawa-hotels
Tel: (800) 780-7234 (905) 723-5271

🛏 **The White House Bed & Breakfast**
494 King Street East
Oshawa ON L1H 1G1
www.bbcanada.com/10408.html
Tel: (905) 579-0062

🏕 **Darlington Provincial Park**
1600 Darlington Park Road
Bowmanville ON L1C 3K3
Tel: (905) 436-2036

🚲 **Bicycles Plus**
843 King Street West Unit 11
Oshawa ON L1J 2L4
www.bicyclesplus.com
Tel: (905) 436-6040

🚲 **Oshawa Library** - Jess Hann Branch
199 Wentworth Street West
Oshawa ON L1J 6P4
www.oshawalibrary.on.ca
Tel: (905) 579-6111 ext. 5860

Ottawa 66 Q62-63 GPS 45.42150,-75.69189:
City

ℹ🛏🛏🍴⭐🛏🚲🚲

ℹ **Ottawa Online Cycling Maps**
ottawa.ca/residents/onthemove/travelwise/
cycling/index_en.html

ℹ **The Capital Pathway**
National Capital Commission - bike paths
www.canadascapital.gc.ca/bins/ncc_web_
content_page.asp?cid=16297-16299-9970-9971-
29551&lang=1

ℹ **Capital Information Kiosk**
90 Wellington Street
Ottawa ON
www.canadascapital.gc.ca
Tel: (866) 811-0055

🛏 **Benner's Bed & Breakfast**
539-541 Besserer Street
Ottawa ON K1N 6C6
www.bennersbnb.com
Tel: (613) 789-8320

🛏 **Auberge King Edward Bed & Breakfast**
525 King Edward Avenue

Ottawa ON K1N 7N3
www.kingedwardottawa.com
Tel: (613) 565-6700

🛏 **Alexander House**
542 Besserer Street
Ottawa ON K1N 6C7
ottawabandb.com
Tel: (613) 797-5355

🛏 **Carleton University Conference Services** -
172 Residence Commons Carleton University
Ottawa ON K1S 5B6
www2.carleton.ca/housing/conference-services
Tel: (613) 520-5611

⭐ **Rideau Canal Locks 1-8**
www.pc.gc.ca/lhn-nhs/on/rideau/index.aspx
Tel: (888) 773-8888 (613) 283-5170

🚲 **Cycos** - rentals
5 Hawthorne Avenue
Ottawa ON K1S 0A9
www.cycosport.ca
Tel: (613) 567-8180

🚲 **Fosters Sports Centre**
305 Bank Street
Ottawa ON
www.fosterssports.ca
Tel: (613) 236-9611

🚲 **Ottawa Public Library**
120 Metcalfe
Ottawa ON K1P 5M2
www.biblioottawalibrary.ca
Tel: (613) 580-2945

Owen Sound 39 Z19 GPS 44.56488,-80.94260:
Town

🍴🛏🚲ℹ⭐🛏🏕🚲🚲

ℹ **Bruce Peninsula Package Route**

ℹ **Owen Sound & Grey County**
www.visitgrey.ca
Tel: (877) 733-4739 (519) 376-3265

🏛 **Grey Roots Museum & Archives**
102599 Grey Road 18 RR#4
Owen Sound ON N4K 5N6
Tel: (877) 473-9766 (519) 376-3690

⭐ **Tom Thomson Art Gallery**
840 First Avenue West
Owen Sound ON N4K 4K4
www.tomthomson.org
Tel: (519) 376 1932

⭐ **Summerfolk Festival** - middle of August
Kelso Beach Park Second Avenue West
Owen Sound ON N4K 4K4
www.summerfolk.org
Tel: (519) 371-2995

⭐ **Inglis Falls Conservation Area** - 80 foot waterfall
and hiking trails
Inglis Falls Road north of Road 18

🛏 **MacLean Estate Bed & Breakfast**
404 9th Street East
Owen Sound ON N4K 1P3
Tel: (519) 416-5326

🛏 **The Highland Manor B&B**
867 4th Ave 'A' West
Owen Sound ON N4K 6L5
www.highlandmanor.ca
Tel: (519) 372-2699

🛏 **Best Western Inn on the Bay**
1800 2nd Avenue East Box 516
Owen Sound ON N4K 5P1
www.bestwesternontario.com/hotels/best-
western-inn-on-the-bay
Tel: (800) 780-7234 (519) 371-9200

🏕 **Owen Sound Campgrounds** -
Harrison Park Campground
75 2nd Avenue East
Kelso Beach Campground
2nd Avenue West
Owen Sound ON
Tel: (519) 371-9734

🍴 **Nathaniel's Restaurant**
215 8th Street East
Owen Sound ON N4K 1L2
Tel: (519) 371-3440

🍴 **Norma Jean's**
243 8th Street East
Owen Sound ON N4K 1L2
Tel: (519) 376-2232

🚲 **Jolley's Alternative Wheels**
939 Second Avenue West
Owen Sound ON N4K 1S2
www.alternativewheels.com
Tel: (519) 371-1812

🚲 **Owen Sound Public Library**
824 First Avenue West

Owen Sound ON N4K 4K4
owensound.library.on.ca
Tel: (519) 376-6623

Paincourt 6 A8 GPS 42.39289,-82.29365: Village

🛏️

Paisley 27 C17 GPS 44.30653,-81.27205: Town

ℹ️🛏️🏛️🍴🚲⛺🚴

🚴 Bruce Peninsula Package Route

🏛️ Treasure Chest Museum
407 Queen Street Box 125
Paisley ON N0G 2N0
Tel: (519) 353-7176

🛏️ Gar-Ham Hall Bed & Breakfast
538 Queen Street North
Paisley ON N0G 2N0
www.bbcanada.com/2770.html
Tel: (519) 353-7243

⛺ Paisley Rotary Campground
416 Water Street
Paisley ON N0G 2N0
Tel: (519) 353-5575

🍴 Marty's Bar & Grill
526 Queen Street
Paisley ON N0G 2N0
Tel: (519) 353-5012

🍴 Back Eddie's
660 Queen Street South
Paisley ON N0G 2N0
www.backeddies.com
Tel: (519) 353-4787

📚 Bruce County Library
274 Queen Street
Paisley ON N0G 2N0
Tel: (519) 353-7225

Paris 16 R24 GPS 43.19068,-80.38164: Town

ℹ️🛏️🍴🚗🚴⭐🚲🚴

ℹ️ Theatre to Theatre Package Route

🚴 Cobblestone buildings - including the 1837 St. James Anglican Church
5 Burwell Street & 165 Grand River Street North

⭐ Paris Fair - Labour Day weekend
139 Silver Street
Paris ON N3L 1V5
Tel: (519) 442-2823

⭐ Paris Farmers Market - Thursday - Syl Apps Community Centre
51 William Street Paris ON

🛏️ Asa Wolverton House B&B
52 Grand River Street South
Paris ON N3L 2B3
www.bbcanada.com/10616.html
Tel: (519) 442-1652

🛏️ Behind The Pines Bed & Breakfast
1 Homestead Road
Paris ON N3L 1P3
http://bbcanada.com/7539.html
Tel: (519) 442-1740

🚲 PM Cycle and Multisport
300 Grand River Street North #3
Paris ON N3L 3R7
Tel: (519) 302-0778

📚 Brant County Library
12 William Street
Paris ON N3L 1K7
www.brant.library.on.ca
Tel: (519) 442-2433

Parry Sound 57 R27 GPS 45.34364,-80.03576: Town

🛏️ℹ️⭐🚲🍴🚗🚴

ℹ️ Georgian Bay Country Tourism
70 Church Street Unit 3
Parry Sound ON P2A 1Y9
www.gbcountry.com
Tel: (888) 229-7257 (705) 746-4213

⭐ Festival of the Sound - music festival - July and August
42 James Street
Parry Sound ON P2A 1T5
www.festivalofthesound.ca
Tel: (866) 364-0061 (705) 746-2410

🛏️ 40 Bay Street Bed & Breakfast
40 Bay Street
Parry Sound ON P2A 1S5
www.40baystreet.com
Tel: (866) 371-2638 (705) 746-9247

🛏️ Comfort Inn

120 Bowes Street
Parry Sound ON
www.comfortinn.com/hotel-parry_sound-canada-CN288?promo=gcicn288
Tel: (877) 424-6423 (705) 746-6221

🛏️ Microtel Inn And Suites
292 Louisa Street
Parry Sound ON P2A 0A1
www.microtelinn.com
Tel: (800) 771-7171 (705) 746-2700

🚲 Ontario Trysport
77 Bowes Street
Parry Sound ON P2A 2L6
ontariotrysport.com
Tel: (877) 844-9887 (705) 746-8179

📚 Parry Sound Public Library
29 Mary Street
Parry Sound ON P2A 1E3
www.pspl.on.ca
Tel: (705) 746-9601

Pelee Island 5 H45 GPS 41.76848,-82.68887:
www.pelee.org The island is very flat and the maximum distance around the outer ring of roads is 30 kilometers (18 miles). The main roads are paved or surface treated in the summer. Roads are quiet, often tree lined and along the shore. Suggested stops are the Pelee Island Winery Pavilion just south of the ferry dock, the Fish Point Nature Preserve (unsafe for swimming), the public beach on the East Shore Road, the museum and trading post at the ferry dock and a hike to the ruins at Lighthouse Point. There is no town on the island and only a few stores and restaurants.

ℹ️🛏️🍴🍷⭐⛺

ℹ️ Erie Shores Package Route

⭐ Pelee Island – Leamington, Kingsville ON - Sandusky, Ohio USA
www.ontarioferries.com/jii/english/index.html
Tel: (800) 661-2220

🍷 Pelee Island Winery - Pelee Island just south of ferry dock
www.peleeisland.com
Tel: (800) 597-3533 (519) 733-6551

🛏️ Anchor & Wheel Inn
The Island Restaurant
11 West Shore Road
Pelee Island ON
www.anchorwheelinn.com
Tel: (519) 724-2195

🛏️ Island Memories Bed & Breakfast
192 North Shore Road
Pelee Island ON
www.island-memories.com
Tel: (519) 724-2667

⛺ East Park Campground
1362 East Shore Road
Pelee Island ON
Tel: (519) 724-2913

Pembroke 81 K51 GPS 45.82648,-77.11221: Town

🛏️ℹ️🍴🚗🚴

ℹ️ Ottawa Valley Tourist Association
9 International Drive
Pembroke ON K8A 6W5
www.ottawavalley.org
Tel: (800) 757-6580 (613) 732-4364

🛏️ Booth House Inn B&B
272 Pembroke Street East
Pembroke ON K8A 3K1
www.bbcanada.com/boothhouseinn
Tel: (613) 735 1151

🛏️ Grey Gables Manor Inn B&B
353 Mackay Street
Pembroke ON K8A 1C8
www.greygablesmanor.com
Tel: (613) 635-7011

🛏️ Best Western Pembroke Inn - restaurant
1 International Drive RR#4
Pembroke ON K8A 6W5
bestwesternontario.com/hotels/best-western-pembroke-inn-and-conference-centre
Tel: (800) 567-2378 (613) 735-0131

🛏️ Travelodge Pembroke
900 Pembroke Street East
Pembroke ON K8A 3M2
www.travelodgepembroke.com
Tel: (800) 578-7878 (613) 735-6868

📚 Pembroke Public Library
237 Victoria Street
Pembroke ON K8A 4K5

Tel: (613) 732-8844

Penetanguishene 41 X27
GPS 44.76812,-79.93536: Town

⭐🛏️🍴🛏️🚲🚴

🚴 Discovery Harbour -1828 British Naval Base Homeport of magnificent replica ships H.M.S. Bee and H.M.S. Tecumseth.
93 Jury Drive
Penetanguishene ON L9M 1G1
www.discoveryharbour.on.ca
Tel: (705) 549-8064

⭐ Kings Wharf Theatre
97 Jury Drive
Penetanguishene ON L9M 1G7
www.draytonentertainment.com
Tel: (855) 372-9866 (705) 549-5555

🛏️ Georgian Terrace Guest House
14 Water Street
Penetanguishene ON L9M 1V6
www.georgianterrace.ca
Tel: (888) 549-2440 (705) 549-2440

🚲 Georgian Cycle
21 Peel Street
Penetanguishene ON L9M 1A5
www.shopmidland.com/georgiancycle
Tel: (705) 549-7388

Perth 49 W58 GPS 44.89894,-76.24833: Town

🚴ℹ️🛏️🍴🚴

🚴 St. Lawrence and Rideau Canal Package Route

ℹ️ Tourist Information: Beautiful Perth
www.beautifulperth.com

🚴 Perth Museum - 1840 Matheson House
11 Gore Street East
Perth ON
Tel: (613) 267-1947

🛏️ Nevis Estate
61 Drummond Street West
Perth ON K7H 2K5
www.nevisestate.com
Tel: (613) 326-0017

🛏️ Perth Manor Boutique Hotel
23 Drummond Street West
Perth ON K7H 2J6
www.perthmanor.com
Tel: (613) 264-0050

🍴 Maximilian Dining Lounge
99 Gore Street East
Perth ON K7H 1J1
Tel: (613) 267-2536

🍴 Bistro 54
54 Foster Street
Perth ON K7H 1S1
Tel: (613) 267-5454

📚 Perth Library
30 Herriott Street
Perth ON K7H 1T2
www.perthunionlibrary.ca
Tel: (613) 267-1224

Petawawa 81 K50 GPS 45.894702,-77.283249: Town

🛏️🍴🚲🛏️

🛏️ Petawawa River Inn & Suites
3520 Petawawa Boulevard
Petawawa ON K8H 1W9
www.petawawariverinnandsuites.ca
Tel: (800) 573-9775 (613) 687-4686

🛏️ Quality Inn & Suites
3119B Petawawa Boulevard
Petawawa ON K8H 1W9
www.petawawaqualityinnandsuites.com
Tel: (866) 477-1130 (613) 687-2855

🚲 GearHeads
3025 Petawawa Boulevard
Petawawa ON K8H 1X9
www.gearheads.ca
Tel: (613) 687-4624

Peterborough 33 C41 GPS 44.30073,-78.32131: City

ℹ️⭐🚴🛏️🍴🚲🚴

ℹ️ Peterborough and The Kawarthas Tourism
1400 Crawford Drive RR#5
Peterborough ON K9J 6X6
www.thekawarthas.net
Tel: (800) 461-6424 (705) 742-2201

ℹ️ Peterborough and The Kawarthas Classics Road

Cycling Routes

- Peterborough Trails & Bikeways
- Lang Hastings TransCanada Trail
- Trent Canal Lock 19, 20, 21 and 22 - Lock 21 is the highest hydraulic lift lock in the world
www.pc.gc.ca/eng/lhn-nhs/on/trentsevern/visit/visit6/lock21.aspx
PO Box 567 Peterborough ON K9J 6Z6
camping permitted at most lock stations with prior approval
Tel: (888) 773-8888 (705) 750-4900
- Little Lake Musicfest - late June to late August
- Benson Bennet Bed & Breakfast
180 Benson Avenue
Peterborough ON K9H 5Y5
Tel: (877) 743-4857 (705) 743-4857
- Moffat House Bed & Breakfast
597 Weller Street
Peterborough ON K9H 2N9
www.moffathouse.ca
Tel: (705) 743-7228 (877) 415-1646
- Best Western Otonabee Inn - restaurant
84 Lansdowne Street East
Peterborough ON
bestwesternontario.com/hotels/best-western-otonabee-inn
Tel: (800) 780-7234 (705) 742-3454
- Wild Rock Outfitters
169 Charlotte Street
Peterborough ON K9J 2T7
www.wildrock.net
Tel: (888) 945-3762 (705) 745-9133
- Peterborough Public Library
345 Aylmer Street North
Peterborough ON K9H 3V7
www.peterborough.library.on.ca
Tel: (705) 745-5382

Philipsburg 22 N21 GPS 43.42126,-80.72067: Village

Pickering 25 J34 GPS 43.83762,-79.08231: City

- Port Restaurant
1289 Wharf Street
Pickering ON L1W 1A2
www.portrestaurant.ca
Tel: (905) 839-7678
- Bay Cycle and Sports
980 Brock Road South
Pickering ON L1W 2A3
www.baycyclesports.com
Tel: (800) 613-3585 (905) 837-1433
- Cycle Life
1050 Brock Road
Pickering ON L1W 3X4
Tel: (905) 837-2906

Picton 35 G51 GPS 44.00922,-77.13897: Town

- Bay of Quinte Package Route
- Bay of Quinte and Northumberland Package Route
- Lake Ontario Trent Canal Package Route
- Prince Edward County Tourism
116 Main Street
Picton ON
www.pec.on.ca
Tel: (800) 640-4717 (613) 476-2421
- Prince Edward County Jazz Festival - late August
Regent Theatre Picton and other locations
224 Main Street Box 500
Picton ON K0K 2T0
www.pecjazz.org
Tel: (877) 411-4761 (613) 476-8416
- Great Canadian Cheese Festival - early June - Fairgrounds
- Taste Community Grown A Celebration of Regional Cuisine - late September - Fairgrounds
- Macaulay Heritage Park - museum
35 Church Street at Union Street
Picton ON
www.pecounty.on.ca/government/rec_parks_culture/rec_culture/museums/macaulay.php
- Black Prince Winery

13370 Loyalist Parkway RR#1
Picton ON K0K 2T0
www.blackprincewinery.com
Tel: (866) 470-9463 (613) 476-4888
- The Picton Harbour Inn
33 Bridge Street
Picton ON
www.pictonharbourinn.com
Tel: (800) 678-7906 (613) 476-2186
- Claramount Inn & Spa - restaurant
97 Bridge Street
Picton ON K0K 3V0
www.claramountinn.com
Tel: (800) 679-7756 (613) 476-2709
- Edgewater B&B
25 Hill Street
Picton ON K0K 2T0
Tel: (613) 476-4256
- Brown's Manor Bed &Breakfast
2 Johnson Street
Picton ON K0K 2T0
www.brownsmanor.com
Tel: (613) 476-0248
- Sandbanks Provincial Park
3004 County Road 12 RR#1
Picton ON K0K 2T0
Tel: (613) 393-3319
Reservations: www.ontarioparks.com
Tel: (888) 668-7275
- Painted Peppercorn
172 Main Street
Picton ON
Tel: (613) 476-8225
- Portabella Restaurant
265 Main Street West
Picton ON
www.portabellaonmain.com
Tel: (613) 476-7057
- Picton Public Library
208 Main Street
Picton ON K0K 2T0
www.peclibrary.org
Tel: (613) 476-5962

Plevna 63 V53 GPS 44.96228,-76.98394: Village

- Dark Sky Preserve Observation Pad
5816 Road 506 just south of Plevna
- Kingston Frontenac Public Library
6638 Buckshot Lake Road
Plevna ON K0H 2M0
Tel: (613) 479-2542

Point Clark 26 F13 GPS 44.06933,-81.75442: Village

- Point Clark Lighthouse c.1859
www.pc.gc.ca/eng/lhn-nhs/on/clark/natcul.aspx

Pointe Fortune 69 P73 GPS 45.56503,-74.45229: Quebec Village

- Traversier Le Passeur - Ferry from Pointe Fortune to Carillon Quebec
www.traversierlepasseur.com
Tel: (450) 537-3412
- Voyageur Provincial Park
1313 Front Road Box 130
Chute-a-Blondeau ON K0B 1B0
Tel: (613) 674-2825
Reservations: www.ontarioparks.com
Tel: (888) 668-7275

Poplar Hill 8 T14 GPS 43.00540,-81.51100: Village

Port Bruce 9 X19 GPS 42.66098,-81.02280: Hamlet

- Ports of Lake Erie Package Route
- Port Bruce Provincial Park
sand beach on Lake Erie, no camping
Port Bruce ON N0J 1T0
www.ontarioparks.com
Tel: (519) 874-4691

Port Burwell 9 X20 GPS 42.64570,-80.80594: Hamlet

- Ports of Lake Erie Package Route
- Port Burwell Marine Museum & Historic

Lighthouse
20 Pitt Street & 17 Robinson Street
Port Burwell ON N0J 1T0
Tel: (519) 874-4807
- Project Ojibwa Oberon Class Submarine
3 Pitt Street Box 250
Port Burwell ON N0J 1T0
Tel: (519) 633-7641
- Grey Gables Bed & Breakfast
22 Erieus Street Box 297
Port Burwell ON N0J 1T0
www.bbcanada.com/3912.html
Tel: (519) 874-4644
- Port Burwell Provincial Park
9 Wilson Lane
Port Burwell ON N0J 1T0
Tel: (519) 874-4691
Reservations: www.ontarioparks.com
Tel: (888) 668-7275
- Elgin County Library
21 Pitt Street
Port Burwell ON N0J 1T0
www.library.elgin-county.on.ca
Tel: (519) 874-4754

Port Colborne 19 U33-34 GPS 42.88509,-79.25198: City

- Grand Niagara Package Route
- Theatre to Theatre Package Route
- Welland Canal Lock 8
- Farmers Market - Friday mornings - Downtown in front of City Hall
66 Charlotte Street
Port Colborne ON
www.portcolborne.com/page/farmers_market
- Port Colborne Historical and Marine Museum
280 King Street
Port Colborne ON
Tel: (905) 834-7604
- Nickel Beach Welland Street at Lake Road
- Showboat Festival Theatre - Roselawn Centre
296 Fielden Avenue
Port Colborne ON
www.roselawncentre.com
Tel: (905) 834-0833
- Canal Days Maritime Heritage Festival - August holiday weekend
www.portcolborne.com/page/canal_days
- Talwood Manor B & B
303 Fielden Avenue
Port Colborne ON L3K 4T5
www.talwoodmanor.com
Tel: (905) 348-5411
- Lakebreeze Bed & Breakfast
234 Steele Street
Port Colborne ON L3K 4X7
www.lakebreezeniagara.com
Tel: (877) 834-1233 (905) 834-1233
- The Smokin Buddha
265 King Street
Port Colborne ON L3K 4G8
Tel: (905) 834-6000
- Canal Side Restaurant & Cooking Store
232 West Street
Port Colborne ON L3K 4E3
Tel: (905) 834-6090
- Sherkston Shores
490 Empire Road
Sherkston ON L0S 1R0
www.sherkston.com
Tel: (877) 482-3224 (905) 894-0972
- Port Colborne Library
310 King Street
Port Colborne ON L3K 4H1
www.portcolbornelibrary.org
Tel: (905) 834-6512

Port Credit 24 M30 GPS 43.55143,-79.58593: see Mississauga

Port Dalhousie 19 Q33 GPS 43.20190,-79.26810: part of St Catharines

- Grand Niagara Package Route
- Theatre to Theatre Package Route
- Lakeside Park - antique carousel and public beach
1 Lakeport Road
St. Catharines ON L2N 5B3
www.stcatharines.ca/en/experiencein/LakesideParkCarousel.asp

Old Port B&B
73 Main Street
St. Catharines ON L2N 4V1
www.bbcanada.com/oldprtbb
Tel: (905) 934-5761

Simcoe Suites
20 Simcoe Street
Port Dalhousie ON L2N 5C7
(905) 935-8842

Port Dover 11 V26
GPS 42.78498,-80.20116: Beach Town

Ports of Lake Erie Package Route
Theatre to Theatre Package Route
Norfolk Tourism
Tel: (800) 699-9038 (519) 426-9497
Bicycling on Norfolk County Trails
Friday the Thirteenth Motorcycle Festival
Lighthouse Festival Theatre
247 Main Street
Port Dover ON
Tel: (888) 779-7703 (519) 583-2221
South Coast Jazz - Port Dover Arena
809 Saint George Street
Port Dover ON N0A 1N0
Tel: (519) 774-2787
Dover House Bed & Breakfast
17 Morgan Street Box 1201
Port Colborne ON N0A 1N0
Tel: (519) 583-3654
Goldora Place B&B
57 Prospect Street
Port Colborne ON N0A 1N6
Tel: (519) 583-3415
Erie Beach Hotel - restaurant
19 Walker Street
Port Colborne ON N0A 1N0
Tel: (519) 583-1391
Schofields Bistro
237 Main Street
Port Dover ON
Tel: (519) 583-3400
Norfolk Public Library
413 Main Street
Port Dover ON N0A 1N0
Tel: (519) 583-0622

Port Elgin 38 B16 GPS 44.43710,-81.38816:
Resort town

Bruce Peninsula Package Route
Port Elgin Pumpkinfest - early October
Spruce Hall Bed & Breakfast
824 Goderich Street
Port Elgin ON N0H 2C0
www.bbcanada.com/2643.html
Tel: (866) 389-4250 (519) 832-9835
Windspire Inn - restaurant
276 Mill Street Box 2366
Port Elgin ON N0H 2C0
www.windspireinn.com
Tel: (888) 389-7111 (519) 389-3898
Port Elgin Super 8
5129 Highway 21
Port Elgin ON N0H 2C0
www.portelginsuper8.com
Tel: (888) 388-3608 (519) 832-2058
Port Elgin Municipal Tourist Camp
584 Bruce Street
Port Elgin ON
Tel: (519) 832-2512
MacGregor Point Provincial Park
1593 Bruce Road 33 RR#1
Port Elgin ON N0H 2C5
Tel: (519) 389-9056
Reservations: www.ontarioparks.com
Tel: (888) 668-7275
Brucedale Conservation Area
137 Sprucedale Drive RR#1
Port Elgin ON N0H 2C0
www.svca.on.ca
Tel: (519) 389-4516
Andre's Swiss Country Dining
442 Goderich Street
Port Elgin ON N0H 2C4
www.andresswissdining.com
Tel: (519) 832-2461
Rick's Bikes (Richard Diotte)
761 Goderich Street
Port Elgin ON

Tel: (519) 832-2744
Bruce County Library
708 Goderich Avenue
Port Elgin ON N0H 2C0
library.brucecounty.on.ca
Tel: (519) 832-2201

Port Hope 33 G41 GPS 43.95012,-78.29161:
Town

Lake Ontario Trent Canal Package Route
All Canadian Jazz Festival - Downtown -
early September
www.allcanadianjazz.ca
Canadian Firefighters Museum
95 Mill Street South
Port Hope ON
www.firemuseumcanada.com
Tel: (905) 885-8985
Capitol Theatre - Restored 1930's atmospheric
theatre
20 Queen Street
Port Hope ON L1A 3Z4
www.capitoltheatre.com
Tel: (800) 434-5092 (905) 885-1071
Carlyle Inn & Bistro
86 John Street
Port Hope ON L1A 2Z2
Tel: (855) 383-3316 (905) 885-5500
The Waddell Hotel - restaurant
1 Walden Street
Port Hope ON L1A 1M8
thewaddell.ca
Tel: (905) 885-2449
Penstowe Bed & Breakfast
98 Ontario Street
Port Hope ON L1A 2V2
www.penstowe.com
Tel: (905) 885-4317
Port Hope Public Library
31 Queen Street
Port Hope ON L1A 2Y8
www.phpl.ca
Tel: (905) 885-4712

Port Lambton 6 W6 GPS 42.65674,-82.50571:
Village

Port Perry 31 E36 GPS 44.10682,-78.94273:
Town

Port Perry Tourist Information
www.discoverportperry.ca
Tel: (905) 985-4971
The Coach House Gallery Bed & Breakfast
425 Lakeshore Drive
Port Perry ON L9L 1N7
Tel: (905) 985-8082
Lakeshore Bed & Breakfast
435 Lakeshore Drive
Port Perry ON L9L 1N7
www.bbcanada.com/lakeshorebb
Tel: (905) 985-7684
Scugog Public Library
231 Water Street
Port Perry ON L9L 1A8
www.scugoglibrary.ca
Tel: (905) 985-7686

Port Robinson 19 S34 GPS 43.03839,-79.21010:
Village

Welland Canal Pedestrian and Bicycle Ferry -
April to December - check schedule in advance
www.thorold.com
Tel: (905) 227-6613 x272

Port Rowan 10 X23 GPS 42.62402,-80.45047:
Village

Ports of Lake Erie Package Route
Bicycling on Norfolk County Trails
Backus Conservation Area -
1798 water powered grist mill and museum
1267 Second Concession Road RR#1
Port Rowan ON N0E 1M0
www.lprca.on.ca/backus.htm
Tel: (519) 586-2201 (877) 990-9932
Seasons House Bed & Breakfast
1040 Bay Street Box 358
Port Rowan ON N0E 1M0

Tel: (800) 646-0668 (519) 586-7096
Rowan Nights Bed & Breakfast
57 Front Rd Box 408
Port Rowan ON N0E 1M0
Tel: (519) 586-8845
Long Point Provincial Park - a UN biosphere
reserve.
350 Erie Boulevard Box 99
Port Rowan ON N0E 1M0
Tel: (519) 586-2133
Reservations: www.ontarioparks.com
Tel: (888) 668-7275
Norfolk Public Library
1034 Bay Street
Port Rowan ON N0E 1M0
www.norfolk.library.on.ca
Tel: (519) 586-3201

Port Severn 41 X29 GPS 44.80303,-79.71502:
Trent Canal Lock 45
Group camping at most lock stations with prior
approval
www.pc.gc.ca/eng/lhn-nhs/on/trentsevern/visit/
visit6.aspx
Tel: (888) 773-8888 (705) 750-4900

Port Stanley 8 X18 GPS 42.66575,-81.21258:
Village

Ports of Lake Erie Package Route
Port Stanley Canfest - Canada Day weekend
Port Stanley Festival Theatre
6-302 Bridge Street
Port Stanley ON
www.portstanleytheatre.ca
Tel: (855) 782-4353 (519) 782-4353
Port Stanley Terminal Rail
309 Bridge Street
Port Stanley ON N5L 1C5
www.pstr.on.ca
Tel: (877) 244-4478 (519) 782-3730
Kettle Creek Inn - restaurant
216 Joseph Street
Port Stanley ON N5L 1C4
www.kettlecreekinn.com
Tel: (866) 414-0417 (519) 782-3388
Windjammer B&B - restaurant
324 Smith Street
Port Stanley ON
www.thewindjammerinn.com
Tel: (519) 782-4173
Elgin County Library
302 Bridge Street
Port Stanley ON N5L 1C3
www.library.elgin-county.on.ca
Tel: (519) 782-4241

Pottageville 30 G30
GPS 43.99192,-79.62307: Hamlet

Powassan 89 G32
GPS 46.08072,-79.36832: Town

Powassan Public Library
324 Clark Street
Powassan ON P0H 1Z0
Tel: (705) 724-3618

Prescott 50 Y64 GPS 44.70942,-75.51842:
Town

St. Lawrence and Rideau Canal Package Route
St. Lawrence Shakespeare Festival
206 King Street West
Prescott ON K0E 1T0
www.stlawrenceshakespeare.ca
Tel: (613) 925-5788
**Forwarders Museum & Tourist Information
Centre**
201 Water Street
Prescott ON
Tel: (613) 925-1861
Fort Wellington
370 Vankoughnet Street
Prescott ON K0E 1T0
www.pc.gc.ca/lhn-nhs/on/wellington/index_E.
asp
Tel: (613) 925-2896
Ashbury Inn on the River B&B
1665 County Road 2 RR#1

Prescott ON K0E 1T0
www.ashburyinnbb.com
Tel: (866) 731-7410 (613) 925-2566

The Colonel's Inn Bed & Breakfast
408 East Street
Prescott ON K0E 1T0
www.bbcanada.com/thecolonelsinn
Tel: (613) 925-2159

Dewar's Inn on the River
1649 Road 2
Prescott ON K0E 1T0
www.dewarsinn.com
Tel: (877) 433-9277 (613) 925-3228

The Red George Pub
197 Water Street West Suite 102
Prescott ON K0E 1T0
Tel: (613) 925-8800

The Wok House
238 King Street West
Prescott ON
Tel: (613) 925-2532

Prescott Public Library
300 Dibble Street West
Prescott ON
www.prescott.ca/residential/library.aspx
Tel: (613) 925-4340

Prince Albert 31 F36 GPS 44.08389,-78.95416:
Village

Providence Bay 72 M9 GPS 45.67664,
-82.26981: Village

Auberge Inn
71 McNevin Street
Providence Bay ON P0P 1T0
www.aubergeinn.ca
Tel: (705) 377-4392 (877) 977-4392

Queenston 19 R35 GPS 43.16362,-79.05350:
Village

Grand Niagara Package Route

Theatre to Theatre Package Route

Brock's Monument - Queenston Heights Park

Laura Secord Homestead
29 Queenston Street
Queenston ON
www.niagaraparks.com/heritage-trail/laura-
secord-homestead.html

MacKenzie Printery & Newspaper Museum
1 Queenston Street
Queenston ON
www.mackenzieprintery.org
Tel: (905) 262-5676

Riverbrink - Samuel E. Weir Museum and Art
Gallery
116 Queenston Street
Queenston ON
www.riverbrink.org
Tel: (905) 262-4510

South Landing Inn
21 Front Street Box 269
Queenston ON L0S 1L0
www.southlandinginn.com
Tel: (905) 262-4634

Queenston Heights Restaurant
14184 Niagara Parkway
Queenston ON
www.niagaraparks.com/dining/queenstonres.php
Tel: (905) 262-4374

Reeces Corners 12 T9 GPS 42.97953,-82.11765:
Village

Country View Motel Resort - camping
RR#1
Wyoming ON N0N 1T0
www.countryviewmotelandrvresort.com
Tel: (519) 845-3394

Renfrew 82 P55 GPS 45.47418,-76.68695: Town

Lochiel Street Bed and Breakfast
270 Lochiel Street South
Renfrew ON K7V 1W8
www.bbcanada.com/8563.html
Tel: (844) 284-3298 (613) 433-3752

Best Western Renfrew Inn - restaurant
760 Gibbons Road
Renfrew ON K7V 4A2
www.bestwesternontario.com/renfrew-hotels
Tel: (800) 780-7234 (613) 432-8109

Martin Cycle and Small Engine
31 Patrick Avenue
Renfrew ON K7V 3G6
Tel: (613) 432-4855

Renfrew Public Library
3 Railway Avenue
Renfrew ON K7V 3A9
www.town.renfrew.on.ca/library
Tel: (613) 432-8151

Renton 10 U25 GPS 42.85948,-80.22011: Village

Rideau Ferry 49 W59 GPS 44.84980,-76.14207:
Village

Ridgetown 7 A11 GPS 42.43957,-81.88657:
Town

Erie Shores Package Route

1875 Ridge House Museum
53 Erie Street South
Ridgetown ON
www.chatham-kent.ca/ridgehouse
Tel: (519) 674-2223

Dempster House
66 Main Street East Box 358
Ridgetown ON N0P 2C0
www.dempsterhouse.on.ca
Tel: (519) 365-3453

Howard Johnson Ridgetown
21198 Victoria Road
Ridgetown ON N0P 2C0
Tel: (800) 330-8713

Chatham Kent Library
54 Main Street
Ridgetown ON N0P 2C0
www.chatham-kent.ca/community+services/
library/Library.htm
Tel: (519) 674-3121

Ridgeway 19 U35 GPS 42.87810,-79.05181:
Town

Fort Erie Historical Museum
402 Ridge Road
Ridgeway ON
www.museum.forterie.ca/historical.html
Tel: (905) 894-5322

Fort Erie Library - Crystal Ridge Branch
89 Ridge Road South
Ridgeway ON L0S 1N0
www.forterie.library.on.ca
Tel: (905) 894-1281

Rockford 39 A19-20 GPS 44.52385,-80.91774:
Village

Rockland 67 P66 GPS 45.54603,-75.29304:
Town

Clarence Rockland Public Library
1525 Avenue du Parc
Rockland ON K4K 1C3
Tel: (613) 446-5680

Rockport 37 C61 GPS 44.38037,-75.93590:
Village

1000 Islands Cruises - Rockport Boat Line
23 Front Street
Rockport ON
www.rockportcruises.com
Tel: (613) 659-3402 (800) 563-8687

Boathouse Country Inn - restaurant
19 Front Street
Rockport ON K0E 1V0
www.boathousecountryinn.com
Tel: (613) 659-2348

Rodney 7 Y13 GPS 42.56803,-81.68309:
Village

Elgin County Library
207 Furnival Road

Rodney ON N0L 2C0
www.library.elgin-county.on.ca
Tel: (519) 785-2100

Rossmore 34 E49 GPS 44.13935,-77.38770:
Village

Rossport 2 GPS 48.83491,-87.51991: Village

St. Catharines 19 Q33 GPS 43.15633,-79.24867:
City

Grand Niagara Package Route

Ontario Travel Information Centre
Westbound QEW
251 York Road
Niagara-on-the-Lake ON L0S 1J0
www.ontariotravel.net
Tel: (905) 684-6354 (800) 668-2746

Welland Canals Centre - St. Catharines Museum
- Lacrosse Hall of Fame
1932 Welland Canals Parkway at Lock 3
St. Catharines ON L2R 7K6
www.stcatharineslock3museum.ca
Tel: (905) 984-8880

Brock University Conference & Event Services
50 Glenridge Avenue
St. Catharines ON L2S 3A1
www.brocku.ca/conference-services/individual
Tel: (905) 688-5550

Ski Pro Shop
278 Geneva Street
St. Catharines ON
www.skiproshop.com
Tel: (905) 934-2682

St. Clair Beach 4 B3 GPS 42.31528,-82.86126:
Hamlet

St. Clements 22 M22 GPS 43.52378,-80.65191:
Village

Region of Waterloo Library
3605 Lobsinger Line
St. Clements ON N0B 2M0
www.rwl.library.on.ca
Tel: (519) 699-4341

St. Davids 19 R35 GPS 43.16062,-79.10156:
Village

Old Firehall Restaurant
268 Four Mile Creek Road at York Road
St. Davids ON
www.oldfirehall.com
Tel: (905) 262-5443

St. Jacobs 22 M22 GPS 43.53920,-80.55360:
Village

St. Jacobs Schoolhouse Theatre
11 Albert Street West
St. Jacobs ON
Tel: (855) 372-9866

St. Jacobs Country Playhouse
40 Benjamin Road
St. Jacobs ON
Tel: (855) 372-9866 (519) 747-7788

Mennonite Story Visitor Centre
1406 King Street North
St. Jacobs ON
Tel: (519) 664-3518

Harvest Moon Restaurant
5 Parkside Drive
St. Jacobs ON N0B 2N0
www.harvestmoonrestaurant.ca
Tel: (519) 664-2373

Stone Crock
1396 King Street
St. Jacobs ON N0B 2N0
Tel: (519) 664-2286 (866) 664-2286

DH Food & Lodging - historic c.1852
1430 King Street Box 389
St. Jacobs ON N0B 2N0
Tel: (519) 664-3731

Queensway Landing Bed & Breakfast
46 Queensway Drive
St. Jacobs ON N0B 2N0
www.bbcanada.com/9444.html

Tel: (519) 664-2824

Baumann Haus B&B
25 Spring Street Box 6
St Jacobs ON N0B 2N0
Tel: (519) 664-1515

Region of Waterloo Library
29 Queensway Drive
St. Jacobs ON N0B 2N0
www.rwl.library.on.ca
Tel: (519) 664-3443

St. Marys 15 Q18 GPS 43.25950,-81.14142: Town

Stonetown Heritage Festival - early July
Tel: (519) 284-2340 x626

Canadian Baseball Hall of Fame and Museum
386 Church Street South
St. Marys ON N4X 1C2
www.baseballhalloffame.ca
Tel: (877) 250-2255 (519) 284-1838

The Westover Inn - restaurant
300 Thomas Street
St. Marys ON N4X 1B1
www.westoverinn.com
Tel: (800) 268-8243 (519) 284-2977

Hathaway House Bed & Breakfast
44 St. Andrew Street South Box 2616
St. Marys ON N4X 1A4
www.hathawaybedandbreakfast.com
Tel: (519) 284-1137

Stone Willow Inn & Wild Stone Bar & Grill - restaurant
940 Queen Street East
St. Marys ON N4X 1B3
www.stonewillow.com
Tel: (800) 409-3366 (519) 284-4140

Little Red's Pub & Eatery
159 Queen Street East
St. Marys ON N4X 1A2
Tel: (226) 661-2233

St. Marys Public Library
15 Church Street Box 700
St. Marys ON N4X 1B4
www.stmarys.library.on.ca
Tel: (519) 284-3346

St. Thomas 8 V17 GPS 42.77894,-81.19315: City

Ports of Lake Erie Package Route

Tourist Information –
St. Thomas and Elgin County
www.elgintourist.com
Tel: (877) 463-5446 x168 (519) 631-1460 x168

Elgin County Railway Museum
225 Wellington Street
St. Thomas ON N5R 2S6
www.ecrm5700.org
Tel: (519) 637-6284

Iron Horse Festival - late August
www.ironhorsefestival.com
Tel: (519) 207-4000

Jumbo Elephant Statue
76 Talbot Street
St. Thomas ON

Cardinal Court Motel
10401 Sunset Road RR#7
St. Thomas ON N5P 3T2
www.cardinalcourt.ca
Tel: (877) 774-8380 (519) 633-0740

Paul's Bicycle Repair & Sports Exchange
115 Ross Street
St. Thomas ON N5R 3X8
Tel: (519) 631-3307

St. Thomas Public Library
153 Curtis Street
St. Thomas ON N5P 3Z7
www.st-thomas.library.on.ca
Tel: (519) 631-6050

St. Williams 10 W24 GPS 42.66786,-80.41552: Village

Burning Kiln Winery
1709 Front Road St
St. Williams ON L0E 1P0
Tel: (519) 586-9858

Saltford 20 J13 GPS 43.74444,-81.69279: Village

Sandfield 73 M11 GPS 45.70471,-81.99865:

Hamlet

Sandford 31 E33 GPS 44.13506,-79.20110: Hamlet

Sarnia 12 T7 GPS 42.97877,-82.40336: City

Ontario Travel Information Centre
Blue Water Bridge
1455 Venetian Boulevard
Sarnia ON N7T 7W7
www.ontariotravel.net
Tel: (800) 668-2746 (519) 344-7403

Sarnia and Lambton County Tourism
1455 Venetian Boulevard
Sarnia ON N7T 7W7
Tel: (800) 265-0316 (519) 336-3232

Bicycle Crossing - Sarnia – Port Huron, Michigan USA
Riders and bicycles are transported at the convenience of the Blue Water Bridge Authority
Tel: (810) 984-3131
For alternatives see Sombra Marine City Ferry and Walpole Island Algonac Ferry

Bayfest Festival of Peforming Arts & Canada Day Celebration
Centennial Park
Sarnia ON
Tel: (866) 450-4474 (519) 337-4474

Imperial Theatre
168 North Christina Street
Sarnia ON N7T 7H8
www.imperialtheatre.net
Tel: (519) 344-7469

Point Edward Casino
2000 Venetian Boulevard
Tel: (519) 383-7770 (888) 394-6244

Best Western Plus Guildwood Inn - restaurant
1400 Venetian Boulevard
Sarnia ON N7T 7W6
www.bestwesternontario.com/hotels/best-western-guildwood-inn
Tel: (800) 780-7234 (519) 337-7577

Super 8 Motel
420 North Christina Street
Sarnia ON N7T 5W1
www.super8.com
Tel: (800) 889-9698

Twin Lakes Retreat Bed & Breakfast
1404 Errol Road East
Sarnia ON N7S 5T2
www.bbcanada.com/11084.html
Tel: (519) 542-8014

The Bicycle Shop
410 Front Street
Sarnia ON
www.thebicycleshopsarnia.ca
Tel: (519) 344-0515

Lambton County Library
124 Christina Street South
Sarnia ON N7T 8E1
www.lclmg.org
Tel: (519) 337-3291

Sauble Beach 38 Z17 GPS 44.62966,-81.26325: Village

Bruce Peninsula Package Route

Sauble Beach Tourism Sandfest - early August

Knights Inn Motel - restaurant
11 Sauble Falls Parkway Box 9 RR#1
Sauble Beach ON N0H 2G0
www.bmts.com/~knightsinn
Tel: (877) 239-9921 (519) 422-2311

Sauble Beach Lodge
11 Sauble Falls Parkway Box 9 RR#1
Sauble Beach ON
Tel: (519) 422-1040

Bruce County Library - Sauble Beach
27 Community Center Drive
Sauble Beach ON
Tel: (519) 422-1283

Sauble Falls 38 Y17 GPS 44.68428,-81.25557: Hamlet

Sauble Falls Provincial Park
Sauble Falls Road RR#3
Wiarton ON N0H 2T0
Tel: (519) 422-1952

Reservations: www.ontarioparks.com
Tel: (888) 668-7275

Sault Ste Marie 2 GPS 46.51797,-84.34797: City

Sault Ste. Marie International Bridge
Bicycles are permitted
Tel: (705) 942-4345 (906) 635-5255

Ontario Travel Information Centre
Sault Ste. Marie International Bridge
261 Queen Street West
Sault Ste. Marie ON P6A 1A3
www.ontariotravel.net
Tel: (705) 945-6941 (800) 668-2746

Tourism Sault Ste. Marie
99 Foster Drive
Sault Ste. Marie ON P6A 5X6
Tel: (800) 461-6020 (705) 759-5442

Algoma Farmers Market - Roberta Bondar Tent Pavilion
Wednesdays afternoon and Saturday morning
Tel: (705) 779-2586

Canadian Bushplane Heritage Centre
50 Pim Street
Sault Ste. Marie ON
www.bushplane.com
Tel: (877) 287-4752 (705) 945-6242

Agawa Canyon Train Tour
129 Bay Street
Sault Ste. Marie ON P6A 6Y2
www.algomacentralrailway.com
Tel: (705) 946-7300 (800) 242-9287

Quality Inn Bay Front
180 Bay St
Sault Ste. Marie ON
www.qualityinnssm.com
Tel: (800) 228-5151 (705) 945-9264

Sleep Inn
727 Bay Street
Sault Ste. Marie ON P6A 6Y3
www.sleepinnssmarie.ca
Tel: (877) 953-7533 (705) 253-7533

Algoma Bicycle Company
360 Queen Street East
Sault Ste. Marie ON P6A 1Z1
Tel: (705) 759-3443

Sault Ste. Marie Public Library
50 East Street
Sault Ste. Marie ON P6A 3C3
www.ssmpl.ca
Tel: (705) 759-5230

Schomberg 30 G30 GPS 44.00281,-79.68410: Town

Schreiber 2 GPS 48.81386,-87.26647: Town

Scone 27 C18 GPS 44.30527,-81.07301: Hamlet

Seaforth 20 M15 GPS 43.55304,-81.39370: Town

Memories Forever B&B
86 Goderich Street West
Seaforth ON N0K 1W0
www.bbcanada.com/7751.html
Tel: (519) 525-7156

Huron County Library
108 Main Street South Box 490
Seaforth ON N0K 1W0
www.huroncounty.ca/library
Tel: (519) 527-1430

Scotland 16 S24 GPS 43.02577,-80.37540: Village

Shabaqua Corner 2 GPS 48.60147,-89.89700: Village

Sharon 30 E-F32 GPS 44.09960,-79.44052: Village

Historic Sharon Temple
18974 Leslie Street
Sharon ON L0G 1V0
www.sharontemple.ca
Tel: (905) 478-2389

🚲 Spoke O'Motion
5-17915 Leslie Street
Newmarket ON N3Y 3E3
www.spokeomotion.com
Tel: (905) 853-9545

Shebandowan 2 GPS 48.62463,-90.07244: Village
🍴

Simcoe 17 U25 GPS 42.83726, -80.30404: Town
ℹ️⭐📖🍴🚲🛏️
ℹ️ Theatre to Theatre Package Route
ℹ️ Ports of Lake Erie Package Route
⭐ Norfolk County Fair & Horse Show - mid October
⭐ Jensen Cheese
37 Evergreen Hill Road Box 311
Simcoe ON N3Y 4L2
Tel: (866) 625-0615 (519) 426-4523
🍴 The Blue Elephant Restaurant
6 Norfolk Street South
Simcoe ON N3Y 2W2
www.blueelephant.ca
Tel: (519) 428-2886
🛏️ Best Western Little River Inn - restaurant
203 Queensway West
Simcoe ON N3Y 2M9
bestwesternontario.com/hotels/best-western-little-river-inn
Tel: (800) 780-7234 (519) 426-2125
📖 Norfolk County Public Library
49 Colborne Street South
Simcoe ON N3Y 4H3
www.ncpl.ca
Tel: (519) 426-5206

Sioux Narrows 2 GPS 49.41902,-94.09607: Village
🛒🔺
🔺 Sioux Narrows Provincial Park
Box 5080
Kenora ON P9N 3X9
Tel: (807) 226-5223
Reservations: www.ontarioparks.com
Tel: (888) 668-7275

Smiths Falls 49 W60: Town
ℹ️🛏️🔺🚲📖
ℹ️ St. Lawrence and Rideau Canal Package Route
ℹ️ Visiting Smiths Falls
www.smithsfalls.ca/visiting-here.cfm
🔺 Rideau Canal Museum, Locks 26, 27, 29 and 31
group camping with prior approval
www.pc.gc.ca/lhn-nhs/on/rideau/index.aspx
Tel: (888) 773 8888 (613) 283 5170
🛏️ Best Western Colonel By Inn
88 Lombard Street
Smiths Falls ON K7A 4G5
www.bestwesternontario.com/hotels/best-western-colonel-by-inn/
Tel: (800) 780-7234 (613) 284-0001
🛏️ Montague House Bed & Breakfast
482 Queen Street
Smiths Falls ON K7A 5B8
Tel: (613) 283-4198
🔺 Rideau Canal Locks 26, 27, 29 and 31
group camping with prior approval
Smiths Falls ON
🚲 Sport X
11 Chambers Street
Smiths Falls ON K7A2Y2
www.sportx.ca
Tel: (613) 284-1632
📖 Smiths Falls Public Library
81 Beckwith Street North
Smiths Falls ON K7A 2B9
www.smithsfallslibrary.ca
Tel: (613) 283-4198

Smithville 18 S31 GPS 43.09392,-79.54890: Town
🛒🍴

Sombra 6 W6 GPS 42.71401,-82.47841: Village
ℹ️🛒🍴⭐🚲🛏️🔺📖
ℹ️ Sombra to Marine City, Michigan USA
Michigan Ferry, Bluewater Ferry
www.bluewaterferry.com
Tel: (877) 892-3879 (519) 892-3879
ℹ️ Bridge to Bay Trail

Marine City to Algonac Michigan USA
www.stclaircounty.org/Offices/parks/btob.aspx
🛒 Sombra Museum
3470 St. Clair Parkway
Sombra ON
www.twp.stclair.on.ca/sombra_museum.htm
Tel: (519) 892-3982
🛏️ Sheboane Bed & Breakfast
2955 St. Clair Gardens
Sombra ON N0P 2H0
www.sheboane.ca
Tel: (519) 892-3389
🔺 Branton Cundick Park
54 West Wilkesport Line
Sombra ON
www.twp.stclair.on.ca/camping.htm
Tel: (519) 892-3968
🔺 Cathcart Park
955 St. Clair Parkway
Sombra ON N0P 2H0
www.twp.stclair.on.ca/camping.htm
Tel: (519) 892-3342
📖 Lambton County Library
3536 St. Clair Parkway
Sombra ON N0P 2H0
www.lclmg.org
Tel: (519) 892-3711

South Baymouth 73 N11
GPS 45.57011,-82.01320: Village
ℹ️🚲🛏️🔺
🚲 Little Schoolhouse and Museum
www.manitoulin-island.com/museums/little_schoolhouse.htm
Tel: (705) 859-2344
ℹ️ Tobermorey-South Baymouth Ferry
Reservations and information
www.ontarioferries.com/chi/english/index.html
Tel: (800) 265-3163
ℹ️ Manitoulin Island Cycling Maps
🛏️ Huron Motor Lodge
24 Water Street
South Baymouth ON P0P 1Z0
www.manitoulin.com/hml
Tel: (800) 387-2756 (705) 859-3131
🛏️ Buckhorn Motel
21076 Hwy 6 Box 40
South Baymouth ON P0P 1Z0
www.buckhornmotel.com
Tel: (705) 859-3635
🛏️ South Bay Guest House
14-15 Given Road
South Baymouth ON P0P 1Z0
www.southbayguesthouse.com
Tel: (705) 671-9611
🔺 John Budd Memorial Park
First Street, 1 km north of ferry dock

South Lancaster 52 T72 GPS 45.13026,-74.49153: Village
🛒🍴🔺
🔺 Glengarry Park Campsite
20800 South Service Road
Lancaster ON K0C 1N0
www.stlawrenceparks.com
Tel: (800) 437-2233 (613) 543-4328

Southampton 38 A16 GPS 44.49774,-81.36985: Town
ℹ️🛒⭐🛏️🍴🔺🚲📖
ℹ️ Bruce Peninsula Package Route
⭐ Saugeen First Nations Pow Wow in August at Saugeen Amphitheatre gardens east on Highway 21
www.saugeenfirstnation.ca
🛏️ Chantry Breezes Bed & Breakfast
107 High Street
Southampton ON N0H 2L0
www.chantrybreezes.com
Tel: (519) 797-1818
🛏️ Southampton Inn
118 High Street
Southampton ON N0H 2L0
www.thesouthamptoninn.com
Tel: (888) 214-3816
🛏️ Huron Haven Motel
21 Huron Street South Box 479
Southampton ON N0H 2G0
www.bmts.com/~huronhaven
Tel: (519) 797-2248
🍴 Walker House
146 High Street
Southampton ON N0H 2L0
Tel: (519) 797-2772

🍴 Forge & Thistle Wee Pub and Dining Room
48 Albert Street South
Southampton ON N0H 2L0
Tel: (519) 483-4848
🔺 Southampton Municipal Tourist Camp
227 Lake Street
Southampton ON N0H 2L0
Tel: (866) 832-2008 x124 (519) 832-2008 x124
🚲 Martin's Bicycle Shop
23 High Street
Southampton ON N0H 2L0
Tel: (519) 797-3200
📖 Bruce County Library
215 High Street
Southampton ON N0H 2L0
www.library.brucecounty.on.ca
Tel: (519) 797-3586

Southwold 8 V16 GPS 42.81031,-81.35703: Village
🛒

Spanish 2 GPS 46.19310,-82.33808: Village
🛒🛏️📖
🛏️ Le Bel Abri Bed & Breakfast
3 Garnier Street
Spanish ON P0P 2A0
www.bbcanada.com/1482.html
Tel: (705) 844-2545
📖 Spanish Public Library
8 Trunk Road
Spanish ON P0P 2A0
www.town.spanish.on.ca
Tel: (705) 844-2555

Sparta 9 W18 GPS 42.70244,-81.07954: Village
🛒🍴📖
🛒 Historic Quaker village - meeting house, blacksmith shop museum

Spencerville 50 X64 GPS 44.84306,-75.54668: Village
🛒ℹ️
🛒 Spencerville Mill Water Street
Tel: (613) 658-5885

Springbrook 46 B47 GPS 44.40001,-77.61396: Village
🛒🍴

Stirling 34 C47 GPS 44.29630,-77.54678: Town
🛒🍴🚲⭐🛏️
🚲 Farmtown Park Hastings County Museum of Agricultural Heritage
437 West Front Street
Stirling ON K0K 3E0
www.agmuseum.ca
Tel: (613) 395-0015
⭐ The Stirling Festival Theatre
41 West Front Street
Stirling ON K0K 3E0
www.stirlingfestivaltheatre.com
Tel: (877) 312-1162 (613) 395-2100
🛏️ La Dolce Vita Bed & Breakfast
54 Wellington Street
Stirling ON K0K 3E0
www.ldvbb.com
Tel: (613) 395-2138

Stockdale 34 D47 GPS 44.20017,-77.62922: Hamlet
🛒

Stoney Point 5 B6 GPS 42.31428,-82.55171: Hamlet
🛒

Stratford 21 P19 GPS 43.37013,-80.98193: City
ℹ️⭐🛏️📖🍴🚲📖
ℹ️ Theatre to Theatre Package Route
ℹ️ Tourist Information – Stratford and Area
www.welcometostratford.com
Tel: (800) 561-7926
ℹ️ Stratford Festival
55 Queen Street
Stratford ON N5A 4M9
www.stratfordfestival.ca
Tel: (800) 567-1600
⭐ Farmers Market - Saturday mornings at fairgrounds
20 Glastonbury Drive
Stratford ON
🛏️ Stratford Festival Accommodation Bureau
www. stratfordaccommodations.com

Tel: (800) 567-1600

🛏️ **Best Western Plus The Arden Park Hotel -**
restaurant
552 Ontario Street
Stratford ON N5A 6W4
Tel: (877) 788-8818 (519) 275-2936

🛏️ **Dufton House B&B**
12 Elizabeth Street
Stratford ON N5A 4Z2
www.duftonhouse.com
Tel: (519) 271-7413

🍴 **Revival House**
70 Brunswick Street
Stratford ON N5A 6V6
Tel: (519) 273-3424

🍴 **The Prune**
151 Albert Street
Stratford ON N5A 3K5
www.oldprune.on.ca
Tel: (519) 271-5052

🚲 **Totally Spoke'D**
29 Ontario Street
Stratford ON
www.totallyspoked.ca
Tel: (519) 273-2001

📚 **Stratford Public Library**
19 St Andrew Street
Stratford ON N5A 1A2
www.stratford.library.on.ca
Tel: (519) 271-0220

Strathroy 8 T14 GPS 42.95577,-81.62230: Town

🛏️🍴📚🏕️📚

🛏️ **Clock Tower Inn** - Strathroy Ale House
71 Frank Street
Strathroy ON N7G 2R5
www.clocktower-inn.com
Tel: (888) 776-8515 (519) 245-5656

🛏️ **Strathroy Motor Inn**
28540 Centre Road
Strathroy ON N7G 3H6
www.strathroymotorinn.com
Tel: (519) 245-4480

🏕️ **Trout Haven Park**
24749 Park Street
Strathroy ON N7G 3H5
www.trouthaven.ca
Tel: (519) 245-4070

📚 **Middlesex County Library**
34 Frank Street
Strathroy ON N7G 2R4
www.middlesex.library.on.ca
Tel: (519) 245-1290

Sudbury 86 See inset map
GPS 46.52209,-80.95303: City

📚🏛️🍴🛏️🛏️

🏛️ **Non Motorized Trails in Greater Sudbury**

⭐ **Sudbury Jazz Fest** - early September

🛏️ **Hampton Inn Sudbury**
2280 Regent Street
Sudbury ON P3E 0B4
Tel: (866) 500-4938 (705) 523-5200

🛏️ **Chateau Guay Motel & Restaurant**
2865 Kingsway
Sudbury ON P3B 2G4
Tel: (705) 566-1501

🛏️ **A1 Southbay Guest House**
1802 South Bay Road
Sudbury ON P3E 6H7
Tel: (877) 656-8324 (705) 671-9611

Sturgeon Falls - West Nipissing 88 D28
GPS 46.36660,-79.93129: Town

🍴📚🛏️

Summerstown 52 U72 GPS 45.05772,-74.56559:
Village

📚🍴

Sweaburg 16 S21 GPS 43.067233, -80.759614:
Hamlet

📚

Sydenham 36 B55 GPS 44.31816,-76.54086:
Village

📚🍴

Tamworth 47 A52 GPS 44.48738,-76.99482:
Town

🏛️📚🛏️🍴🛏️📚

🏛️ **Lake Ontario Trent Canal Package Route**

🛏️ **At Home Bed & Breakfast**
12 Ottawa Street
Tamworth ON K0K 3G0
www.athomebedandbreakfast.ca
Tel: (613) 379-2035

📚 **Lennox & Addington Library**
1 Ottawa Street
Tamworth ON K0K 3G0
www.lennox-addington.on.ca/library/about-
the-library.html
Tel: (613) 379-3082

Tara 39 A18 GPS 44.47652,-81.14525: Village

📚📚

📚 **Bruce County Public Library**
69 Yonge Street
Tara ON
www.library.brucecounty.on.ca/telib
Tel: (519) 934-2626

Teeswater 26 G16 GPS 43.99034,-81.30226: Town

⭐📚🍴📚

⭐ **Teeswater Creamery/Gay Lea Retail Store**
21 Clinton Street North
Teeswater ON N0G 2S0
www.gaylea.com
Tel: (519) 392-6864

📚 **Bruce County Public Library**
2 Clinton Street South
Teeswater ON
www.library.brucecounty.on.ca/telib
Tel: (519) 392-6801

Tehkummah 73 M11 45.64955,-82.00350: Village

📚🛏️🏕️

🏕️ **Gordons Park Bed & Breakfast & Campground**
18777 Highway 6
Tehkumah ON P0P 2C0
www.gordonspark.com
Tel: (705) 859-2470

Terra Cotta 23 K28 GPS 43.71651,-79.93595: Village

📚🍴

Terrace Bay 2 GPS 48.78335,-87.09792: Town

📚🍴🛏️🏕️📚

🛏️ **Coach House Motel** - restaurant
Simcoe Plaza
Terrace Bay ON
Tel: (807) 825-9113

🏕️ **Rainbow Falls Provincial Park** - west on
Highway 17
1004 Highway 17 Box 280
Terrace Bay ON P0T 2W0
Tel: (807) 824-2298
Reservations: www.ontarioparks.com
Tel: (888) 668-7275

🏕️ **Neys Provincial Park** - east on Highway 17
1004 Highway 17 Box 280
Terrace Bay ON P0T 2W0
Tel: (807) 229-1624
Reservations: www.ontarioparks.com
Tel: (888) 668-7275

📚 **Terrace Bay Library**
1010B Highway 17 Box 369
Terrace Bay ON
www.terracebay.ca/?pgid=78
Tel: (807) 825-3315 x222

Thamesville 7 Y11 GPS 42.55182,-81.97105:
Town

📚🍴📚

📚 **Chatham Kent Public Library**
3 London Road
Thamesville ON N0P 2K0
www.chatham-kent.ca/community+services/
library/hours+and+locations/Thamesville+Library.
htm
Tel: (519) 692-4251

Thedford 13 R12 GPS 43.16396,-81.85515:
Town

📚🍴

Thessalon 2 GPS 46.26541,-83.54646: Village

📚🛏️🏕️📚🍴

🛏️ **Carolyn Beach Motel** - restaurant
1 Lakeside Drive Box 10
Thessalon ON P0R 1L0
www.carolynbeach.ca
Tel: (800) 461-2217 (705) 842-3330

🏕️ **Lakeside Park**
Highway 17B at Stanley Street

Thessalon ON
Tel: (705) 842-2523

📚 **Thessalon Public Library**
187 Main Street
Thessalon ON P0R 1L0
www.thesslibcap.com
Tel: (705) 842-2306

Thornbury (Blue Mountains) 40 Z23-24
GPS 44.56179,-80.45293: Town

⭐📚🍴📚

⭐ **Apple Harvest Festival** - October

📚 **The Blue Mountains Public Library**
173 Bruce Street South
Thornbury ON N0H 2P0
Tel: (519) 599-3681

Thorndale 15 S18 GPS 43.10513,-81.14118: Town

🛏️🍴🛏️📚

🛏️ **Silver Rock Bed & Breakfast**
21814 Fairview Road
Thorndale ON N0M 2P0
www.angelfire.com/on/hamilton
Tel: (519) 461-0331

📚 **Middlesex County Library**
21790 Fairview Road
Thorndale ON N0M 2P0
www.middlesex.library.on.ca
Tel: (519) 461-1150

Thorold 19 R34 GPS 43.12429,-79.19772:
City

📚🏛️🍴🛏️🚲📚

🏛️ **Thorold Tourism** Lock - view of Welland Canal
Locks 4,5,6 & 7
50 Chapel Street South
Thorold ON L2V 2C6
www.thoroldtourism.ca
Tel: (888) 680-9477

🛏️ **The Inn At Lock 7**
24 Chapel Street South
Thorold ON L2V 2C6
www.innatlock7.com
Tel: (877) 465-6257 (905) 227-6177

🛏️ **Robinsong Bed & Breakfast**
41 Welland Street South
Thorold ON L2V 2B6
www.bbcanada.com/robinsong
Tel: (905) 680-2427

🚲 **Clarkson Cycle**
103A Pine Street South
Thorold ON
clarksoncycle.com
Tel: (905) 227-0810

🚲 **Canal City Cycle** - rentals
50 Front Street North
Thorold ON
Tel: (905) 964-8056

📚 **Thorold Public Library**
14 Ormond Street North
Thorold ON L2V 1Y8
www.thoroldpubliclibrary.ca
Tel: (905) 227-2581

Thunder Bay 2 GPS 48.38170,-89.24548:
City

📚🍴🛏️📚🏛️🏕️🚲📚

🏛️ **Ontario Travel Information Centre**
7671 Highway 61
Neebing ON P7C 5V5
www.ontariotravel.net
Tel: (807) 964-2094 (800) 668-2746

🏛️ **Fort William Historical Park**
recreated fur trading post
1350 King Road
Thunder Bay ON P7K 1L7
www.fwhp.ca
Tel: (807) 473-2344

🛏️ **McVicar Manor Bed & Breakfast**
146 Court Street North
Thunder Bay ON P7A 4V2
www.bbcanada.com/3918.html
Tel: (807) 344-9300

🛏️ **The Little Pearl Bed & Breakfast**
268 Pearl Street
Thunder Bay ON P7B 1E6
www.thelittlepearl.ca
Tel: (807) 346-8700

🛏️ **Best Western Crossroads Motor Inn**
655 West Arthur Street

Thunder Bay ON P7E 5R6
www.bestwesternontario.com/hotels/best-
western-crossroads-motor-inn
Tel: (800) 780-7234 (807) 577-4241

🛏 Super 8 Motel
439 Memorial Avenue
Thunder Bay ON P7B 3Y6
www.super8.com
Tel: (800) 889-9698 (807) 344-2612

⛺ Thunder Bay KOA
162 Spruce River Road
Thunder Bay ON P7B 5E4
www.koa.com/where/on/55120/reserve
Tel: (800) 562-4162 (807) 683-6221

⛺ Kakabeka Falls Provincial Park
32 kilometers west on Highway 11/17 Box 252
Kakabeka Falls ON P0T 1W0
Tel: (807) 473-9231
Reservations: www.ontarioparks.com
Tel: (888) 668-7275

🍽 Bistro One
555 Dunlop Street
Thunder Bay ON
www.bistroone.ca
Tel: (807) 622-2478

🍽 Caribou Restaurant & Wine Bar
727 Hewitson Street
Thunder Bay ON P7B 6B5
Tel: (807) 628-8588

🚲 Fresh Air Experience
710 Balmoral Street
Thunder Bay ON P7C 5V3
www.freshairexp.com
Tel: (877) 311-9393 (807) 623-3800

📖 Thunder Bay Waverley Resource Library
285 Red River Road
Thunder Bay ON P7B 1A9
www.tbpl.ca
Tel: (807) 344-3585

Tilbury 5 C7 GPS 42.26166,-82.43200: Town
⭐🛏📖🍽

⭐ 175 year old clock and local history murals in
shopping district

⭐ L&K Antiques
Highway 401 exit 56
4625 Richardson Side Road South
Tilbury ON N0P 2L0
l-kantiques.tripod.com
Tel: (519) 682-3592

🛏 Katharine's Bed & Breakfast
8 Carlyle Street
Tilbury ON
www.bbcanada.com/3088.html
Tel: (519) 682-3706 (519) 401-3061

🍽 Uncle Chow's Restaurant
8 Mill Street West
Tilbury ON N0P 2L0
Tel: (519) 682-1984

Tillsonburg 9 U21 GPS 42.861942, -80.727507:
Town
📖🛏🍽

📖 Annandale National Historic Site & tourist
Information
30 Tillson Avenue
Tilsonburg ON N4G 2Z8
www.tillsonburg.ca/site/1251/default.aspx

🛏 Howard Johnson Tillsonburg
92 Simcoe Street
Tillsonburg ON N4G 2J1
www.hojotillsonburg.ca
Tel: (866) 942-7366 (519) 842-7366

🛏 The Mill Tales Inn - restaurant
20 John Pound Road
Tillsonburg ON
www.milltalesinn.webs.com
Tel: (519) 842-1782

📖 Tillsonburg Public Library
2 Library Lane
Tillsonburg ON N4G 2S7
Tel: (519) 842-5571

Tobermory 54 S14 GPS 45.25382,-81.66509:
Village
📖ℹ🍽⭐🛏⛺📖

⭐ Fathom Five National Marine Park -
diving centre to explore shipwrecks
Box 189
Tobermory ON
www.pc.gc.ca/amnc-nmca/on/fathomfive/index.
aspx

⭐ Tobermory to South Baymouth Manitoulin
Island - ferry service
www.ontarioferries.com/chi/english/index.html
Tel: (800) 265-3163

⭐ Blue Heron Cruises - Flowerpot Island &
shipwrecks
24 Carlton Street, Little Tub Harbour
Tobermory ON N0H 2R0
Tel: (855) 596-2999 (519) 596-2999

🛏 Harbourside Motel
24 Carlton Street, Little Tub Harbour
Tobermory ON N0H 2R0
www.blueherronco.com/motel.htm
Tel: (855) 596-2999 (519) 596-2999

🛏 Blue Bay Motel
32 Bay Street Box 58
Tobermory ON N0H 2R0
www.bluebay-motel.com
Tel: (519) 596-2392

🛏 Innisfree Bed & Breakfast
46 Bay Street
Tobermory ON N0H 2R0
www.tobermoryaccommodations.com
Tel: (888) 996-8190 (519) 596-8190

⛺ Tobermory Village Campground - 3 km south
7159 Highway 6
Tobermory ON N0H 2R0
www.tobermoryvillagecamp.com
Tel: (519) 596-2689

⛺ Bruce Peninsula National Park
407 Cyprus Lake Road at Highway 6
Tobermory ON N0H 2R0
www.pc.gc.ca/pn-np/on/bruce/index_E.asp
Tel: (877) 737-3783 (519) 596-2233

📖 Bruce County Library
22 Bay Street
Tobermory ON
library.brucecounty.on.ca/tolib
Tel: (519) 596-2446

Toledo 49 Y60 GPS 44.74629,-76.00128: Hamlet
📖

Toronto 24 K32 GPS 43.64899,-79.35356: Capital
city of Ontario
ℹ⭐📖🍽🛏🚲📖

ℹ Toronto Online Cycling Map
www.toronto.ca/cycling/map/index.htm

ℹ Ontario Travel Information Centre
Union Station - Main Hall near the Skywalk
65 Front Street West
Toronto ON M5G 2C2
www.ontariotravel.net
Tel: (416) 314-5899 (800) 668-2746

ℹ Toronto Tourism
www.seetorontonow.com
Tel: (800) 363-1990 (416) 203-2500

ℹ GO Transit Service Union Station
Bicycles permitted Saturday, Sunday, holidays,
weekday off-peak, and travelling opposite to
peak direction. Toronto to Niagara seasonal GO
TRAIN
www.gotransit.com
Tel: (888) 438-6646 (416) 869-3200

ℹ TTC subway, streetcar & bus transit
www3.ttc.ca
Tel: (416) 393-4636

ℹ Toronto Island Ferry - Docks 9 Queens Quay
West south end of Bay Street
Tel: (416) 397-2628

⭐ International Dragon Boat Race Festival -
Centre Island - late June
Toronto ON
Tel: (416) 595-0313 x23

⭐ Luminato Festival of Arts and Creativity -
mid June
180 Shaw Street Suite 301
Toronto ON M6J 2W5
Tel: (416) 368-3100

⭐ Toronto Pride Week - late June
14 Dundonald Street
Toronto ON M4Y 1K2
Tel: (416) 927-7433

⭐ Toronto Buskerfest - Downtown Yonge Street -
late August

⭐ Toronto Caribbean Carnival - August holiday
weekend

⭐ Word on the Street National Book and
Margazine Festival - late September
Harbourfront Centre
Toronto ON
Tel: (416) 504-7241

🛏 Novotel Toronto Centre

45 The Esplanade
Toronto ON M5E 1W2
www.novotel.com/gb/hotel-0931-novotel-
toronto-centre/index.shtml
Tel: (416) 367-8900 (800) 221-4542

🛏 Radisson Hotel Admiral
249 Queens Quay West
Toronto ON M5J 2N5
www.radisson.com/torontoca_admiral
Tel: (800) 967-9033 (416) 203-3333

🛏 Toronto Bed & Breakfast - Reservation Service
www.torontobandb.com

🛏 Neill-Wycik College - economical student
residence May to August
96 Gerrard Street East
Toronto ON M5B 1G7
www.neill-wycik.com
Tel: (800) 268-4358 (416) 977-2320

🚲 Cycle Solutions
444 Parliament Street
Toronto ON M5A 3A2
www.cycle-solutions.ca
Tel: (416) 972-6948

🚲 Cycle Solutions
615 Kingston Road
Toronto ON M4E 1R3
www.cycle-solutions.ca
Tel: (416) 691-0019

🚲 Wheel Excitement - rentals
249 Queen's Quay West Unit 106
Toronto ON M5J 2N5
www.wheelexcitement.ca
Tel: (416) 260-9000

🚲 Mountain Equipment Co-Op
400 King Street West
Toronto ON M5V 1K2
www.mec.ca
Tel: (888) 847-0770 (416) 340-2667

📖 Toronto Public Library
www.torontopubliclibrary.ca
171 Front Street East
Toronto ON
Tel: (416) 393-7655
2161 Queen Street East
Toronto ON
Tel: (416) 393-7703

Tory Hill 61 V41 GPS 44.97280,-78.2747: Village
⛺ Silent Lake Provincial Park
1589 Silent Lake Park Road
Bancroft ON K0L 1C0
Tel: (613) 339-2807
Reservations: www.ontarioparks.com
Tel: (888) 668-7275

Tottenham 30 F29 GPS 44.02287,-79.80578:
Town
📖ℹ📖

📖 New Tecumseh Public Library
18 Queen Street North
Tottenham ON L0G 1W0
www.ntpl.ca
Tel: (905) 936-2291

Turkey Point 10 W24 GPS 42.68459,-80.33105:
Village
🛏🍽⛺

⛺ Turkey Point Provincial Park
194 Turkey Point Road Box 5
Turkey Point ON N0E 1T0
Tel: (519) 426-3239
Reservations: www.ontarioparks.com
Tel: (888) 668-7275

Tweed 46 A49 GPS 44.47550,-77.31102: Town
ℹ📖🛏🍽📖

ℹ Lake Ontario Trent Canal Package
Route

🛏 Park Place Motel
43 Victoria Street South
Tweed ON K0K 3J0
Tel: (866) 478-3134 (613) 478-3134

🛏 Holiday House Bed & Breakfast
42 St Edmund's Road RR#4
Tweed ON K0K 3J0
www3.sympatico.ca/edward.zak
Tel: (866) 272-7613 (613) 478-5025

📖 Tweed Public Library
255 Metcalf Street Box 628
Tweed ON K0K 3J0
www.tweedlibrary.ca
Tel: (613) 478-1066

Uxbridge 31 E34 GPS 44.10616,-79.12386: Town

⭐🏨🍴📚

⭐ **Thomas Foster Memorial**
9449 Concession 7 on Road 1 north of Road 11
www.uxbridge.com/people/tfoster.html
Tel: (905) 640-3966

⭐ **Leaskdale Manse Museum** - home of LM
Montgomery, author of the Anne of Green
Gables
Road 1 at Leaskdale Road
www.uxbridge.com/people/maud.html

🏨 **Just Mary Home Suite Home B&B**
49 Main Street North
Uxbridge ON L9P 1J7
www.bbcanada.com/justmary
Tel: (905) 852-5349

📚 **Uxbridge Public Library**
9 Toronto Street
Uxbridge ON L9P 1P7
www.uxlib.com
Tel: (905) 852-9747

Vankleek Hill 68 P71 GPS 45.52099,-74.65144:
Town

🏨🍴⭐

⭐ **Beau's Brewery**
10 Terry Fox Drive
Vankleek Hill ON
Tel: (866) 585-2337 (613) 678-2799

Varna 20 M14 GPS 43.53387,-81.59593: Village
🏨

Vernonville 33 F44 GPS 44.04707,-77.98319:
Hamlet

Verona 36 A54 GPS 44.48005,-76.69421: Town
ℹ️🏨🍴

ℹ️ **Lake Ontario Trent Canal Package Route**

Victoria Harbour 41 X29 GPS 44.75070,
-79.77444: Village

🏨🍴📚

📚 **Tay Township Public Library**
145 Albert Street
Victoria Harbour ON L0K2A0
Tel: (705) 534-3581

Vienna 9 W20 GPS 42.67992,-80.78888: Village
🏨🍴📚

📚 **Edison Museum of Vienna** - Home of Captain
Samuel Edison, Thomas Edison's grandfather
14 Snow Street
Vienna ON N0J 1Z0
www.edisonmuseum.ca
Tel: (519) 874-4999

Villa Nova 10 T25 GPS 42.94285,-80.16037:
Village

🏨

Virgil 19 Q34 GPS 43.22119,-79.12422: Town
🏨🍴

Vittoria 10 V24 GPS 42.76215,-80.32357: Village
🏳️ Capital of London District 1815 to 1825

Wallaceburg 6 X7 GPS 42.59297,-82.39503:
Town

ℹ️🏨🏳️⭐📚

⭐ **WAMBO Wallaceburg Antique Motor and Boat
Outing** - in early August
www.kent.net/wambo/

📚 **Wallaceburg District Museum**
505 King Street
Wallaceburg ON
www.kent.net/wallaceburg-museum
Tel: (519) 672-8962

🏨 **Days Inn**
76 McNaughton Avenue
Wallaceburg ON N8A 1R9
www.daysinnwallaceburg.com
Tel: (866) 627-0781 (519) 627-0781

📚 **Chatham Kent Public Library**
209 James Street
Wallaceburg ON N8A 2N4
www.chatham-kent.ca/community+services/
library/hours+and+locations/Wallaceburg+Library.
htm
Tel: (519) 627-5292

Wallacetown 8 X15 GPS 42.63405,-81.46614:
Vllage

🏨🍴

Walpole Island First Nation Bkejwanong
6 X6 GPS 42.59442,-82.49857: Community

ℹ️ www.bkejwanong.com

ℹ️ **Walpole Island – Algonac, Michigan USA Ferry
Bicycle Crossing**
100 Tahgahoning Road
Walpole Island ON N8A 4K9
www.walpolealgonacferry.com
Tel: (519) 365-5183

🚲 **Bay to Bridge Trail** - Marine City to Algonac,
Michigan USA
www.stclaircountyparks.org

⭐ **Three Fires Confederacy of Potawatami, Ottawa
and Ojibwa people Pow Wow** - late July

Walters Falls 39 A21 GPS 44.48807,-80.70750:
Village

🏨🍴

🏨 **The Falls Inn & Spa**
140 Front Street West
Walters Falls ON N0H 2S0
Tel: (519) 794-4388

Warkworth 33 D44 GPS 44.20073,-77.88984:
Village

ℹ️⭐🏨📚

ℹ️ **Bay of Quinte & Northumberland Package
Route**

⭐ **Warkworth Long Lunch** - late August
www.warkworth.ca/annual-events/longlunch

🏨 **Thornton Inn**
44 Main Street Box 420
Warkworth ON K0K 3K0
www.thorntoninn.com
Tel: (705) 924-3980

📚 **Town Hall Centre for the Arts** - Trent Hills
Library
40 Main Street
Warkworth ON K0K 3K0
www.trenthillslibrary.ca
Tel: (705) 924-3116

Warsaw 45 G42 GPS 44.430061, -78.1373: Village
🏨🏨🍴🏕️

🏕️ **Warsaw Caves Conservation Area**
289 Caves Road
Warsaw ON
www.warsawcaves.com
Tel: (705) 652-3161 (877) 816-7604

🏨 **Sunflower Bay B&B**
967 Water Street Box 36
Warsaw ON K0L 3A0
www.sunflowerbay.ca
Tel: (705) 652-0403

Warwick 13 T11 GPS 43.00288,-81.94458:
🏨

Wasaga Beach 41 A27 GPS 44.52080,-80.01579:
Village, public beach

🏨📚

🏨 **Saga Resort**
88 Main Street South
Wasaga Beach ON L9Z 2K9
www.sagaresort.com
Tel: (800) 263-7053 (705) 429-2543

🏨 **Donato House Hotel**
1080 Mosley Street
Wasaga Beach ON L9Z 2G1
www.donatohouse.com
Tel: (877) 429-4411

📚 **Wasaga Beach Public Library**
120 Glenwood Drive
Wasaga Beach ON L9Z 2K5
www.wasagabeach.library.on.ca
Tel: (705) 429-5481

Washago 42 X32 GPS 44.74965,-79.33452: Village
🏨🍴

Waterdown 23 P27 GPS 43.33523,-79.89295:
former town in the city of Hamilton

🏨🍴🚲📚

🚲 **Bicycle Works**
316 Dundas Street East
Waterdown ON
www.thebicycleworks.ca
Tel: (905) 689-1991

📚 **Hamilton Public Library** – Waterdown Branch
25 Mill Street North
Waterdown ON L0R 2H0
www.inform.hamilton.ca/record/HAM0563

Tel: (905) 689-6269

Waterford 17 T25 GPS 42.93160, -80.28958:
Town

ℹ️🏨🍴📚

ℹ️ **Ports of Lake Erie Package Route**

ℹ️ **Theatre to Theatre Package Route**

ℹ️ **Bicycling on Norfolk County Trails**

📚 **Norfolk County Public Library**
15 Main Street South
Waterford ON N0E 1Y0
www.ncpl.ca
Tel: (519) 426-3506

Waterloo and Kitchener 22 N23
GPS 43.46339,-80.52076: Adjacent cities in
Waterloo region

ℹ️ℹ️🏨🏕️🚲📚⭐

ℹ️ **Waterloo Region**
Tel: (800) 265-6959

ℹ️ **Waterloo Regional Cycling Network**

⭐ **Uptown Waterloo Jazz Festival** - mid July
www.uptownwaterloojazz.ca
Tel: (226) 220-3036

⭐ **Kitchener Blues Festival** - early August
250 King Street West Box 26039
Kitchener ON
Tel: (519) 571-2555

⭐ **Kitchener Waterloo Octoberfest** - Thanksgiving
weekend in October
Kitchener ON
Tel: (888) 294-4267 (519) 570-4267

🏨 **Marshall Woods B&B**
194 Marshall Street
Waterloo ON N2J 2V1
www.marshallwoods.com
Tel: (519) 883-0273

🏨 **Sugarbush Guest House B&B**
2 Wildwood Place
Waterloo ON N2L 4B1
www.sugarbushguesthouse.com
Tel: (888) 725-4660 (519) 725-4660

🏨 **Comfort Inn Waterloo**
190 Weber Street North
Waterloo ON N2J 3H4
www.waterloocomfortinn.com
Tel: (877) 363-1938 (519) 747-9400

🏨 **Hotel Laurier** - affordable student accommodation
75 University Avenue West
Waterloo ON N2L 3C5
www.wlu.ca/conferences
Tel: (519) 884-0710 x2771

🏕️ **Laurel Creek Conservation Area**
625 Westmount Road
Waterloo ON
www.grandriver.ca
Tel: (866) 668-2267 (519) 884-6620

🚲 **McPhail's Cycle & Sports**
98 King Street North
Waterloo ON N2J 2X4
www.mcphailscycle.com
Tel: (519) 886-4340

📚 **Waterloo Public Library**
35 Albert Street
Waterloo ON N2L 5E2
www.wpl.ca
Tel: (519) 886-1310

Waupoos 35 G52 GPS 44.00130,-77.00103:
Hamlet

🍴🍷⭐

🍷 **Waupoos Estate Winery** - Gazebo Restaurant
3016 Road 8 RR#4
Picton ON K0K 2T0
www.waupooswinery.com
Tel: (613) 478-8338

🍷 **County Cider Company & Estate Winery**
657 Bongards X Road Box 6241
Picton ON K0K 2T0
www.countycider.com
Tel: (613) 476-1022

🍷 **Devils Wishbone Winery**
1014 Road 7 RR#4
Picton ON K0K 2T0
www.devilswishbone.com
Tel: (613) 476-1199

⭐ **Fifth Town Artisan Cheese**
4309 Road 8 RR#4
Picton ON K0K 2T0

www.fifthtown.ca
Tel: (800) 584-8696 (613) 476-5755
🍴 **The Duke of Marysburgh Pub & Bistro**
2470 Road 8
Picton ON
www.dukeofmarysburgh.com
Tel: (613) 476 8991

Wawa 2 GPS 47.99098,-84.77267: Town
🛈🛏🍴🚲⛺📖
🛏 **Northern Lights Motel & Chalets**
1014 Highway 17 North
Wawa ON P0S 1K0
www.nlmotel.com
Tel: (705) 856-1900
🛏 **Best Northern Motel and Restaurant**
Highway 17 South
Wawa ON P0S 1K0
www.bestnorthern.ca
Tel: (800) 434-8240 (705) 856-7302
⛺ **Lake Superior Provincial Park**
Box 267
Wawa ON P0S 1K0
Tel: (705) 856-2284
Reservations: www.ontarioparks.com
Tel: (888) 668-7275
📖 **Wawa Public Library**
40 Broadway Avenue
Wawa ON P0S 1K0
www.mtpl.on.ca
Tel: (705) 856-2062

Webbwood 84 E12 GPS 46.26913,-81.89021: Village
🍴

Welland 19 T33-34 GPS 42.99348,-79.23924: City
🛏🍴⭐🛏📖
⭐ **Welland Rose Festival** - June
www.wellandrosefestival.on.ca
Tel: (905) 732-7673
⭐ **Niagara Food Festival** - early September
🛏 **Anderson's Bed & Breakfast**
324 Kingsway Road
Welland ON L3B 3N9
www.bbcanada.com/3336.html
Tel: (905) 732-3730
🛏 **Best Western Rose City Suites**
300 Prince Charles Drive
Welland ON L3C 7B3
www.bestwesternniagara.com
Tel: (888) 670-7234 (905) 732-0922
📖 **Welland Public Library**
50 The Boardwalk
Welland ON L3B 6J1
www.welland.library.on.ca
Tel: (905) 734-6210

Wellesley 22 M21 GPS 43.47665,-80.76454: Town
🛏🍴⭐📖
⭐ **Apple Butter and Cheese Festival** - September
www.wellesleyabcfestival.ca
⭐ **Wellesley Apple Products**
3800 Nafziger Road North
Wellesley ON
www.wellappleproducts.com
Tel: (519) 656-2400
🍴 **Nith River Chop House**
1193 Queen's Bush Road
Wellesley ON N0B 2T0
www.nithchophouse.com
Tel: (519) 656-9057
📖 **Region of Waterloo Library**
1137 Henry Street
Wellesley ON N0B 2T0
www.rwl.library.on.ca
Tel: (519) 656-2001

Wellington 34 G49 GPS 43.95130,-77.35130: Village
🛈🛏🛏🍴🍷📖
🛈 **Bay of Quinte and Northumberland Package Route**
🛈 **Lake Ontario Trent Canal Package Route**
🛏 **Breeze Off The Lake Bed & Breakfast**
449 Main Street
Wellington ON K0K 3L0
www.breezeoffthelake.ca
Tel: (613) 399-2960

🛏 **Drake Devonshire** - restaurant
24 Wharf Street
Wellington ON K0K 3L0
www.drakedevonshire.ca
Tel: (613) 399-3338
🛏 **Lakeside Village Inn**
349 Main Street
Wellington ON K0K 3L0
www.lakesidevillageinn.ca
Tel: (800) 524-6980 (613) 399-2034
📖 **Prince Edward County Library**
261 Main Street
Wellington ON
www.peclibrary.org
Tel: (613) 399-2023
🍷 **Karlo Estates Winery**
561 Danforth Road
Wellington ON K0K 3L0
www.karloestates.com
Tel: (613) 399-3000
🍷 **Hubbs Creek Vineyard**
562 Danforth Road
Wellington ON K0K 3L0
www.hubbscreekvineyard.com
Tel: (647) 521-2395
🍷 **By Chadsey's Cairns Winery**
17432 Loyalist Parkway
Wellington ON K0K 3L0
www.bychadseyscairns.com
Tel: (613) 399-2992
🍷 **Keint-he Winery & Vineyards**
49 Hubbs Creek Road
Wellington ON K0K 3L0
www.keint-he.ca
Tel: (613) 399-5308
🍷 **Sandbanks Estates Winery**
17598 Loyalist Parkway
Wellington ON K0K 2T0
www.sandbankswinery.com
Tel: (613) 399-1839
📖 **Prince Edward County Library**
261 Main Street
Wellington ON K0K 2T0
www.peclibrary.org
Tel: (613) 399-2023

Wendover 67 N67 GPS 45.57034,-75.14541: Village
🛏

West Guilford 60 T38 35 G50
GPS 45.11666, -78.6: Village
🛏🍴

West Lake 34 G49 35 G50
GPS 43.94216,-77.24350: Resort area
🛏🛏🍴⛺
🛏 **Isaiah Tubbs Resort** - restaurant
642 County Road 12
Picton ON K0K 1T0
www.isaiahtubbs.com
Tel: (800) 724-2393 (613) 393-2090
⛺ **Sandbanks Provincial Park**
3004 Road 12 RR#1
Picton ON K0K 2T0
Tel: (613) 393-3319
Reservations: www.ontarioparks.com
Tel: (888) 668-7275

West Lorne 8 X14 GPS 42.60471,-81.60800: Village
🛏🍴📖
📖 **Egin County Library**
160A Main Street
West Lorne ON N0L 2P0
www.library.elgin-county.on.ca
Tel: (519) 768-1150

West Montrose 22 M22
GPS 43.58756,-80.48192: Village
🛏🛏🎒
🎒 **Ontario's last remaining covered bridge** -
Connecting Hill Street, Covered Bridge Drive
and Rivers Edge Drive crossing the Grand River

Westport 48 Y57 GPS 44.67968,-76.39745: Town
🛈🛏🛏🎒🛏📖
🛈 **St. Lawrence and Rideau Canal Package Route**
🎒 **Rideau District Museum**

29 Bedford Street
Westport ON K0G 1X0
www.village.westport.on.ca/about-westport/
rideau-district-museum
Tel: (613) 273-2502
🛏 **A Victorian Reflection Bed & Breakfast**
16 Church Street
Westport ON K0G 1X0
www.avictorianreflection.com
Tel: (613) 273-8383
🛏 **The Cove Country Inn** - restaurant
2 Bedford Street
Westport ON K0G 1X0
www.coveinn.com
Tel: (888) 298-3466 (613) 273-3636
🍴 **Tangled Garden Café**
7 Church Street
Westport ON K0G 1X0
www.tangledgardencafe.com
Tel: (613) 273-7733
📖 **Westport Public Library**
3 Spring Street
Westport ON K0G 1X0
www.village.westport.on.ca/about-westport/
westport-public-library
Tel: (613) 273-3223

Wheatley 5 E7 GPS 42.09454,-82.46295: Town
🛈🛏🛏📖⛺📖
🛈 **Erie Shores Package Route**
🛏 **By The Bay B&B**
493 Gregory Line RR#1
Wheatley ON N0P 2P0
www.dentsbythebay.com
Tel: (866) 298-4322 (519) 825-7729
🛏 **Blue Heron Getaway Bed & Breakfast**
216 Erie Street South Box 430
Wheatley ON N0P 2P0
Tel: (888) 813-4445 (519) 916-5123
⛺ **Wheatley Provincial Park**
21116 Klondyke Road Box 640
Wheatley ON N0P 2P0
Tel: (519) 825-4659
Reservations: www.ontarioparks.com
Tel: (888) 668-7275
🍴 **Car Barn Restaurant and Tavern**
23 Talbot Street East
Wheatley ON
Tel: (519) 825 4946
📖 **Chatham Kent Library**
35 Talbot Street West
Wheatley ON N0P 2P0
www.chatham-kent.ca/community+services/
library/Library.htm
Tel: (519) 825-7131

Whitby 25 H36 GPS 43.89926,-78.94255: City
🛏🍴🛏🚲
🛏 **Residence Inn**
60 Consumers Drive
Whitby ON L1N 9S3
www.marriott.com/hotels/travel/yyzwy-
residence-inn-whitby
Tel: (866) 277-9165 (905) 444-9756
🚲 **Impala Bicycles**
1818 Dundas Street East
Whitby ON K7G 2G2
www.impalabicycles.com
Tel: (866) 652-2453 (905) 434-4530

White River 2 GPS 48.59312,-85.27481: Village
🛏🍴🛏⛺
🛏 **White River Motel**
Box 608
White River ON P0M 3G0
www.whiterivermotel.com
Tel: (800) 822-5887 (807) 822-2333
⛺ **White Lake Provincial Park**
west on Highway 17 Box 340
White River ON P0M 3G0
Tel: (807) 822-2447
Reservations: www.ontarioparks.com
Tel: (888) 668-7275

Whitefish Falls 84 G13 GPS 46.11509,-81.72925: Village
🛏🍴

Whitney 79 P41 GPS 45.49919,-78.24499: Village

Algonquin East Gate Motel
Box 193
Whitney ON K0J 2M0
www.algonquineastgatemotel.com
Tel: (613) 637-2652

Algonquin Provincial Park
Highway 60 Box 219
Whitney ON K0J 2M0
Tel: (705) 633-5572
Reservations: www.ontarioparks.com
Tel: (888) 668-7275

South Algonquin Public Library
33 Medical Centre Road
Whitney ON K0J 2M0
www.olsn.ca/southalgonquin
Tel: (613) 637-5471

Wiarton 39 X18 GPS 44.74013,-81.13978: Town

Bruce Peninsula Package Route

Bruce County Tourism
578 Brown St Box 129
Wiarton ON N0H 2T0
www.explorethebruce.com
Tel: (800) 268-3838 (519) 534-5344

Wiarton Willy - statue Bluewater Park world famous albino groundhog weather forecaster
www.wiarton-willie.org

Wiarton Willy Inn
Highway 6 south
Wiarton ON N0H 2T0
www.wiartonwillys.com
Tel: (888) 534-3907 (519) 534-3907

Pacific Inn & Lucille's Dining
624 Berford Street
Wiarton ON N0H 2T0
www.pacificinnwiarton.com
Tel: (519) 534-1370

Maplehurst B&B
277 Frank Street Box 803
Wiarton ON N0H 2T0
www.bbcanada.com/1898.html
Tel: (519) 534-1210

Green Door Café
563 Berford Street
Wiarton ON N0H 2T0
www.thegreendoorcafe.com
Tel: (519) 534-3278

Bruce County Library
578 Brown Street
Wiarton ON N0H 2T0
www.library.brucecounty.on.ca
Tel: (519) 534-2602

Wilberforce 61 U41 GPS 45.03678,-78.22264: Village

House in the Village Bed & Breakfast
2293 Loop Road
Wilberforce ON L1N 9S3
Tel: (705) 448-2018

Haliburton Public Library
1101 Holmes Road
Wilberforce ON
Tel: (705) 448-2510

Wilton 36 C54 GPS 44.31709,-76.73006: Village

Wilton Cheese Factory
287 Simmons Road
Odessa ON K0H 2H0
www.wiltoncheese.com
Tel: (613) 386-7314

Windsor 4 B1-2 GPS 42.31782,-83.03391: City

Erie Shores Package Route

Ontario Travel Information Centre -
Detroit-Windsor Tunnel
110 Park Street East
Windsor ON N9A 3A9
www.ontariotravel.net
Tel: (800) 668-2746 (519) 973-1338

Tunnel Bus - Bicycles disassembled are permitted on the Tunnel Bus at the driver's discretion [avoid busy times].
Information at (519) 944 4111 or email: tw@city.windsor.on.ca
Bicycles and pedestrians are prohibited on the Ambassador Bridge. For an alternative use the Pelee Island Ferry from Leamington and Kingsville to Sandusky, Ohio.

Windsor and Essex County Tourism
333 Riverside Drive West Suite 103
Windsor ON N9A 7C5
www.visitwindsoressex.com
Tel: (800) 265-3633 (519) 225-6530

Windsor Trails Map

Ojibway Nature Centre - Carolinian forest and large tallgrass prairie park
5200 Matchette Road
Windsor ON N9C 4E8
www.ojibway.ca
Tel: (519) 966-5852

Art in the Park - early June
Willistead Manor
1899 Niagara Street
Windsor ON

Fiesta Latina - mid August
music and dance celebration

Carousel of the Nations - June
multicultural festival

Caesars Windsor
377 Riverside Drive East
Windsor ON N9A 7H7
www.caesars.com/caesars-windsor/casino
Tel: (800) 991-7777

Hampton Inn & Suites by Hilton Windsor
1840 Huron Church Road
Windsor ON N9C 2L5
hamptoninn3.hilton.com/en/hotels/ontario/
hampton-inn-and-suites-by-hilton-windsor-
YQGCNHX/index.html
Tel: (519) 972-0770

Inn on the River Bed & Breakfast
3857 Riverside Drive East
Windsor ON N8Y 1B1
www.windsorinnontheriver.com
Tel: (866) 635-0055 (519) 945-2110

Comfort Inn & Suites Ambassador Bridge
2330 Huron Church Road
Windsor ON N9E 3S6
www.choicehotels.ca/en/comfort-inn-&-suites-
ambassador-bridge-windsor-hotel-cn901
Tel: (800) 424-6423 (519) 972-1100

Courtesy Bicycles
3154 Sandwich Street West
Windsor ON N9C 1A6
www.courtesybicycles.ca
Tel: (519) 252-0080

Windsor Public Library
3312 Sandwich Street
Windsor ON N9C 1B1
www.windsorpubliclibrary.com
Tel: (519) 255-6770

Wolfe Island 36 E56-57
GPS 44.17999,-76.43677

Wolfe Island Information
www.wolfeisland.com

Wolfe Island Ferry Kingston via Wolfe Island to Cape Vincent New York
Tel: (800) 268-4686 (613)548-7227

Hornes Ferry Cape Vincent New York to Port Alexandria Wolfe Island
Tel: (613) 385-2402 (315) 783-0638

Blue Horizon
1767 5th Line Road
Wolfe Island ON K0L 1L0
www.bbcanada.com/bluehorizon
Tel: (613) 385-2900

Dreamcatcher's Inn
1277 Main Street
Marysville ON K0H 2Y0
www.dreamcatchers-inn.com
Tel: (613) 385-2635

Kingston Frontenac Public Library
10 Highway 95
Kingston ON K0H 2Y0
www.kfpl.ca
Tel: (613) 385-2112

Woodstock 16 R21 GPS 43.13011,-80.75656: City

Ports of Lake Erie Package Route

Tourist Information -
Woodstock and Oxford County
www.tourismoxford.ca
Tel: (519) 539-9800 x3355

Springbank Snow Countess Monument -
Dundas Street at Springbank Avenue

Best Western Plus Woodstock Inn & Suites
811 Athlone Avenue
Woodstock ON N4V 0B6
bestwesternontario.com/hotels/best-western-
plus-woodstock-inn-and-suites
Tel: (519) 537-2320

Holiday Inn Express Hotel & Suites
510 Norwich Avenue
Woodstock ON N4S 3W5
www.hiexpress.com
Tel: (800) 345-8082

Pittock Conservation Area
725138 Pittock Park Road
Woodstock ON
www.thamesriver.on.ca
Tel: (519) 539-5088

Pedal Power Bikes & Boards
590 Dundas Street
Woodstock ON N4S 1C8
www.pedalpower.ca
Tel: (519) 539-3681

Woodstock Public Library
445 Hunter Street
Woodstock ON N4S 4G7
www.woodstock.library.on.ca
Tel: (519) 539-4801

Wooler 34 E46 GPS 44.15687,-77.70042: Village

Yarker 36 C54 GPS 44.37174,-76.77110: Village

Lennox & Addington Public Library
2824 County Road # 6
Yarker ON K0K 3N0
www.lennox-addington.on.ca
Tel: (613) 377-1673

Zurich 20 N14 GPS 43.42113,-81.62515: Town

Zurich Bean Festival - late August

Brokenshire House Bed & Breakfast
19 Rosalie Street
Zurich ON N0M 2T0
www.bbcanada.com/3901.html
Tel: (519) 236-4734

CPSIA information can be obtained
at www.ICGtesting.com
Printed in the USA
BVHW021940260320
576099BV00002B/6